COSMOPOLITANISM IN CONTEXT

Is it possible and desirable to translate the basic principles underlying cosmopolitanism as a moral standard into effective global institutions? Will the ideals of inclusiveness and equal moral concern for all survive the marriage between cosmopolitanism and institutional power? What are the effects of such bureaucratization of cosmopolitan ideals?

This book examines the strained relationship between cosmopolitanism as a moral standard and the legal institutions in which cosmopolitan norms and principles are to be implemented. Five areas of global concern are analyzed: environmental protection; economic regulation; peace and security; the fight against international crimes; and migration.

ROLAND PIERIK is Associate Professor in Political and Legal Philosophy at the University of Amsterdam, where he researches political and legal philosophy and public policy.

WOUTER WERNER is Professor in Public International Law at VU University, Amsterdam, where his main fields of interest are international legal theory; the interplay between international law and international politics; and conflict and security law.

COSMOPOLITANISM IN CONTEXT: PERSPECTIVES FROM INTERNATIONAL LAW AND POLITICAL THEORY

ROLAND PIERIK AND WOUTER WERNER

CAMBRIDGE
UNIVERSITY PRESS

CAMBRIDGE UNIVERSITY PRESS
Cambridge, New York, Melbourne, Madrid, Cape Town,
Singapore, São Paulo, Delhi, Mexico City

Cambridge University Press
The Edinburgh Building, Cambridge CB2 8RU, UK

Published in the United States of America by Cambridge University Press, New York

www.cambridge.org
Information on this title: www.cambridge.org/9781107693098

First published 2010
First paperback edition 2013

A catalogue record for this publication is available from the British Library

Library of Congress Cataloguing in Publication Data
Cosmopolitanism in context : perspectives from international law and
political theory / [edited by] Roland Pierik, Wouter Werner.
p. cm.
Includes bibliographical references.
ISBN 978-0-521-19194-4
1. Cosmopolitanism. I. Pierik, Roland H. M. II. Werner, W. G.
(Wouter G.), 1966– III. Title.
JZ1308.C678 2010
306–dc22
2010014630

ISBN 978-1-107-69309-8 Paperback

CONTENTS

Part IV International Criminal Court

Part V International migration

Part VI Conclusion

1

Cosmopolitanism in context: an introduction

ROLAND PIERIK AND WOUTER WERNER

This book deals with the strained relationship between cosmopolitanism as a moral standard and the real existing institutions in which cosmopolitan ideals are to be implemented.

Cosmopolitanism is an age-old normative ideal which contends that all kosmopolitês, all citizens of the world, share a membership in one single community, the cosmopolis, which is governed by a universal and egalitarian law. Martha Nussbaum describes such cosmopolitans as persons "whose primary allegiance is to the worldwide community of human beings."[1] This cosmopolitan notion of a common humanity translates normatively into the idea that we have moral duties towards all human beings since "every human being has a global stature as the ultimate unit of moral concern."[2] From ancient philosophy onwards, the cosmopolis has been portrayed as a perfect order, guided by divine or natural reason, and contrasted to actual men-ruled polises that were failing ideals of justice and law. Cicero, for example, described true cosmopolitan law as:

> right reason in agreement with nature; it is of universal application, unchanging and everlasting; it summons to duty by its commands, and averts from wrongdoing by its prohibitions … We cannot be freed from its obligations by senate or people, and we need not look outside ourselves for an expounder or interpreter of it.[3]

In similar fashion, some contemporary cosmopolitan thinkers seek to ground cosmopolitanism on naturalist arguments, albeit with slight modifications and variations. Buchanan, for example, speaks of a "natural duty of (cosmopolitan) justice," which he characterizes as "not a

[1] Martha Nussbaum, "Patriotism and Cosmopolitanism," in *For Love of Country: Debating the Limits of Patriotism*, ed. Joshua Cohen (Boston: Beacon Press, 1996), p. 4.

[2] Thomas Pogge, *World Poverty and Human Rights* (Oxford: Polity Press, 2002), p. 169.

[3] Cicero, *De re publica*, ed. Clinton W. Keyes (Cambridge, Mass., London: Loeb Classical Library, 1977), p. 211 (§3.22).

rock-bottom, basic moral principle, though it is close to it."[4] Tan speaks of the "duty of justice" which he regards as a "natural duty" and understands as the requirement "to support and comply with just institutions that exist and apply to us" and the duty to further just arrangements that are *not yet established*.[5] It should be noted, however, that other cosmopolitan thinkers have sought to found moral cosmopolitan principles on alternative or supplementary grounds, such as the existence of a global basic structure of interdependence[6] or the existence of a global consensus on basic human rights.[7] Despite the sometimes diverging foundations, contemporary moral cosmopolitan thought shares three basic features.[8] First, *normative individualism*: human beings or persons are taken to be "self-originating sources of valid claims"[9] and, as such, as the ultimate units of concern. In this way, moral cosmopolitanism differs from moral approaches that take ethnic or religious communities, the family, the state, traditions, etc. as moral concerns in and of themselves. For cosmopolitanism, such issues are not valuable intrinsically, but only instrumentally in the role they play in making people's lives better. Secondly, *all-inclusiveness* (at least when applied to human beings): the status as ultimate unit of concern applies to every living human being equally and not merely to a sub-set thereof, e.g. compatriots, men, or Christians. The basic rights and interests of each individual are of equal importance – although beyond these basic rights and interests cosmopolitanism tolerates differences between individuals. Third and finally, *generality*: the special status of persons has global force

4 Allen Buchanan, *Justice, Legitimacy, and Self-Determination: Moral Foundations for International Law* (Oxford: Oxford University Press, 2004), p. 87.

5 Kok-Chor Tan, *Justice without Borders: Cosmopolitanism, Nationalism and Patriotism* (Cambridge: Cambridge University Press, 2004), p. 60, quoting John Rawls, *A Theory of Justice* (Oxford: Oxford University Press, 1971), p. 115, emphasis is by Tan.

6 Charles Beitz, *Political Theory and International Relations*, 2nd edn. (Princeton: Princeton University Press, 1999), pp. 143–53; Pogge, *World Poverty and Human Rights*, p. 20. Similar arguments are made by others, i.e. Buchanan, *Justice, Legitimacy, and Self-Determination*, pp. 83–85; Simon Caney, *Justice Beyond Borders: A Global Political Theory* (Oxford: Oxford University Press, 2005), p. 4.

7 Buchanan, *Justice, Legitimacy, and Self-Determination*.

8 Thomas Pogge, "Cosmpolitanism," in *A Companion to Contemporary Political Philosophy*, ed. Robert E. Goodin, Philip Pettit, and Thomas Pogge (Oxford: Blackwell, 2007), p. 316; Caney, *Justice Beyond Borders*, pp. 3–6; Tan, *Justice without Borders*, pp. 93–98. Pogge also discusses impartiality as a forth feature of cosmopolitanism which, we think, is already sufficiently dealt with in the first three features.

9 This much quoted phrase is coined by John Rawls, "Kantian Constructivism in Moral Theory," *Journal of Philosophy* 77, no. 9 (1980), p. 543.

and thus generates obligations binding on all. Persons are the ultimate units of concern for everyone, not only for their compatriots. In short, cosmopolitanism emphasizes the *moral worth* of persons, the *equal* moral worth of *all* persons and the existence of derivative *obligations to all* to preserve this equal moral worth of persons.

However, endorsing cosmopolitan moral ideals is one thing, having real existing institutions that effectively protect them is quite another. From its inception, moral cosmopolitanism has been confronted with the question as to whether it is possible and desirable to translate universal moral standards into real existing institutions. This question covers two interrelated sub-questions. In the first place, it raises the question of institutional design: is it possible to translate the moral ideals of cosmopolitanism into legal rights and duties and to design institutions that will effectively protect those rights and enforce those duties? In this context, it is worth mentioning that cosmopolitan thinkers generally dismiss the idea of a world government as either utopian or dangerous – "a universal despotism which saps all man's energies and ends in the graveyard of freedom."[10] With a world government beyond the bounds of the possible or the desirable, many cosmopolitans have explored other ways of implementing cosmopolitan standards. Such attempts, however, always take place in a world which is a far cry from the ideal world of moral cosmopolitanism. This raises the second, related question: what happens when cosmopolitan standards are actually translated into positive law; into legal rights, duties, and powers? This question becomes all the more important in the realm of international law, with its close relations to the world of international (power) politics and the still pivotal role for state sovereignty. Is it possible for moral cosmopolitanism to become institutionalized and still to retain its critical stance towards power? What are the effects of institutionalizing moral cosmopolitanism on power politics? Will cosmopolitanism help to civilize politics or will it end up as yet another justification for imperialistic designs?

The questions that run through the different chapters of this book all relate to the problematique described above. Is it possible to translate the ideals of moral cosmopolitanism into institutions that operate in

[10] Immanuel Kant, "Perpetual Peace," in *Political Writings*, ed. Hans Reiss (Cambridge: Cambridge University Press, 1991), p. 94. See however Thomas Pogge who argues that the idea of world government is dismissed too easily: Pogge, "Cosmpolitanism," p. 315.

the non-ideal world of positive law, economic inequalities, established mechanisms of exclusion, and power politics? To what extent have the ideals of moral cosmopolitanism been incorporated into existing international institutions? What are the effects of such incorporation, both for the critical potential of moral cosmopolitanism and for the functioning of those institutions themselves? It goes without saying that such questions cannot be answered in the abstract. They require a more context-sensitive approach, which takes into account the specific aspects of a problem and the working of real existing institutions. For this reason, this book studies the (possible) role of cosmopolitanism in five different areas of international law and politics: the protection of the global environment, the World Trade Organisation (WTO), the United Nations (UN) system of collective security, the International Criminal Court (ICC), and transboundary migration. These topics are selected because they represent some of the most important issues that beset the world community and thus provide insight in the effects (or lack thereof) of cosmopolitan thinking in relevant sectors of international law and politics.

Moral unity and institutional fragmentation

Institutional questions have played a relatively marginal role in contemporary cosmopolitan political philosophy. Moral cosmopolitan thinkers have concerned themselves primarily with the *justificatory basis* of institutions, and remained largely agnostic about the *form* in which these institutions are organized.[11] Moreover, questions as to how cosmopolitan ideals are to be translated into positive legal rights, obligations, and legal powers have often been bracketed. Cosmopolitanism philosophers have not completely ignored institutional questions though. As a minimum, they have strongly articulated which institutional arrangements are to be excluded. On the one hand, moral cosmopolitanism has rejected institutional frameworks which exclusively privilege the institutions of the sovereign state.[12] Thus, cosmopolitans take the well-being of individuals as fundamental and see the values of national states as derivative.[13] For some cosmopolitans, states only have instrumental value, in so far as they can contribute to

[11] Tan, *Justice without Borders*, p. 94.

[12] Charles Beitz, "Rawls's Law of Peoples," *Ethics* 110, no. 4 (2000), p. 677.

[13] "Social and Cosmopolitan Liberalism," *International Affairs* 75, no. 3 (1999), p. 520.

the primary cosmopolitan ideal of treating all world citizens as moral equals. Others present the more moderate view that certain associations, including states, can be valued independently of cosmopolitan ideals, but that these non-derivative ideals ought to be constrained by ideals of cosmopolitan justice. Thus, what is admissible in the name of states is defined by reference to independently arrived at principles of cosmopolitan justice.[14]

In this sense, cosmopolitanism challenges mainstream approaches like realism or Rawls's "society of states" approach. On the other hand, as was noted above, moral cosmopolitanism generally rejects the constitution of a single world government – including a world police – empowered to enforce the cosmopolitan law worldwide.[15] Instead, it advocates a structure of overlapping and countervailing powers, composed of local, national, regional, and global institutions in different areas.[16]

Cosmopolitanism thinking thus situates itself in an inherently unstable in-between position: it simultaneously emphasizes the moral unity of the world *and* the need to protect a plurality of national and international institutions. The tension between moral unity and institutional fragmentation is not unique for political philosophical theories of cosmopolitanism. International legal thinking has equally struggled with the relation between universal values (human rights, global security, sustainable development, etc.) and the (still) decentralized and fragmented structures of global governance. The tension between moral cosmopolitanism and institutional practice becomes even more pronounced if we take into account that cosmopolitanism is intrinsically underdetermined, conflicting, and not self-executing – just like any other normative ideal (or maybe even more so). Cosmopolitanism thus constantly raises the question who is in a position to prioritize conflicting values and who has the power to determine and enforce their meaning in concrete circumstances. As Koskenniemi has pointed out, the result is that world unity is constantly pushed beyond the horizon:

> A deep-structured cosmopolitism maintains that, deep down, the world is already united ... The problem is that the claimed deep-structural

[14] Tan, *Justice without Borders*.

[15] Charles Beitz, "International Liberalism and Distributive Justice: A Survey of Recent Thought," *World Politics* 51, no. 2 (1999). Beitz, "International Liberalism and Distributive Justice," p. 287.

[16] Buchanan, *Justice, Legitimacy, and Self-Determination*, pp. 55–56.

> principles vary, are conflicting, indeterminate, and receive meaning and applicability only through formal decision-making structures. Re-enter government to make the choice; re-enter intergovernmental negotiation to set the balance. Cosmopolis must wait ...[17]

While the tension between moral unity and institutional fragmentation is not new to cosmopolitan thinking, at least two developments have given it new force and meaning.

In the first place, the ideals of moral cosmopolitanism have increasingly found their way into international legal institutions. The establishment of the International Criminal Court, for example, is based on the idea that some crimes, by their very nature, affect the world community as a whole, as they are, in Hannah Arendt's words, "crimes against the human status," "without which the very words 'mankind' or 'humanity' would be devoid of meaning."[18] In similar fashion, the Court's Statute is based upon the idea that "all peoples are united by common bonds, their cultures pieced together in a shared heritage" and that prosecuting international crimes is necessary to protect the "delicate mosaic" that holds the peoples of the world together.[19] At the same time, the Court has to give concrete meaning and force to these ideas in a world characterized by geographical, ideological, and political cleavages, while being largely dependent on factors that are beyond the control of the Court (most importantly the willingness of States and the Security Council to cooperate with the Court).

However, the codification of cosmopolitanism ideals is not confined to the area of international criminal law. Similar elements can be found in areas such as the protection of the global environment, human rights law, peace and security law, the law of sustainable development, or the law of the sea. For some international lawyers, these developments indicate a change in international law that cannot, or at least not without great difficulty, be explained in terms of the inter-State paradigm.[20] The incorporation of cosmopolitan (or "community") values, they argue, challenges the established doctrines and methods of interpretation of international law, moving it from a civil law type of order between

[17] Martti Koskenniemi, "Legal Cosmopolitanism: Tom Franck's Messianistic World," *New York University Journal of International Law and Politics* 35 (2003), p. 476.

[18] Hannah Arendt, *Eichmann in Jerusalem. A Report on the Banality of Evil* (London: Faber and Faber, 1963), pp. 'Eichmann in Jerusalem' (1963), pp. 268–69.

[19] Preamble ICC.

[20] See, *inter alia*: Bruno Simma, "From Bilateralism to Community Interest in International Law," *Recueil des Cours* 250, no. VI (1994).

sovereign states towards a legal order where a variety of subjects are organized under an overarching legal structure that upholds the interests of the international community as such.[21] Speculations about a fundamental transformation of the international legal order, however, are not confined to academic literature. Maybe the most outspoken legal expression of this idea was given by the International Criminal Tribunal for the Former Yugoslavia (ICTY) in the *Tadic* case. In what reads as a rather unapologetic form of cosmopolitan legal reasoning, the ICTY concluded that international law had moved beyond its state-centric confines into the realm of cosmopolitan justice:

> A State-sovereignty-oriented approach has been gradually supplanted by a human-being-oriented approach. Gradually the maxim of Roman law *hominum causa omne jus constitutum est* (all law is created for the benefit of human beings) has gained a firm foothold in the international community as well.[22]

The rise of cosmopolitanism in international law has given new impetus to the questions identified above. If international law indeed seeks to promote the well-being of human beings, as the ICTY seemed to believe, what are the consequences in practice? How does the incorporation of moral cosmopolitanism affect the interpretation and enforcement of law, the way in which political struggles are fought out, the exercise of power? Who is empowered to determine what is in the "benefit of all human beings" in concrete circumstances, who is authorized (or powerful enough) to prioritize the conflicting demands that follow from such abstract maxims?

In light of recent developments in international law, some age-old questions concerning the relation between moral cosmopolitanism and the reality of legal and political institutions thus gained renewed force and relevance. However, there is a second reason for re-examining these questions. From the late 1990s onwards, cosmopolitan thinking has made a sort of comeback in liberal political philosophy. The revival of cosmopolitanism had to do with the rapid developments in international law and politics described above, but also with a more internal-academic event: the publication of John Rawls's papers on international justice, culminating in *The Law of Peoples* in 1999. In

[21] *Ibid.*, p. 217.

[22] *Prosecutor* v. *Dusko Tadic*, Decision on the Defence Motion for Interlocutory Appeal on Jurisdiction, 2 October 1995.

terms of the central *problematique* of this book, Rawls's theory of international justice can be regarded as an attempt to balance normative individualism with the realities of world politics. In his earlier work, Rawls had already articulated a moral position that essentially boiled down to an equal moral concern for individuals: only human beings are self-originating sources of valid claims, while a person's social and natural circumstances such as race, gender, or talents are "arbitrary from a moral point of view." Their effects on an individual's life chances, therefore, ought to be nullified.[23] At the same time, however, Rawls was cautious not to present his principles as full-fledged cosmopolitan claims. He confined his theory of justice to a "self contained" domestic society, seen as "a closed system isolated from others."[24] *The Law of Peoples* did not fundamentally alter this position. The starting point for Rawls's theory of international justice is not the individual as such, but peoples, organized in sovereign states. As a consequence, his basic rules for international conduct come very close to some core principles of existing international (and essentially inter-state) law: sovereignty, self-determination, non-intervention, self-defence, *pacta sunt servanda*; all mitigated by the need to protect the basic rights of individuals.

Well before the 1990s, Rawls's theory of justice had already spurred debates on the possibility and desirability of universalizing his domestic basic principles of justice. Cosmopolitan critics argued that Rawls failed to see the radical implications of his *Theory of Justice*, namely, that it can only be consistently conceived as a theory of *cosmopolitanism* justice. They held that nationality is just another "deep contingency" (like genetic endowment, race, gender, and social class in the domestic theory), one more potential basis of institutional inequalities that are inescapable and present from birth.[25] And since there is no reason within Rawls's model to treat nationality differently, cosmopolitans advocated the application of his principles of justice, not only within a single society but also between individuals across societies. Not surprisingly, these authors remained less than convinced by Rawls's rather traditional, 'Westphalian' approach in *The Law of Peoples*. They argue that their interpretation is the only consistent reading of Rawls's normative axiom of normative individualism that views *human beings*, instead of *compatriots*, are self-originating sources of valid claims, and

[23] Rawls, *A Theory of Justice*, p. 15. [24] *Ibid.*, pp. 457–58.

[25] Thomas Pogge, *Realizing Rawls* (Ithaca: Cornell University Press, 1989), p. 247.

thus deny Rawls's separated approach of domestic and global justice.[26] Indeed, it is fair to say that those cosmopolitans who currently dominate the debate – Charles Beitz, Thomas Pogge, Alan Buchanan, Simon Caney, Kok-Chor Tan, among others – share a simultaneous acceptance *and* refutation of Rawls's work.[27] They all subscribe by and large to a liberal egalitarian position as formulated in Rawls's *two principles* as the normative foundation of their cosmopolitan theories:

> (1) Each person is to have an equal right to the most extensive basic liberties compatible with a similar system of liberty for all; and (2) Social and economic inequalities are to be arranged so that they are both: (a) to the greatest benefit of the least advantaged [the difference principle], and (b) attached to offices and positions open to all under conditions of fair equality of opportunity. [28]

At the same time they refute Rawls's own account of global justice as elaborated in the *Law of Peoples* as too limited, unrawlsian, and merely rules for an already vanished Westphalian world.[29]

However, the ambitious project advocated by cosmopolitans raises fundamental questions concerning the relation between moral cosmopolitanism and institutional reality. Is it really possible to translate the principles of normative individualism into effective global institutions? Will the ideals of inclusiveness and equal moral concern for all survive the marriage between cosmopolitanism and institutional power? As was set out above, cosmopolitanism also has to find a delicate balance between the desiderata of moral universalism and the practicalities of a decentralized and fragmented international world. This means that the cosmopolitan project is always vulnerable to (at least) two types

[26] Allan Buchanan defends a comparable *Natural Duty of Justice*. Buchanan, *Justice, Legitimacy, and Self-Determination*, pp. 86–87.

[27] Allen Buchanan, "Rawls's Law of Peoples: Rules for a Vanished Westphalian World," *Ethics* 110, no. 4 (2000).

[28] Rawls, *A Theory of Justice*, p. 302. Thomas Pogge explicitly dissociates from Rawls's original position and the two principles. See Thomas Pogge, "Three Problems with Contractarian–Consequentialist Ways of Assessing Social Institutions," *Social Philosophy and Policy* 12, no. 2 (1995).

[29] John Rawls, *The Law of Peoples* (Cambridge, Mass.: Harvard University Press, 1999), pp. 115–20. As is well-known, Rawls himself disagrees with this cosmopolitan reading of his domestic work. In his 1999 *Law of Peoples* he presents his favourite extension of the principles of justice for the domestic society to international relations for a *Society of Peoples*. For his criticism of the cosmopolitan interpretation of his work see Costas Douzinas, *Human Rights and Empire: The Political Philosophy of Cosmopolitanism* (Routledge-Cavendish, 2007), p. 177 and p. 176 respectively.

of critique: that of becoming part and parcel of imperialistic politics and that of becoming a pie in the sky.[30] An example of the first type of critique can be found in the work of Douzinas. Douzinas argues that, throughout history, different versions of cosmopolitanism have started as universalistic critiques of local injustices, only to end up as ideologies of imperial rule. Liberal cosmopolitanism, Douzinas argues, does not fare much better as it functions as the "geopolitical framework of the new millennium" and, in its institutionalized form "risks becoming the normative gloss of globalised capitalism at its imperial stage."[31] Scratch a cosmopolitan and you'll find an imperialist just below the surface.[32]

Others have questioned the reality of the cosmopolitan agenda. They argue that "cosmopolitanism seems to have a hard time gripping the imagination"[33] since humanity as a whole is too large and abstract to evoke genuine passions of unity, loyalty, and obligation.[34] In addition, they criticize the impreciseness of cosmopolitanism. Saladin Meckled-Garcia, for example, has argued that cosmopolitan theories of justice generally fail to specify which agent(s) should deliver justice and by which actions they should do so. "Purported principles that do not specify relevant agents must at least be said to be *incomplete* – they are not really principles at all, but descriptions of a desirable state of affairs."[35]

Such critiques force cosmopolitan theories to take a closer and more in-depth look at the institutional implications of their attempts to realize Rawls on a global scale. In order to avert the risks of becoming enlisted in hegemonic projects or being rendered irrelevant for the solution of real life problems, cosmopolitanism has to tackle what Buchanan has called the 'lack of institutional focus' of political philosophers: the tendency to concentrate on principles that govern separate moral issues without due attention for the question what it means if such principles are institutionalized so as to govern a practice that covers many cases:

[30] Note that these critiques bear family resemblances to the critiques that are often raised against mainstream international law. For a discussion see Martti Koskenniemi, *From Apology to Utopia, The Structure of International Legal Argument* (Cambridge: Cambridge University Press, 2005).

[31] Douzinas, *Human Rights and Empire*, p. 177 and p. 176 respectively.

[32] Ronald Beiner as quoted in Catherine Lu, "The One and Many Faces of Cosmopolitanism," *The Journal of Political Philosophy* 8, no. 2 (2000), p. 251.

[33] Nussbaum, "Patriotism and Cosmopolitanism," p. 8.

[34] Lu, "The One and Many Faces of Cosmopolitanism," p. 248.

[35] Saladin Meckled-Garcia, "On the Very Idea of Cosmopolitan Justice: Constructivism and International Agency," *Journal of Political Philosophy* 16, no. 3 (2008), p. 252.

> The simple but neglected point is that one cannot go from a moral argument for the soundness of a particular course of action in a single (usually highly idealized) type of case to a general principle that is suitable for institutionalization. Institutions matter, and if moral principles provide guidance for institutional reform, they must take institutions seriously.[36]

Only if such institutional questions are taken seriously is it possible to assess whether the program of normative individualism is indeed transferable to the global level.

Two caveats are in place on our use of the concept of 'cosmopolitanism.' The book builds on the dominant interpretation of cosmopolitanism in contemporary political philosophy: i.e. cosmopolitanism as a subspecies of liberalism. This does not imply that all cosmopolitan defenses must be liberal (religious thinkers, for instance, have argued for the equal moral standing of moral persons but have argued for illiberal interpretations of those principles) or that all liberal defenses are cosmopolitan (Rawls's *Law of Peoples* is the most obvious argument against the cosmopolitan claim that liberal principles should not be applied to the world as a whole). Rather, it implies that liberalism has become the most important lens through which cosmopolitanism is read in contemporary political philosophy and in international practice. It is, therefore, worthwhile to study the way in which liberal ideals have been translated into existing legal institutions and to examine whether the critical potential of cosmopolitanism has survived its incorporation in the world of law and politics.

Morover, note that this book focuses on cosmopolitanism as normative theory of justice. This means that we will not discuss *cultural cosmopolitanism*, which argues that the good life is not confined to one single cultural tradition but, instead, draws on and integrates various aspects of different cultures.[37] Cosmopolitanism as a cultural phenomenon usually refers to open-mindedness and sophistication, while rejecting nationalism, parochialism, and narrow-mindedness. Although cultural and moral cosmopolitanism refer to similar basic ideas – one's focus should not be restricted to one single cultural tradition but to the world as a whole – they do not coincide. A cultural cosmopolitan does

[36] Buchanan, *Justice, Legitimacy, and Self-Determination*, p. 23.

[37] For a discussion see, *inter alia* Samuel Scheffler, "Conceptions of Cosmopolitanism," *Utilitas* 11 (1999); Jeremy Waldron, "Minority Cultures and the Cosmopolitan Alternative," in *The Rights of Minority Cultures*, ed. Will Kymlicka (Oxford: Oxford University Press, 1995); Kwame Anthony Appiah, *Cosmopolitanism: Ethics in a World of Strangers* (New York: W.W. Norton, 1996).

not need to agree with the basic characteristics of moral cosmopolitanism, i.e. individualism, equality, and obligations to all.

Structure of the book and overview of the chapters

As was set out above, this book discusses the strained relationship between moral cosmopolitanism and institutional reality in five key areas of international law and politics: the protection of the global environment; the World Trade Organization; the United Nations' system of collective security; the International Criminal Court; and transboundary migration.

Part I of this book deals with environmental protection. The chapter by Ellen Hey, 'Global environmental law and global institutions, a system lacking "good process"', discusses the mismatch between substantive and procedural aspects of global environmental law. While substantive legal provisions have codified some core ideas of moral cosmopolitanism, institutional and decision-making structures lag seriously behind. The way in which global environmental law empowers institutions such as the World Bank, Hey argues, disfavours developing States. In this way, the incorporation of moral cosmopolitan elements in substantive law is undermined by the inequality that underlies structures of decision-making. In order to remedy the shortcomings of global environmental law, Hey advocates an interactionist decision-making processes based on procedural fairness, including notions such as transparency, participatory entitlements, and inclusive mechanisms of accountability.

Simon Caney takes a different approach towards problems of environmental degradation in his chapter "Human rights and global climate change." Rather than starting from existing legal instruments, his chapter starts out from the (moral) cosmopolitan assumption that all persons are entitled to protection of their fundamental interests. Caney applies this assumption to the problem of global warming, arguing in favour of a precautionary approach which seeks to prevent the ill effects of global climate change for present and future generations. In the last part of his chapter, Caney develops some methodological devices that help to determine the required level of protection against the (uncertain) outcomes of global climate change. In this way, he provides building-blocks to translate the desiderata of moral cosmopolitanism into a system of positive rights and duties in the area of global warming.

Part II takes up issues related to the World Trade Organisation (WTO). The chapter by Thomas Pogge, "Incentives for pharmaceutical research: must they exclude the poor from advanced medicines?," constitutes an attempt to bridge the gap between moral cosmopolitanism and the realities of contemporary economic life. Based on the cosmopolitan ideal of equal moral concern for the basic needs of all, Pogge critiques the devastating effects of the existing regime for the protection of intellectual property on the global poor. In addition, Pogge's chapter contains concrete proposals for international legal reform, which do justice to the basic interests of the poor and yet contain incentives and rewards for innovation in the pharmaceutical industry.

A different aspect of the WTO regime is discussed in Tomer Broude's chapter, "The WTO/GATS Mode 4, International labor migration regimes and global justice." Broude examines the possible justificatory bases of the legal regime of labor migration (GATS Mode 4). On the basis of an analysis of different theories of global justice, including cosmopolitanism, Broude distils some basic principles that could be used to asses international labor migration regimes. These principles include global distributive justice, human rights protection, effectiveness, and room for emergency safeguards. GATS Mode 4, however, falls short of any of the principles identified by Broude. Those seeking to design a morally sound and practically workable institutional framework for labor migration, he argues, should therefore look beyond the current framework of GATS Mode 4.

Part III discusses issues of collective security and intervention, albeit from two rather divergent angles. Nicholas Tsagourias studies the evolution of the UN system of collective security in his chapter "Cosmopolitan legitimacy and UN collective security." Tsagourias views the UN system as an uneasy compromise between cosmopolitan values on the one hand and state sovereignty and national interest on the other. While the UN system of collective security was built upon cosmopolitan premises, the realities of world politics have forced the UN to constantly reinvent itself in order to retain its legitimacy. Tsagourias analyzes the history of the UN system as a series of attempts to re-establish legitimacy in the face of new challenges. A prime example is the way in which the UN Security Council was transformed from a centralized body that takes the lead in enforcement actions to an institution that dispenses legitimacy to actions initiated by states. Tsagourias's chapter thus demonstrates how an organization based on cosmopolitan principles adapts to a world still largely dominated by sovereign states.

Tan's chapter, "Enforcing cosmopolitan justice: the problem of intervention," contains a reply to those critics who have argued that cosmopolitanism undermines the UN Charter as it is dangerously interventionist by nature. This critique has been voiced by scholars working in a plurality of different traditions, including Rawlsians, mainstream international lawyers, critical theorists, and realists. Tan argues, however, that such critiques are unfounded. While cosmopolitanism takes the way in which states treat their own citizens as a benchmark for their legitimacy, it does not thereby permit all types of responses. If it comes to humanitarian intervention, Tan argues, cosmopolitanism does not deviate much from Rawlsian approaches or from international lawyers who regard interventions legitimate if they are necessary to avert humanitarian emergencies.

Part IV studies the International Criminal Court as an attempt to institutionalize the ideals of moral cosmopolitanism. Both Steven Roach and Victor Peskin, however, caution against overly optimistic readings of the ICC. In his chapter "Rawls's *Law of the Peoples* and the International Criminal Court" Roach criticizes cosmopolitan scholars for side-stepping the realities of inter-state politics. While subscribing to the ideals of moral cosmopolitanism, Roach advocates a more gradual approach in order to realize those ideals. In this context, he argues that Rawls's *Law of Peoples* offers a better starting point than the more ambitious cosmopolitan projects for global justice. In order to illustrate his argument, Roach discusses state cooperation as the "most crucial link between the institutional power of the ICC and the promotion of cosmopolitan ideals …" Roach advocates an interactionist and evolutionary approach to the ICC, which allows for a gradual extension of the ideals of moral cosmopolitanism.

The ambivalent relation between the ICC and state power also figures prominently in Victor Peskin's chapter "An ideal becoming real? The International Criminal Court and the limits of cosmopolitan justice." Peskin analyzes how states have shaped and limited the powers of the ICC and how they continue to affect the functioning of the Court in practice. In this context, he argues that the ICC, which was meant to protect indisputable values and to remain aloof from politics, has actually become part and parcel of domestic and international political struggles. Where Roach witnessed a potential for the gradual spread of cosmopolitan values, Peskin warns against the danger that the Court's dependency on state cooperation will eventually undermine the cosmopolitan ideals of equality and inclusiveness.

Part V is concerned with the issue of international migration. Thomas Spijkerboer presents a critical analysis of contemporary discourses on migration in his chapter "A distributive approach to migration law." According to Spijkerboer, current debates are based on a false dichotomy of cosmopolitanism vs. state sovereignty and persistently ask the wrong question. In the area of migration, Spijkerboer argues, both cosmopolitan approaches and sovereignty-based approaches focus almost exclusively on questions of admission, and end up basically defending existing immigration schemes. Neither of the two approaches pays sufficient attention to what Spijkerboer regards as the most relevant question: how to deal with aliens who are already in the community? His chapter advocates an alternative look on migration issues, which is centered around questions of redistribution and a recognition of the fact that the outsider is part of "our" community.

In contrast to Spijkerboer, Jorge Valadez maintains that questions regarding border control remain important. His chapter, 'Is immigration a human right?', formulates a moderate cosmopolitan justification for the regulation of national borders. Valadez criticizes radical cosmopolitan approaches which define immigration as an individual human right. Such approaches, Valadez argues, neglect the real-life contexts in which migration takes place, undermine the right of self-determination of political communities, and worsen the living conditions of already vulnerable groups. Instead, Valadez advocates a moderate cosmopolitanism which recognizes the importance of self-determination, the need to protect the human rights of those within the territorial boundaries of a political community, and the principle of fair participation in the global system. In the last part of the chapter, Valadez translates these principles into more concrete policy recommendations, thus seeking to bridge the gap between moderate cosmopolitanism and immigration policies.

PART I

Environmental protection

2

Human rights and global climate change

SIMON CANEY

It is now widely accepted that the world's climate is undergoing some profound and long-standing changes. One of the most authoritative sources of information about global climate change is the Intergovernmental Panel on Climate Change (IPCC). In its most recent report, the Fourth Assessment Report, the IPCC confirmed that the Earth's climate is getting warmer and is projected to increase in temperature. It concluded that the Earth has warmed by 0.74 degrees Celsius in the last 100 years and that, furthermore, that "[t]he rate of warming averaged over the last 50 years (0.13°C ± 0.03°C per decade) is nearly twice that for the last 100 years."[1] It devises six different scenarios. According to these six scenarios the likely increase in temperature ranges from 1.1°C to 6.4°C and the likely increase in sea-level ranges from 0.18 metres to 0.59 metres.[2] The IPCC's reports reflect the research of hundreds of climate scientists and represent the most comprehensive and thorough account of the causes and impacts of climate

This research was conducted as part of an Arts and Humanities Research Council research project on "Global Justice and the Environment" and was completed during the tenure of an ESRC Climate Change Leadership Fellowship. I thank the AHRC and the ESRC for their support. I am grateful also to Edward Page for illuminating discussions on the issues examined here. An earlier version of this paper was presented at the Centre for the Study of Social and Global Justice, University of Nottingham (February 2007) and the Symposium on Global Justice, Sovereign Power, and International Law, VU University Amsterdam (March 2007). I am grateful to those present for their questions, and thank, in particular, Mathew Humphrey, Roland Pierik, Matthew Rendall, David Stevens, and Wouter Werner. Sections I, II, and III §1 of this paper draw on Caney "Global Justice, Rights and Climate Change," *Canadian Journal of Law and Jurisprudence* 19, no. 2 (2006), pp. 255–278.

1 Susan Solomon, Dahe Qin and Martin Manning "Technical Summary," in *Climate Change 2007: The Physical Science Basis. Contribution of Working Group I to the Fourth Assessment Report of the Intergovernmental Panel on Climate Change*, ed. Susan Solomon, Dahe Qin, Martin Manning, *et al.* (Cambridge: Cambridge University Press, 2007), p. 36.

2 Solomon *et al.* "Technical Summary," p. 70. It is important to bear in mind that the sea-level projections exclude "future rapid dynamical changes in ice flow."

change as well as what mitigation and adaptation is necessary. It does bear noting, however, that some distinguished climate scientists predict more dramatic changes to the Earth. Stefan Rahmstorf, to give one example, argues that sea levels may rise by more than the IPCC's projections. He argues that by 2100 they may have increased by between 0.5 to 1.4 metres compared to 1990 levels.[3] James Hansen similarly has long drawn attention to the possibility of more serious climate scenarios.[4] In what follows I shall follow the projections produced by the IPCC. I note these other accounts to show that according to some, the IPCC's conclusions may be too conservative.

These changes raise a number of ethical questions. Do future generations have a right not to suffer the ill effects of global climate change? What rights do people have to consume fossil fuels? How much carbon dioxide are people entitled to emit? Some have advocated a human right to a healthy environment and related concepts are affirmed in international law. One important starting point is the 1972 Stockholm Declaration of the United Nations Conference on the Human Environment. Principle 1 of the Declaration maintains that:

> Man has the fundamental right to freedom, equality and adequate conditions of life, in an environment of a quality that permits a life of dignity and well-being, and he bears a solemn responsibility to protect and improve the environment for present and future generations.[5]

A somewhat weaker statement can be found in the Rio Declaration on Environment and Development. Principle 1 of the latter states: "Human beings are at the centre of concerns for sustainable development. They are entitled to a healthy and productive life in harmony with nature."[6] This, notably, eschews the language of rights though it, nonetheless, posits that people are entitled to a healthy environment. In this paper, I wish to argue, along cosmopolitan lines that climate change jeopardizes

[3] Stefan Rahmstorf "A Semi-Empirical Approach to Projecting Future Sea-Level Rise," *Science* 315, no. 5810 (2007), pp. 368–70.

[4] See James Hansen "A Slippery Slope: How Much Global Warming Constitutes 'dangerous anthropogenic interference'?," Climatic Change 68, no. 3 (2005), pp. 269–79.

[5] See www.unep.org/Documents.multilingual/Default.asp?DocumentID=97&ArticleID=1503.

[6] See www.un.org/documents/ga/conf151/aconf15126-1annex1.htm. For a discussion of environmental rights in international law see Patricia Birnie and Alan Boyle *International Law and the Environment* 2nd edn. (Oxford: Oxford University Press, 2002) pp. 252–61 and Philippe Sands Principles of International Environmental Law 2nd edn. (Cambridge: Cambridge University Press, 2003), pp. 294–97.

a number of fundamental human rights.[7] The current consumption of fossil fuels is, I argue, unjust because it generates outcomes in which people's fundamental interests are unprotected and, as such, undermines certain key rights. I further argue that this is unjust whether those whose interests are unprotected are fellow citizens or foreigners and whether they are currently alive or will be born in the future. In this sense, I defend a cosmopolitan perspective on climate change.[8]

This chapter has the following structure. In Section I, I introduce some important methodological preliminaries. Section II introduces the key normative argument – it argues that global climate change damages some fundamental human interests and results in a state of affairs in which the rights of many are unprotected: as such it is unjust. The remaining sections address some complexities that arise because of the particular nature of global climate change. Thus Sections III–IV examine whether the human rights approach can adequately deal with the inter-temporal character of climate change. Section V takes into account the fact that climate change results in risks and uncertainties (rather than known outcomes), and Section VI explores the level of protection from climate harms that persons should be able to claim as a matter of right.

I Methodological preliminaries

Having briefly sketched the nature of global climate change, I want now to address some important methodological preliminaries before then turning to normative argument. We would do well to bear two general points in mind.

First, it may be useful to start by indicating how I shall approach the topics under consideration. How should one reason about global environmental justice in general and global climate change in particular? My answer in response to this has two components. First, global environmental problems, such as climate change, raise questions concerning

[7] See also Tim Hayward *Constitutional Environmental Rights* (Oxford: Oxford University Press, 2005) and James Nickel "The Human Right to a Safe Environment: Philosophical Perspectives on its Scope and Justification," *Yale Journal of International Law* 18, no. 3, pp. 281–95.

[8] It is though deliberately a rather minimal kind of cosmopolitanism and I hope, for that reason, that it will appeal to those who may repudiate more ambitious kinds of cosmopolitanism (for example, those that endorse a kind of global egalitarianism). For my earlier defence of a cosmopolitan political morality see *Justice Beyond Borders: A Global Political Theory* (Oxford: Oxford University Press, 2005).

the distribution of environmental burdens and benefits. They raise, that is, questions of distributive justice. As such we have *pro tanto* reason to draw on the considerable literature on distributive justice and explore its relevance and applicability to environmental concerns. If this is a plausible way of thinking about the distribution of burdens and benefits then there is a *pro tanto* reason to employ it to address the distribution of global environmental burdens and benefits.[9]

However, and this is the second point, in doing so we must accommodate the special features of global environmental problems. What might these special features be? To answer this note that analyses of distributive justice have tended to focus on the distribution of *income and wealth* between the *contemporary* members of one *country*. Each of the underlined terms needs to be adjusted in order to derive principles of global environmental justice. To use the terminology employed by John Rawls we need to address three "problems of extension."[10] *First*, we need to revisit the standard notions of burdens and benefits. In analyses of distributive justice, some think that justice is concerned with "primary goods."[11] Others think that justice is concerned with a persons' "welfare" or the "resources" at their disposal.[12] The point here is that we need to have an answer to the question: in what way does the environment matter for a theory of justice? Does it matter, for example, because it impacts on our level of income and wealth? We can call this first issue – the issue of which environmental goods and bads are to be incorporated into a theory of justice and why – the

[9] For a similar methodological precept see Brian Barry "Sustainability and Intergenerational Justice," in *Fairness and Futurity: Essays on Environmental Sustainability and Social Justice*, ed. Andrew Dobson (Oxford: Oxford University Press, 1999), pp. 93–94: cf. further pp. 96–100.

[10] This term comes from Rawls. See John Rawls "The Law of Peoples," in *Collected Papers* ed. Samuel Freeman (Cambridge, Mass.: Harvard University Press, 1999), p. 531 and Rawls *Political Liberalism* (New York: Columbia University Press, 1993), pp. 20–21. Rawls mentions four problems of extension, namely the challenge of extending his theory to deal with the international domain, future generations, those who are sick, and non-human animals and the natural world, "The Law of Peoples," p. 531. See also Rawls's discussion of constructivism and the problems of extension in "The Law of Peoples," pp. 531–33.

[11] John Rawls *Justice as Fairness: A Restatement* (Cambridge, Mass.: Harvard University Press, 2001), pp. 57–61 and 168–76.

[12] See Ronald Dworkin *Sovereign Virtue: The Theory and Practice of Equality* (Cambridge, Massachusetts: Harvard University Press, 2000), pp. 11–64 (on welfare) and 65–119 (on resources). For an alternative view see G.A. Cohen "On the Currency of Egalitarian Justice," *Ethics* 99, no. 4 (1989), pp. 906–44. For an analysis of these different metrics as they bear on climate change see Edward Page *Climate Change, Justice and Future Generations* (Cheltenham: Edward Elgar Publishers, 2006) ch. 3.

first extension (E-1). *Second*, standard theories of distributive justice focus on the distribution of burdens and benefits between the members of a state. Climate change, however, is a matter of global justice and so we face the question of whether the same principles of justice that apply within the state also obtain at the global level. Or whether none travel, as it were, from the domestic to the global context? Or do some (but not all) principles that apply domestically also apply globally? Our question here, then, is what guidance can domestic principles of distributive justice give to the global environmental question that we face. On the cosmopolitan approach that I defend, the same rights that apply within the state also apply at the global level. We might term this the problem of the second extension (E-2). There is a *third*, and final way, in which global climate change requires revisions to the standard principles of justice. Orthodox treatments of justice focus on the distribution of burdens and benefits between contemporaries. However, global climate change raises questions of inter-generational justice in two distinct ways. First, the ill effects of the high greenhouse gas emissions of current generations will often be borne by future generations. Second, part of the problem facing current and future generations arises because of the policies of past generations. As such we, and future people, inherit problems caused by others. Let us refer to this third challenge – that is, the challenge of ensuring that a theory of justice can deal with the inter-generational aspects of global climate change – the third extension (E-3).

To pull all these points together, we might say that a theory of justice that addresses global climate change should draw on the theories and principles of justice that emanate from the orthodox literature on distributive justice but they must also be revised and extended where that is necessary to deal with the distinctive aspects of global climate change and in particular the three issues just identified (the environmental extension, the international extension and the inter-generational extension).

A second preliminary point that should be noted is that we need to study global climate change (and, indeed, other environmental problems) in conjunction with global economic problems. It is, I think, misplaced to study them in isolation. This holds for three reasons. *First*, the ill effects of global climate change will be felt predominantly by the poor. In the first place many of the global poor are employed in industries, such as agriculture, which would suffer from drought. To give another example, climate change will result in raised sea-levels which will, in turn, adversely affect the inhabitants of Bangladesh. According to Sir John Houghton, if sea levels rise by fifty cm then ten per cent of Bangladesh's habitable land will be lost to the sea and with that 6 million Bangladeshis; and if sea levels rise by one metre then twenty per cent of the land will be lost and 15 million would be affected. Furthermore, sea levels are due to rise by one metre by 2050 (though only thirty cm of this is due to global climate change) and by just under two metres by 2100 (with seventy cm of this being due to global climate change).[13] This will hit its agricultural sector very heavily and, as such, severely threatens the Bangladesh economy which is heavily dependent on its agriculture. Houghton records, for example, that "half the country's economy comes from agriculture and eighty-five per cent of the nation's population depends on agriculture for its livelihood. Many of these people are at the very edge of subsistence."[14] In addition to the fact that the global poor tend to earn their living in ways which are more exposed to the ill effects of global climate change, it also bears noting that the global poor are likely to be disproportionately at risk for a further reason: namely they are more at risk from diseases like malaria and cholera. Further to this, the global poor are less able to adapt to the health-threatening and life-threatening effects of global climate change. So the first point is that global warming will penalize the (future) global poor, worsening their condition further.[15]

A *second* reason why it is inappropriate to analyze global climate change in isolation from global economic justice is that the principles and policies frequently suggested for dealing with global climate change will impact adversely on some people's economic entitlements. For

[13] Sir John Houghton *Global Warming: The Complete Briefing* (Cambridge: Cambridge University Press, 2004) 3rd edn., p. 150.

[14] Houghton *Global Warming*, pp. 150–51. Note also that as well as losing land to the sea, the remaining land will be exposed to greater risks from "storm surges" and will be ruined by saline intrusion (pp. 151–52).

[15] For more on this see Joel B. Smith, Hans-Joachim Schellnhuber, and M. Monirul Qader Mirza "Vulnerability to Climate Change and Reasons for Concern: A Synthesis," in *Climate Change 2001: Impacts, Adaptation, and Vulnerability – Contribution of Working Group II to the Third Assessment Report of the Intergovernmental Panel on Climate Change* ed. James J. McCarthy, Osvaldo F. Canziani, Neil A. Leary, *et al.* (Cambridge: Cambridge University Press, 2001), pp. 916, 940–41 and 957–58; David S.G. Thomas and Chasca Twyman "Equity and Justice in Climate Change Adaptation Amongst Natural-Resource-Dependent Societies," *Global Environmental Change* 15, no. 2 (2005), pp. 115–24; and Richard S.J. Tol, Thomas E. Downing, Onno J. Kuik, *et al.* "Distributional Aspects of Climate Change Impacts," *Global Environmental Change* 14, no. 3 (2004), pp. 259–72. For further discussion see Page *Climate Change, Justice and Future Generations*, p. 35.

example, a large majority of experts on global warming argue that the appropriate response to global climate change is for humans to engage in a policy of 'mitigation'; that is, they should cut back on their fossil fuel consumption.[16] But this may hinder some people's ability to protect their fundamental interests. To give a concrete illustration: levying a charge on imported goods to reflect the carbon emissions involved in their transportation may hit farmers in developing countries very severely. We need therefore a (provisional) account of persons' economic entitlements to assess whether mitigation makes fair or unfair demands of people.

A *third* reason for not analyzing global climate change and economic justice separately is that some of the measures normally suggested for improving the condition of the world's worst off often accelerate global climate change. (This is, in a way, a corollary of the last point.) For example, those who celebrate the importance of economic growth as a means of eradicating poverty may unwittingly cause environmental degradation unless steps are taken to ensure that any development that takes place is clean.

For these three reasons it would be inappropriate to conduct an analysis of the normative issues surrounding global climate change in isolation from an analysis of the nature of global economic justice (and indeed vice versa).[17]

II The main argument

The preceding points provide a necessary background. Let us turn now to the normative issues. In what follows I wish to argue that persons are entitled to the protection of their fundamental interests from the harmful effects of global climate change and it is unjust for other persons to act in ways which would leave people's fundamental interests at risk from the changing climate.

The main argument proceeds as follows. It begins first with the premise that:

(1) A person has a right to X when X is a fundamental interest that is sufficient to impose obligations on others.

[16] See, for example, Sir Nicholas Stern in *The Economics of Climate Change: the Stern Review* (Cambridge: Cambridge University Press, 2007).

[17] It is also, note, similarly inappropriate to analyze the just way to deal with global climate change in isolation from other environmental issues (like, for example, the appropriateness of using nuclear energy).

Here I affirm Joseph Raz's well-known "interest theory" of rights.[18] In Raz's view, rights serve to protect fundamental interests. This claim does make sense of our use of the notion of rights. We ascribe rights to protect highly valued interests (such as liberty of conscience, association, and expression) and our standard ascription of rights is guided by our account of what persons' most important interests are. This is true even of rights that might, at first glance, seem rather trivial such as, for example, the right to decide whether or not to dye one's own hair. What underlies our affirmation of this right is a commitment to a powerful interest – the interest in being autonomous and having the recognized ability to make our own decisions. A system of rights that was indifferent to persons' "higher order interests" (as Rawls calls them)[19], and that was constructed without regard to its impact on persons' fundamental interests would surely be implausible. Indeed it is difficult to think of how one could derive a system of rights that took no account of persons' interests. However, it should also be noted that identifying interests is not sufficient for establishing a right. As Raz's account rightly stresses, interests can ground rights only if they are "sufficient" to generate duties that others must honour.[20] For these reasons we should accept (1).

The next premise in the argument maintains:

(2) Global climate change damages persons' fundamental interests.

This makes both normative and empirical claims for it affirms some fundamental interests and then contends that global climate change damages them. To support (2) we need, then, to identify some vital human interests and ascertain any ways in which climate change harms them. Consider, then, the following interests:

(a) the interest in access to food and water;
(b) the interest in not suffering involuntary loss of life;
(c) the interest in avoiding involuntary threats to persons' health;
(d) the interest in avoiding involuntary displacement; and
(e) the interest in not being deprived of the capacity to develop.

Each of these, I submit, is an important interest.

There is, moreover, extensive evidence from the most recent report of the IPCC (the Fourth Assessment Report) and from other authoritative

[18] See Jozeph Raz *The Morality of Freedom* (Oxford: Clarendon Press, 1986), ch. 7 in general and the formulation on p. 166 in particular.

[19] Rawls *Political Liberalism*, pp. 74ff and 106.

[20] See Raz *The Morality of Freedom*, p. 166.

sources that each of these interests is undermined by the processes of climate change currently underway. Consider first (a) the interest in access to food and water: Temperature increases can lead to drought, desertification, and crop failure and, as such, result in malnutrition and deprivation. According to recent estimates, a temperature increase of 2.5°C will result in an extra 45–55 million people suffering from hunger by the 2080s; a temperature increase of 3°C will result in an increase of 65–75 million people of those who are threatened by hunger; and a temperature increase of 3–4°C will result in an increase of 80–125 million in that category.[21]

Consider now (b): climate change will result in freak weather events and in death from heat stress and, as such, threaten our most fundamental interest – the interest in not suffering involuntary loss of life. If we turn now to, (c), the interest in avoiding involuntary threats to persons' health, the IPCC reports that climate change will generate increased risks of both water-borne and vector-borne diseases.[22] Turning now to (d), the rising sea-levels that accompany climate change are projected to lead to displacement from small island states (including the Maldives, Tuvalu and Kiribati) and from coastal settlements.[23] As reported above (I§2), Bangladesh may be particularly badly affected.

Finally, it is worth drawing attention to the ways in which climate change undermines another core interest (e) – what I have termed "the interest in not being deprived of the capacity to develop." By this I am not claiming (but also, crucially, not denying) that people have an interest in being enabled to develop. My suggestion is the more modest one that persons have an interest in others not acting in ways which harm

[21] Bill Hare "Relationship between Increases in Global Mean Temperature and Impacts on Ecosystems, Food Production, Water and Socio-economic Systems," in *Avoiding Dangerous Climate Change* ed. Hans Joachim Schellnhuber, Wolfgang Cramer, Nebojsa Nakicenovic, *et al.* (Cambridge: Cambridge University Press, 2006) p. 179.

[22] See Ulisses Confalonieri, *et al.* "Human Health" in *Climate Change 2007: Impacts, Adaptation and Vulnerability. Contribution of Working Group II to the Fourth Assessment Report of the Intergovernmental Panel on Climate Change* ed. M.L. Parry, O.F. Canziani, J.P. Palutikof, *et al.* (Cambridge: Cambridge University Press, 2007), pp. 391–431; R.S. Kovats, D. Campbell-Lendrum, and F. Matthies "Climate Change and Human Health: Estimating Avoidable Deaths and Disease," *Risk Analysis* 25, no. 6 (2005), pp. 1409–18; *Climate Change and Human Health: Risks and Responses* ed. A.J. McMichael, *et al.* (Geneva: World Health Organization, 2003).

[23] See Nobuo Mimura, *et al.* "Small Islands," in *Climate Change 2007: Impacts, Adaptation and Vulnerability. Contribution of Working Group II to the Fourth Assessment Report of the Intergovernmental Panel on Climate Change* ed. M.L. Parry, O.F. Canziani, J.P. Palutikof, *et al.* (Cambridge: Cambridge University Press, 2007).

their ability to develop. Climate change, however, clearly does this. For example, raised sea-levels and increased storm surges can destroy vital infrastructure and thereby harm people's capacity to develop. It is worth noting this interest for it may be true of some that climate change does not result in their loss of life or malnutrition or increased poor health or involuntary displacement. And yet they may be adversely affected because their capacity to develop economically has been impaired by others.

For all these reasons, (2) is, I think, a plausible premise: climate change threatens a number of important human interests.[24]

Before we can conclude that there is a right not to suffer from the ill effects of global climate change we need the following premise:

(3) Adequate protection of the interest in not suffering from the ill effects of global climate change does not impose unduly demanding obligations on others.

Two points should be made here. First, (3) is supported by the fact that the interests at stake – e.g. interests in access to food, not being threatened by malaria, cholera, or dengue – are vital ones, the satisfaction of which is normally required for a decent standard of living. In virtue of this they can be said to be sufficient to be the sort of interests that ground rights. But would the correlative obligations be unduly demanding? In which case, is it the case that notwithstanding the importance of the interests there is no right? This is where a second point comes in. It is appropriate here to acknowledge that people obviously have other interests than the interests cited above and, moreover, these interests can involve high fossil fuel consumption. Persons need to be able to use electricity to keep warm, transport goods, cook food, and so on. They might have an interest in using land which will require deforestation and thus contribute to global warming. As such we face the question: Might the interests in "not suffering from climate change" be trumped by the interests in 'using natural resources to support

[24] We should, of course, note that some question the scientific orthodoxy on global climate change. One well-known skeptic is Bjørn Lomborg *The Skeptical Environmentalist: Measuring the Real State of the World* (Cambridge: Cambridge University Press, 2001), ch. 24. More recently a fairly skeptical position was expressed in the recent report of the House of Lords Select Committee on Economic Affairs – *The Economics of Climate Change Volume 1: Report*, the second report of Session 2005–06 (London: the Stationery Office, 6 July 2005) published by the Authority of the House of Lords, HL Paper 12-I.

oneself'?[25] The most effective and appropriate reply to this concern, I believe, is that, in practice, the vital interests adduced in the objection and the vital interests adduced in support of premise (2) can be jointly satisfied. It is, of course, crucial that people have sufficient energy to keep warm, that they can grow crops to support themselves and so on. But the level of greenhouse gas (GHG) emissions that these activities require would not in themselves cause harmful climate change. What do contribute to dangerous climate change are the fossil-fuel intensive practices of the highly affluent industrialized world; and it is certainly possible to cut back on many of their high emission activities without compromising the fundamental interests invoked by the objection. Put in more concrete terms, one can both cut back on emissions and yet protect the vital interests adduced by the objection by cutting back on energy-inefficient cars, reducing the volume of air travel, eliminating poor building insulation, decreasing transportation of goods, using renewable energy sources, and so on. And given the vital nature of the interests cited in support of premise (2) and the *relatively* trivial nature of many climate endangering activities, it is fair to conclude that adequate protection of the interest in not suffering from the ill effects of global climate change does not impose unduly demanding obligations on others.[26] (3) should, thus, be accepted.

Now if we hold that persons have a right to X if X is an interest that is sufficient to generate duties that others must honour (assumption (1)), and if we hold that global climate change jeopardizes fundamental interests (assumption (2)) and that the latter interests are sufficient to generate obligations in others (assumption (3)), it logically follows that:

(C) Persons have a right not to suffer from the ill effects associated with global climate change.

[25] Of course, someone might respond that even if the two sets of interests clash this does not entail that there is not a human right not to suffer from climate change. She might allow that there can be conflicting rights. In this vein she might hold both that the interests adduced in support of premise (2) justify a right not to suffer from dangerous climate change and that the interests mentioned earlier in this paragraph justify a right to activities which generate high levels of greenhouse gas emissions. So the competing interests justify competing rights. This might save the idea that there is a prima facie right not to suffer from climate change but it is small solace if, all things considered, the right to engage in activities which issue high levels of GHGs always takes priority.

[26] See the instructive discussion in Henry Shue "Subsistence Emissions and Luxury Emissions," *Law and Policy* 15, no. 1 (1993), pp. 39–59.

Having outlined the argument it is worth considering how it deals with the three challenges identified earlier. Three points in particular should be made. First, it is fairly clear that the argument presented so far can meet (E-1). It can show why changes to the environment matter – the environmental changes in question harm fundamental interests (E-1). Second, it is also evident that the above argument can meet (E-2). The core premise appeals to the interests that persons have as *humans* and hence can be extended globally (E-2). The argument does not claim either that one subgroup of persons (*Norwegians*, say) has these interests or that it is only their interests that matter. The claim, rather, is that *all* persons possess these interests and, as such, are the bearers of these rights. The above argument thereby justifies a set of *cosmopolitan* rights. The third extension – the inter-generational extension – is, however, much less straightforward and hence requires fuller analysis. For this reason we will explore in later sections whether the argument presented above can be extended to deal with future generations.

More generally, in the remainder of this chapter we shall consider four remaining complications and concerns that need to be addressed. The first two concern whether this argument can be extended to the interests of people in the future (Sections III–IV); a third concerns how this argument deals with risk and uncertainty (Section V); and a fourth concerns how we specify the level of protection to which persons are entitled (Section VI).

III Challenge 1 – future people

One important issue, then, is whether we can legitimately extend the argument developed in Section II to future people. Or does the argument apply only to current generations?

Prior to answering this question it bears noting that some of the ill effects of global climate change are already being felt by current generations. The World Health Organization (WHO) reported in 2004, for example, that in 2000 there were 77,000 deaths due to malnutrition that is attributable to climate change and 47,000 deaths were due to diarrhoea that is attributable to climate change. In addition, the year 2000 saw 27,000 deaths resulting from malaria that stemmed from climate change. Indeed, according to the WHO, the overall total of deaths in 2000 that stemmed from climate change is 166,000 people.[27] So

[27] See Anthony J. McMichael, *et al.* "Chapter 20: Global Climate Change" in *Comparative Quantification of Health Risks: Global and Regional Burden of Disease Attribution to*

although climate change has moral relevance, in part, because of its impact on future people this does not exhaust its moral relevance.

With this duly noted we can turn to the question: can the rights-centered approach defended earlier be extended to future generations? Following the methodological strictures announced above in Section I, the appropriate strategy would seem to be to present the basic case for rights not to suffer from the ill effects of global climate change and then to examine what morally relevant difference, if any, the inter-generational dimension makes.[28]

Let us begin, then, by noting that the premises of the above argument refer to the interests of persons and that the argument itself is animated by a commitment to the impartial treatment of all persons. Given this we have a reason to assume that its conclusions apply to *all* persons, including future persons. If persons, in virtue of their humanity, have interests then this should apply to those who are alive and those who will be born. This point of view is nicely expressed by Joel Feinberg in his seminal paper on "The Rights of Animals and Unborn Generations":

> Five centuries from now men and women will be living where we live now. Any given one of them will have an interest in living space, fertile soil, fresh air, and the like, but that arbitrarily selected one has no other

Selected Major Risk Factors ed. Majid Ezzati, Alan D. Lopez, Anthony Rodgers, *et al.* (Geneva: World Health Organization, 2004), p. 1606. This report has full discussions of climate change induced effects on heat stress, diarrhoea, malnutrition, extreme weather events, and vector borne diseases (pp. 1562–1605).

[28] A similar (though different) strategy is taken by Page in his recent book on climate change. He begins by setting out the case for thinking that anthropogenic climate change that damages the well-being of future people is unjust and then considers counter-arguments which claim that persons lack obligations to future people. Page *Climate Change, Justice and Future Generations* esp. ch. 5 and 6. Page's initial argument for the injustice of climate change is as follows: (P1) "the changes in the climate system that are being brought about by human action threaten the well-being of members of future generations"; (P2) "human action that threatens the well-being of members of future generations is unjust and unethical"; therefore, (P3) "the changes in the climate system that are being brought about by human action are unjust and unethical," *Climate Change, Justice and Future Generations*, p. 9. After the word "ethical," there is a footnote (fn. 40) which attributes this argument to a number of other thinkers. I am in broad agreement with this argument (which Page terms the "Inter-generational Responsibility Argument," p. 9) but note three differences between it and the argument mounted here. First, the Inter-generational Responsibility Argument (IRA) does not invoke the rights of future people, whereas that is a key element in the argument given in Section II. (cf. Page's discussion of the rights of future people in *Climate Change, Justice and Future Generations* pp. 142–150). Second, the IRA argues that threatening the well-being of future people is unjust without examining how onerous that requirement might be on

> qualities we can presently envision very clearly. We don't even know who his parents, grandparents, or great-grandparents are, or even whether he is related to us. Still, whoever these human beings may turn out to be, and whatever they might reasonably be expected to be like, they will have interests that we can affect, for better or worse, right now. That much we can and do know about them. The identity of the owners of these interests is now necessarily obscure, but the fact of their interest-ownership is crystal clear, and that is all that is necessary to certify the coherence of present talk about their rights.[29]

There would seem, then, to be a case for ascribing interests (and hence rights) to future people.

Some dispute this claim and reject all talk of the ascription of rights to future generations. Wilfred Beckerman and Joanna Pasek, for example, maintain that future generations cannot be said to have anything and so cannot be said to have rights. Only entities that currently exist can have rights. As they put the point: "the general proposition that future generations cannot have anything, including rights, follows from the meaning of the present tense of the verb 'to have'. Unborn people simply cannot *have* anything. They cannot have two legs or long hair or a taste for Mozart."[30]

Prior to evaluating this argument we might note that if the above reasoning were correct then it would undermine not simply a rights-centered approach but also the welfarist approach that is dominant among economists. That is, if the claim that "unborn people cannot

earlier generations, whereas that is a key element of the argument of Section II. Third, the IRA, as presented here, limits itself to "the changes in the climate system *that are being brought about by human action*" (p. 9: my emphasis), whereas my argument in Section II applies to all dangerous climate change whether anthropogenic or not.

29 Joel Feinberg, "The Rights of Animals and Unborn Generations," *Rights, Justice, and the Bounds of Liberty: Essays in Social Philosophy* (Princeton: Princeton University Press, 1980), p. 181: cf. further especially pp. 180–83. See, further, the illuminating treatments by Robert Elliott "The Rights of Future People," *Journal of Applied Philosophy*, 6., no. 2 (1989), pp. 159–69, and Lukas H. Meyer "Past and Future: The Case for a Threshold Notion of Harm," in *Rights, Culture, and the Law: Themes from the Legal and Political Philosophy of Joseph Raz* ed. Lukas H. Meyer, Stanley L. Paulson, and Thomas W. Pogge (Oxford: Oxford University Press, 2003), pp. 143–59.

30 *Justice, Posterity, and the Environment* (Oxford: Oxford University Press, 2001), p. 16. See Beckerman and Pasek *Justice, Posterity, and the Environment*, pp. 11–28. See also Ruth Macklin "Can Future Generations Correctly be Said to Have Rights?" and Robert T De George "The Environment, Rights, and Future Generations," both in *Responsibilities to Future Generations: Environmental Ethics* ed. Ernest Partridge (Buffalo, New York: Prometheus Books, 1981). I have omitted a footnote from this passage (fn. 11) in which Beckerman and Pasek cite work by De George, Macklin, and others.

have anything" establishes that they cannot have rights then it would also equally establish that they cannot have utility functions either. Thus if Beckerman and Pasek are right, then, we should also conclude that consequentialist analyses cannot be applied to future generations, and must include only the utility functions of existing people.[31]

A defender of a welfarist approach is likely to reply that future people will have utility functions. But, as many defenders of rights have noted, exactly the same point can be made by defenders of rights. This point is made by Robert Elliott who persuasively defends what he terms the "Concessional View."[32] This eschews the claim that future people currently hold rights and asserts instead that future people will have rights. A corollary of this is that other persons are under a duty not to act in ways which prevent people from being able to enjoy these rights. This, however, has the implication that people alive at t1 are under a duty not to act in ways which prevent people at t1+50 from being able to enjoy their rights. A rights-centered analysis can thus cope with the inter-generational character of climate change. It holds that members of the current generation are under a duty not to act in ways which will undermine or violate the rights that future people will have.[33] And when applied to the case of climate change this entails that current generations should reduce greenhouse gas emissions to such a level that their behavior does not create threats which will undermine or violate the rights that future people will have.

IV Challenge 2 – pure time discounting

Consider now a second issue. On some accounts, the inter-temporal character of climate change is morally significant, not because rights cannot be ascribed to future generations, but because a defensible public policy should adopt a positive pure time discount rate. That is to

[31] Compare with Joerg Chet Tremmel "Establishing Intergenerational Justice in National Constitutions," in *Handbook of Intergenerational Justice* ed. Joerg Chet Tremmel (Cheltenham: Edward Elgar, 2006), p. 200.

[32] Elliott "The Rights of Future People," especially pp. 160 and 162ff.

[33] Elliott "The Rights of Future People," p. 162. See, further, Simon Caney "Human Rights, Responsibilities and Climate Change" in *Global Basic Rights* ed. Charles Beitz and Robert Goodin (Oxford: Oxford University Press, 2009), pp. 234–36. For instructive discussions see Feinberg "The Rights of Animals and Unborn Generations," pp. 181–82; Meyer "Past and Future: The Case for a Threshold Notion of Harm," p. 145; and Axel Gosseries "On Future Generations," Future Rights," *Journal of Political Philosophy*, 16, no. 4 (2008), especially pp. 455–58.

say, governments should accord diminishing weight to the interests of people the further off in time they are. A number of prominent economists have taken this view.[34] Others, though, have adopted a zero pure time discount view.[35] Note that a great deal hangs on this issue, for the less weight that is given to future generations the weaker is the case for mitigating dangerous climate change.

I suggest that the human rights jeopardized by dangerous climate change should not be subject to a positive pure time discount rate. The reasoning underpinning the rights – namely that there are basic interests which justify the imposition of duties on others – accords no moral relevance to time. It refers only to (a) the centrality of the interests and (b) the reasonableness of the demands on others and, given these two factors, if two persons have the same interest and the protection of these interests imposes the same costs on others then they should both enjoy a right of exactly the same weight. Temporal location in itself has no deep moral significance. There is, therefore, no case for attributing a lesser standing to the rights of some rather than others.

Many are, however, strongly committed to discounting. What arguments might one adduce for a positive pure time discount rate? Two arguments are often advanced.

Argument 1: First, some argue that people generally prefer pleasures to occur earlier in time rather than later. From this (alleged) fact that people act on pure time preference they conclude that current generations should/are entitled to adopt a positive pure time discount rate. There are two obvious problems with this. First, even if many do prefer

[34] See William D. Nordhaus "A review of the *Stern Review on the Economics of Climate Change*," *Journal of Economic Literature* 45, no. 3 (2007), pp. 686–702; Martin L. Weitzman "A review of the *Stern Review on the Economics of Climate Change*," *Journal of Economic Literature*, 45, no. 3 (2007), pp. 703–24.

[35] For an eloquent statement of this position by a utilitarian see Henry Sidgwick's discussion in *The Methods of Ethics*. Sidgwick writes: "it may be asked, How far we are to consider the interests of posterity when they seem to conflict with those of existing human beings? It seems, however, clear that the time at which a man exists cannot affect the value of his happiness from a universal point of view; and that the interests of posterity must concern a Utilitarian as much as those of his contemporaries, except in so far as the effect of his actions on posterity – and even the existence of human beings to be affected – must necessarily be more uncertain," *Methods of Ethics* (Indianapolis: Hackett Publishing Company, 1981 [1907]), Book IV ch. I §2, p. 414. See also Frank Ramsey "A Mathematical Theory of Saving," *Economic Journal*, 38, no. 152 (1928), p. 543. For a brilliant modern discussion see Parfit *Reasons and Persons* (Oxford: Oxford University Press, 1984), pp. 480–86. A zero pure time discount rate is also famously adopted by Stern in *The Economics of Climate Change*, especially pp. 35–37 and 50–60.

that pleasures occur earlier in their life rather than later this preference does not entail that it is obligatory to do so or even that it is permissible to do so. One cannot derive a moral duty (or permission) to discount just from the fact that many prefer to do so. Second, as Thomas Schelling observes, one cannot move from the case of discounting within a person's life to determining whether discounting between generations is appropriate. That I might want a unit of pleasure to occur earlier in my life rather than later in my own life does not establish that it is permissible that I enjoy a unit of pleasure in my life rather than that some future person enjoy that same quantity.[36]

Argument 2: Consider now a second, more promising, argument against a zero discount rate: the view that it is excessively demanding. It may demand one generation make a large sacrifice and thereby reduce its members to a pitiful level if by doing so it would benefit successive generations by an amount that is greater than the burden that its members suffer. This, it seems, is unreasonably demanding. This troubling conclusion, they point out, can, however, be avoided if we posit a positive pure time discount rate. A zero pure time discount rate, however, leaves us committed to imposing heavy sacrifices on any generation to promote the well-being of its successors.[37]

This argument is, however, also unpersuasive for, on its own, a zero pure time discount rate does *not* impose unduly demanding requirements on current generations. It may do so if, for example, we combine it with a maximizing consequentialism. This might indeed require large sacrifices of current generations. But I am not defending a maximizing consequentialism or indeed a view that maximizes anything. Rather I am arguing that current generations should respect the human rights of current and future people and this makes far less onerous demands.

[36] Thomas Schelling "Intergenerational Discounting," *Energy Policy* 23 nos. 4/5, p. 396. See Simon Caney "Climate Change, Human Rights and Discounting," *Environmental Politics* 17, no. 4 (2008), especially p. 544.

[37] For a classical statement of this objection see Tjalling Koopmans "Objectives, Constraints, and Outcomes in Optimal Growth Models," *Econometrica* 35, no. 1 (1967), (especially his discussion of what he terms "the paradox of the indefinitely postponed splurge" (p.8)). See also Lomborg *The Skeptical Environmentalist*, p. 314 and David Pearce, Ben Groom, Cameron Hepburn, and Phoebe Koundouri "Valuing the Future: Recent Advances in Social Discounting," *World Economics* 4, no. 2 (2003), pp. 124–25. Kenneth Arrow also makes a similar point: see his "Discounting, Morality, and Gaming," in *Discounting and Intergenerational Equity* ed. Paul R. Portney and John P. Weyant (Washington DC: Resources for the Future, 1993), pp. 14–16.

The view that human rights should be subject to a zero discount rate is, therefore, not vulnerable to concerns about unfairly demanding duties.[38]

Furthermore, even if we set this aside, and even if we work with a maximizing consequentialism, it is not clear that a zero pure time discount rate would necessarily generate excessively demanding demands. It may appear this way if we focus solely on the claims that, (i), current generations should maximize well-being and, (ii), they should adopt a zero pure time discount rate. However, once we add two other considerations into the picture the situation changes. Suppose, for example, that, as many economists assume, (iii), future generations will be wealthier than earlier generations. Suppose also that, (iv), the principle of diminishing marginal utility applies. Now if we combine (iii) and (iv) there is a strong case for devoting resources to current generations over future generations. Given that they are likely to be less affluent than future generations current generations would benefit more than future people for each extra unit of wealth. Thus whereas (i) combined with (ii) may give us reason to devote resources to future generations, (iii) combined with (iv) adds a corrective tendency in the other direction (giving us reason to devote resources to current generations). In short, when we put the pure time discount rate into a broader context it is not self-evident that the ensuing policy will be unduly demanding.

The claim that the human rights jeopardized by climate change should not be subject to a positive pure time discount rate thus remains intact.

V Challenge 3 – risk and uncertainty

Having considered two issues concerning the scope of the rights defended in Section II we may turn now to consider a third complication. This complication arises because the harms referred to by the climate scientists are not presented as certainties but as risks or uncertainties.

[38] As Broome expresses the point "[i]f excessive sacrifice should be avoided, that fact should be incorporated into the value function in a different way. A natural way would be to fix some minimum level of well-being below which no generation should fall," *Counting the Cost of Global Warming* (Cambridge: The White Horse Press, 1992), p. 106. As he notes, this point has also been made by Rawls and Parfit. See Rawls's argument that the problem is with a maximizing view and to add discounting is just an "ad hoc" solution (*A Theory of Justice* (Oxford: Oxford University Press, 1999) Revised edition, p. 262) and Parfit's discussion in *Reasons and Persons*, pp. 484–85. For further discussion see Caney "Climate Change, Human Rights and Discounting," especially pp. 548–50.

This observation could change how we define the rights in question. More radically, it might undermine the plausibility of a rights-centered approach altogether. Many writers are, for example, skeptical of the ability of a rights approach to cope with risk and uncertainty. Dennis McKerlie, for example, writes that: "the rights view cannot answer questions about risk."[39] Moreover, even Robert Nozick acknowledges that: "[a]ctions that risk crossing another's boundary pose serious problems for a natural-rights position."[40]

In what follows I hope to show that a rights-oriented approach can cope with risk and uncertainty *and* that when applied to climate change it defends a broadly precautionary perspective. This last point calls for some clarification for the precautionary principle (or as some prefer to call it the "precautionary approach") has been formulated in different ways and it is important to be clear what I am claiming here. One version of the precautionary principle is affirmed in Principle 15 of the Rio Declaration on Environment and Development. This states that:

> In order to protect the environment, the precautionary approach shall be widely applied by States according to their capabilities. Where there are threats of serious or irreversible damage, lack of full scientific certainty shall not be used as a reason for postponing cost-effective measures to prevent environmental degradation.[41]

A similar but non-identical statement appears in Article 3.3 of the United Nations Framework Convention on Climate Change (UNFCCC). This states that:

> The Parties should take precautionary measures to anticipate, prevent or minimize the causes of climate change and mitigate its adverse effects. Where there are threats of serious or irreversible damage, lack of full scientific certainty should not be used as a reason for postponing such measures, taking into account that policies and measures to deal with climate change should be cost-effective so as to ensure global benefits at the lowest possible cost. To achieve this, such policies and measures should take into account different socio-economic contexts, be comprehensive, cover all relevant sources, sinks and reservoirs of greenhouse gases and adaptation, and comprise all economic sectors. Efforts to address climate change may be carried out cooperatively by interested Parties.[42]

[39] David McKerlie "Rights and Risk," *Canadian Journal of Philosophy* 16, no. 2 (1986), p. 251.
[40] Robert Nozick *Anarchy, State and Utopia* (Oxford: Blackwell, 1974), p. 74.
[41] See www.un.org/documents/ga/conf151/aconf15126–1annex1.htm.
[42] See http://unfccc.int/resource/docs/convkp/conveng.pdf. Instructive analyses of the status of the precautionary principle in international environmental law can be

My claim, here, is animated by a similar thought to those contained in both of these formulations. Nonetheless, as we shall see, it differs from both. For example, by contrast with both of these statements it puts human rights at its core.

How, though, might one employ the concept of human rights to deal with the risks and uncertainties associated with the projected impacts? One response might be to argue that persons have a right not to be exposed to *any* risk of a harm from other people.[43] A second response might be to argue that persons have a right not to be exposed to an *unreasonably high level of* a risk of a harm from other people. So this second view requires us to specify what constitutes an unreasonably high probability of a harm.[44] One might then apply either of these views to climate change and thereby seek to develop a rights-oriented response to climate change.

Here, however, I propose an alternative approach – one that focuses on the duties of major social and political institutions not to risk the rights of those whose lives they affect. Stated baldly, its key claim is this: *actors should not pursue a course of action which runs a non-negligible risk of violating the human rights of others when they can pursue alternative courses of action without compromising their or other people's human rights*. To carry on with the risky behaviour in such circumstances (simply because one enjoys the benefits, say, of air travel or airconditioning or wasteful energy use) when one could do otherwise without loss of human rights is to treat others without due respect for their rights. It is perhaps arguable that one might be entitled to expose others to risk when that is necessary to uphold one's own rights.[45] However, to expose others to non-negligible risk of violating their human rights when there are no equivalent extenuating circumstances (such as 'this activity is

found in Jonathan B. Weiner "Precaution," in *The Oxford Handbook of International Environmental Law* ed. Daniel Bodansky, Jutta Brunnée, and Ellen Hey (Oxford: Oxford University Press, 2007), pp. 597–612, Birnie and Boyle *International Law and the Environment*, pp. 115–21; Sands *Principles of International Environmental Law*, pp. 266–79.

43 See David McCarthy "Rights, Explanation, and Risks," *Ethics*, 107, no. 2 (1997), pp. 205–25. McCarthy defends what he terms the "Risk Thesis" where this holds that "we have the right that other people not impose risks of harm upon us," p. 208.

44 This second view is discussed and criticized by McCarthy, "Rights, Explanation, and Risks," especially pp. 212–14) and McKerlie, "Rights and Risk," especially pp. 247–48.

45 Relatedly, the fact that one policy exposes others to risk of a serious harm is not on its own sufficient to condemn that policy. (It might, for example, be the case that all the other options are even worse.) This is a point stressed by Cass Sunstein in *Laws of Fear: Beyond the Precautionary Principle* (Cambridge: Cambridge University Press, 2005), pp. 26–34.

necessary to protect the rights of others/ourselves') is to show an unjustified and reckless disregard for them.

Now the *proposed* principle has quite clear implications for climate change because we have good reason to accept that:

(1) If greenhouse gases continue to be emitted so that their atmospheric concentration exceeds a certain level then there is a high probability that continued emissions will jeopardize the fundamental *human rights* of many people; and
(2) Humanity can reduce emissions to such a level that they do not produce a high probability of a *human rights*-endangering climate, without compromising other human rights.[46]

Thus, given the claim that:

(3) Actors should not pursue a course of action which runs a non-negligible risk of violating the *human rights* of others when they can pursue alternative courses of action without compromising their or other people's *human rights,*

it follows (from (1), (2) and (3)) that:

(4) Humanity should reduce greenhouse levels to such a level that they do not produce a high probability of a *human rights*-endangering climate.

Consider now (1) and (2) in more detail. (1) is based on the recognition that once the concentration of greenhouse gases in the atmosphere

[46] My invocation of (1) and (2) in support of a precautionary policy is in line with Stephen Gardiner's excellent treatment of the precautionary principle in "A Core Precautionary Principle," *Journal of Political Philosophy* 14, no. 1 (2006), pp. 33–60. Gardiner draws on Rawls's maximin principle to construct what he terms the "Rawlsian Core Precautionary Principle" (p. 48). The latter holds that precaution is appropriate when (i) there is uncertainty, (ii) people do not particularly value increases above the kind of minimum guaranteed by the maximin principles and (iii) people strongly object to falling below a minimum standard (p. 47). As he says, this interpretation of the precautionary principle entails that we should adopt a precautionary approach to global climate change (p. 55). See also Gardiner's judicious analysis of the precautionary principle in "Ethics and Global Climate Change," *Ethics* 114, no. 3 (2004), especially p. 577 and Henry Shue's illuminating "Deadly Delays, Saving Opportunities: Creating a More Dangerous World?" in *Climate Ethics* ed. Stephen Gardiner, Simon Caney, Dale Jamieson, and Henry Shue (New York: Oxford University Press, 2009). My proposal differs from both by giving a central place to the concept of human rights. For a fuller statement of my approach (on which I draw here) see Caney "Climate Change and the Future: Time, Wealth and Risk," *Journal of Social Philosophy* 40, no. 2 (2009), pp. 177–81.

passes a certain point then additional emissions increasingly jeopardize the human rights of some. The level (or, more likely, the range of atmospheric concentration) at which this occurs need not detain us here.[47] The key point is that after a certain point, additional emissions will increasingly risk dangerous climate change. Furthermore, the Fourth Assessment Report finds that, given the past and current levels of emissions, it is already "likely" that, in this century, there will be droughts, more frequent intense cyclones, and extreme sea-level rises. Heatwaves and extreme precipitation are said to be "very likely" and increased temperatures are "virtually certain."[48] (1) is, thus, very plausible.

Consider now (2). (2) claims that humanity can mitigate dangerous climate change without undermining any fundamental human rights. This claim needs to be unpacked. Note, first, that (2) makes reference to "humanity." It does so because whether the emission of greenhouse gases risks damaging human rights or not depends on the total volume of greenhouse gases emitted by *all humanity*. Thus (2) claims that *humanity* can avert causing dangerous climate change without compromising people's human rights in the process. Now note that my affirmation of (2) depends on two further specific assumptions. First, it assumes, (i), that the largest part of this burden should be met by affluent members of the world, and *not* by the global poor. (If we were to attribute a large share of the burden to the global poor then it would not be the case that they can mitigate without compromising their or other people's rights.) Elsewhere I have defended this normative claim about how the burden of mitigation should be shared by appealing to a combination of the "Polluter Pays" Principle and an "Ability to Pay" Principle.[49] I here assume that that analysis is correct and thus that the global poor are not required to make onerous sacrifices to mitigate climate change. Second, note also that (2) assumes, (ii), that the advantaged members of the world can mitigate without loss of human rights. They can do so, for example, by adopting greater energy efficiency (via, for example, better insulated homes), by using other energy sources (like renewable energy

[47] It is often said to be between 450 and 550 ppm CO_2 equivalent (CO_2e). See, for example, Stern *The Economics of Climate Change*, ch. 8. See, though, James Hansen, *et al.* "Target atmospheric CO_2: Where should humanity aim?" *The Open Atmospheric Science Journal*, 2 (2008), pp. 217–31.

[48] Solomon et al "Technical Summary," in *Climate Change 2007: The Physical Science Basis*, p. 52.

[49] See Caney "Climate Change, Justice and the Duties of the Advantaged," *Critical Review of International Social and Political Philosophy*, 12, no. 2 (2009) and "Human Rights, Responsibilities and Climate Change."

sources) and by expending less energy on non-vital interests.[50] (2) is, therefore, also highly plausible.

In short, then, we have seen that there is an intuitively plausible way of combining risk and rights (principle (3)) and, moreover, that when this is combined with two facts about climate change ((1) and (2)) it supports a precautionary approach to anthropogenic climate change. Humanity (most notably the global advantaged) are under a duty not engage in behavior which (a) imposes a non-negligible risk of harming the human rights of others when (b) they can abstain from this behavior without loss of their own (or others') human rights.

VI Challenge 4 – what is the fair level of protection?

Thus far we have addressed three questions that arise from the claim that climate change is unjust, in part, because it jeopardizes human rights. In this last section, we turn to consider a fourth issue, namely: *How much* protection does the right not to suffer from climate change require? To what level of protection from climate change are people entitled as a matter of right?

Prior to answering this question, two points need to be observed. First, note that the question "how much protection does the right not to suffer from climate change require?"' cannot be given a fully adequate answer without considering the claims of later generations. What rights current people can claim will depend, in part, on our provisional assumptions about what it is fair to leave future people (and vice versa). The reason for this is straightforward: the resources involved in upholding the rights of some (at t1) affect the resources available to uphold the rights of others (at t2) and, by the same token, the reverse is also true. Our answer to the question at hand thus inescapably has an inter-generational character. Second, our answer to the question at hand must be consistent with the conclusions reached in section IV: that is, the human rights in question should not be subject to a positive pure time discount rate. Thus it would be inappropriate to accord

[50] For two important discussions of how greenhouse gas emissions can be reduced (both of which draw attention to some ways in which the duty to mitigate can be met without compromising human rights) see Jon Creyts, *et al. Reducing U.S. Greenhouse Gas Emissions: How Much at What Cost? U.S. Greenhouse Gas Abatement Mapping Initiative Executive Report December 2007* (McKinsey and Company, 2007), and Stephen Pacala and Robert Socolow "Stabilization Wedges: Solving the Climate Problem for the Next 50 Years with Current Technologies," *Science* 305, no. 5686 (2004), pp. 968–72.

lesser weight to the human rights of some *purely on the basis of considerations about their place in time.*

With these duly noted, let us turn directly to the question of how the level of protection (from the possible ill effects of climate change) should be handled between people who live in different generations.

Some might suggest that persons in one generation should act so that all future people have the same risks as they themselves have. On this egalitarian view members of any one generation have a duty (i) not to leave the world worse off than it was when they reached adulthood but they also have a duty (ii) not to leave it any better off either.[51]

This uncompromising egalitarianism has an intuitive appeal but it runs into problems because it ignores the different challenges facing different generations and the different costs to different generations of maintaining this equality. To see this consider some examples:

> I: First, suppose that members of one generation, G1, face an incredibly low risk of suffering from climate-related harm. Indeed the risks are so low that the members of G1 think that it would not be at all be unfair to face higher risks. Now suppose that to ensure that members of future generations enjoy such exceptionally low risks would require an enormous sacrifice on G1. Here it seems unreasonable to insist on equality because it would impose *enormously onerous burdens* on the contemporary generation to reduce the risks of future generations to what is an unnecessarily low level. Egalitarianism here asks too much of current generations.
>
> II: Suppose, now, that one generation, G1, faces unduly high risks. Suppose, however, that G1 could act in such a way that would lower this risk for future generations (but not for itself), and suppose, moreover, that G1 could do so without imposing undue costs on itself. In such circumstances G1 should surely lower the risks for its successors. In doing so, however, it would produce an inequality for it would render successor generations better off than itself and this violates equality. The case for doing so, however, seems strong: the inequality would *greatly benefit* later generations and generates *minimal* costs on G1. Egalitarianism here asks too little of current generations.[52]

[51] For this kind of view see Brian Barry "The Ethics of Resource Depletion," in *Liberty and Justice: Essays in Political Theory Volume 2* (Oxford: Clarendon Press, 1991), p. 263.

[52] This last point is, of course, one version of the "levelling down" objection. For a much fuller exploration of this objection (in the context of an evaluation of the appropriateness of adopting an egalitarian approach to climate change) see Edward Page's instructive discussion in *Climate Change, Justice and Future Generations*, especially pp. 80–82 and in "Justice Between Generations: Investigating a Sufficientarian Approach," *Journal*

The key point that these examples bring out is that any adequate principle of inter-generational justice must factor in both the costs to any current generation, on the one hand, and the benefits to future people, on the other, and it needs to find some way of giving both their due. An inter-generational principle of equality, I have argued, does not perform that role.

Drawing on the failings of the egalitarian approach, I want to consider an alternative answer. This takes its cue from a suggestion made by Rawls. Rawls writes:

> The parties can be required to agree to a savings principle subject to the further condition that they must want all *previous* generations to have followed it. Thus the correct principle is that which the members of any generation (and so all generations) would adopt as the one their generation is to follow and as the principle they would want preceding generations to have followed (and later generations to follow), no matter how far back (or forward) in time.[53]

This approach has two virtues. First, it takes on board the interests of both present generations and also past generations and it requires people to balance both. People can advance their own interests (because the rule selected has to be one that they can live with) and hence they will not select an unduly demanding rule. At the same time, people are constrained to take into account the interests of others (because the rule selected has to be one that they are willing for others to have adopted) and hence they will not select an unduly undemanding rule. The Rawlsian procedure thus compels people to think of both the demands that a principle of inter-generational principle of justice imposes and also the benefits it can yield. As such it compels people to think in an impartial fashion. Put otherwise, we might say that the Rawlsian procedure takes into account the point of view of both the duty-bearers (people have to choose a principle they could comply with) and the

of Global Ethics 3, no. 1 (2007), especially pp. 5–7. Page explores the resources available to egalitarians to meet this objection but finds them ultimately unpersuasive and favours a sufficientarian approach (most clearly in "Justice Between Generations"). The "levelling down" objection has received much discussion. For an influential analysis see Parfit's seminal treatment of it in "Equality and Priority," *Ratio* 10, no. 3 (1997), pp. 211 and 218–20.

53 Rawls *Political Liberalism*, p. 274. A footnote (fn. 12) has been omitted. As Rawls notes there, the account here differs somewhat from the original treatment in *A Theory of Justice*. The position captured in the text above is, however, in the revised edn. of *A Theory of Justice*, p. 255 and in *Justice as Fairness: A Restatement*, p. 160.

rights-bearers (people have to choose a principle that they would want others to have adopted). The Rawlsian procedure thus succeeds where the egalitarian principle fails.

Second, the Rawlsian procedure, by contrast with the strict egalitarian formula discussed above, is flexible for it can take into account the differing circumstances faced by different generations. Persons in the Rawlsian contract act so that the principle of inter-generational justice is not too demanding and to do that they must take on board the different circumstances that members of different generations enjoy. As such it will not be vulnerable to the type of counter-examples that apply to the egalitarian view.

On this basis, then, I propose that the right not to suffer from the ill effects of global climate change should be understood to mean that each generation should bestow on following generations the level of protection that it is willing to apply to others and which it would want preceding generations to have applied to it.

VII Conclusion

Some affirm a very minimal set of rights and would be skeptical of extending this set to include "environmental" rights of any kind. In this paper I have argued that the kinds of considerations that we normally invoke to defend human rights entail that persons have a human right not to suffer from the ill effects of global climate change. More precisely, I have argued that persons have human rights to a decent standard of health, to economic necessities, and to subsistence. I have further argued that anthropogenic global climate change undermines these human rights. In the remainder of the paper I have sought to defend this claim against critics and to render it more precise. In particular I have considered the arguments of those who dispute whether future people hold these rights and those who argue that the rights of future people should be subject to a positive discount rate. Neither challenge is, however, persuasive. The paper then concludes by trying to accommodate the risky and uncertain nature of climate change and by seeking to determine the fair level of protection that current and future people can claim as a matter of right.

3

Global environmental law and global institutions: a system lacking "good process"

ELLEN HEY

Introduction

This chapter illustrates the extent to, and manner in which, international environmental law has moved beyond the inter-state paradigm, central to classical international law, hence the term "global environmental law." It makes the point that while elements that signify a departure from the inter-state paradigm can be identified in terms of both substantive law and institutional and decision-making patterns, global environmental law harbors a mismatch between these two interrelated aspects of law. On the one hand, substantive law reflects ideals associated with moral cosmopolitanism; on the other hand, the institutional and decision-making patterns take away from those ideals by the manner in which they empower global institutions. In global environmental law this development is particularly apparent in the South–North context. In this context, general principles that mark a departure from the discretionary role of states and instead reflect ideals of moral cosmopolitanism have been introduced. Concomitantly, global institutions, the World Bank in particular, have been endowed with discretionary public powers, powers that are exercised with regard to developing states and individuals and groups in developing states, in particular. This development entails that the ensuing legal system does not meet standards of justice, irrespective of whether justice is conceptualized as international, that is inter-state, justice, or in terms of moral

Ellen Hey is Professor and Head of the Department of Public International Law, Erasmus University Rotterdam. I am grateful to Jutta Brunnée for sharing with me her thoughts on further development of the interactional theory of international law and to Jutta Brunnée, Roland Pierik, and Wouter Werner for valuable comments on earlier versions of this essay. Thanks are due to Michelle Rodenburg, my student assistant, for helping me find materials for this essay. The usual disclaimer applies.

cosmopolitanism, focusing on attaining justice for individuals.[1] This essay, then, suggests that global environmental law, due to its institutional and decision-making patterns, ultimately does not focus on the equal moral worth of all persons and does not reflect the ideal that this understanding of persons results in the generation of obligations binding on all.[2] This chapter, due to the often limited focus on institutional aspects, questions whether theories of moral cosmopolitanism offer the most fruitful perspective from which to address the mismatch between substantive law and the institutional and decision-making patterns applicable in global environmental law.

The institutional and decision-making patterns, in addition to the substantive aspects, of global environmental law merit the attention of legal scholars and political theorists alike. The focus of analysis should include the manner in which these patterns continue to foster inequality between developing and developed states and between individuals and groups in these states[3] (part of "the dark, non-progressive side of international law"), despite the "narratives of progress and development" that the substantive aspects of global environmental law promise.[4] This chapter suggests that interactional decision-making processes, which can be established and maintained through law by focusing also on law's communicative function and can foster justice, may serve to illuminate global environmental law.[5] By implication, this chapter assumes that

[1] For a similar point made with regard to "global administrative law" see B.S. Chimni, "Cooption and Resistance: Two Faces of Global Administrative Law" (2005); IILJ Working Paper No. 2005/16, available at: http://iilj.org/publications/2005-16Chimni.asp (accessed 14 February 2010). On international and global justice see Chris Brown, "From International to Global Justice?" in *Oxford Handbook of Political Theory*, ed. John S. Dryzek, Bonnie Honig, and Anne Phillips (Oxford: Oxford University Press, 2006), p. 621.

[2] See the introduction to this book.

[3] See Anthony Anghie, "Colonialism and the Birth of International Institutions," *NYU Journal of International Law and Politics*, 34 (2002), p. 513; Thomas Pogge, "The Influence of the Global Order on the Prospects for Genuine Democracy in Developing Countries" *Ratio Juris* 14 (2001), p. 326; Thomas Pogge, "Incentives for Pharmaceutical Research: Must They Exclude the Poor from Advanced Medicines?," this book.

[4] The quoted words are from Hilary Charlesworth and David Kennedy, "Afterword: and forward – there remains so much we do not know," in *International Law and its Others*, ed. Anne Orford (Cambridge: Cambridge University Press, 2006), p. 406.

[5] See Jutta Brunnée and Stephen Toope, "International Law and Constructivism: Elements of an Interactional Theory of International Law" *Columbia Journal of Transnational Law* 39 (2000); Wibren van der Burg, "The Morality of Aspiration: A Neglected Dimension of Law and Morality," in *Rediscovering Fuller, Essays on Implicit Law and Institutional Design* ed. Willem J. Witteveen and Wibren van der Burg (Amsterdam: Amsterdam University Press, 1999), p. 169. Van der Burg, expanding upon Fuller, illustrates how the

individuals, society, and law have the potential to engage in continuously ongoing mutually (re)constitutive processes in which identities, preferences, and law can be defined and redefined, if decision-making processes meet standards of procedural fairness.[6] This essay, moreover, makes the point that national public law offers a discourse in which these deficiencies can be conceptualized.[7]

I first proceed to outline the interactional understanding of justice that underlies this chapter. Thereafter, the focus is on substantive developments in global environmental law that reflect concerns associated with distributive justice. Subsequently, institutional and decision-making patterns in global environmental law are considered. As will appear, there is a mismatch between the substantive aspects of global environmental law and the related institutional and decision-making patterns. The former focus on the functional role of states,[8] by, even if

continuum between the morality of duty and the morality of aspiration, posited but not explained by Fuller, can be conceived if thought of in terms of functions of law. He distinguishes four functions of law: protective and instrumental, and communicative and regulatory. Amongst other things, he makes the point that the communicative and regulatory roles of law relate to, respectively, the morality of aspiration and the morality of duty.

[6] See Phillip Allot, *Eunomia, New Order for a New World* (Oxford: Oxford University Press, 1990) and Allot, "The Concept of International Law," *European Journal of International Law* 10 (1999), p. 31. Allot regards law as an important element in the self-constituting interactive process of a society and proposes his theory of constitutionalism, which suggests that it is possible for a society, also global society, to develop a concept of the public domain in which only public, or as Allot calls it, social, power is exercised in the public interest and subject to limits and the requirement of accountability and thus able to address abuse of power (*Eunomia*, various places e.g. 297–339; "The Concept"). Also see Amartya Sen, *Development as Freedom* (Oxford: Oxford University Press, 1999). Sen emphasizes the constructive role of political freedom by illustrating that political and civil rights, especially those guaranteeing open debate, perform important roles in "the processes of generating informed and reflected choices" (p. 153) and in informing those exercising public powers about what their actions might be directed at, p. 152.

[7] The point made is that the discourse and concepts of national public law are useful in conceptualizing contemporary developments in international/global law, not that international/global law is an external extension of domestic public law, an argument which was made, in particular, by nineteenth century German lawyers. See Martti Koskenniemi, *The Gentle Civilizer of Nations, The Rise and Fall of International Law 1870–1960* (Cambridge, Cambridge University Press 2002), pp. 179–265.

[8] The distinction between the functional and discretionary role of states in international environmental law refers to the distinction between states exercising delegated powers in the interest of humankind (comparable to Allot's social powers, see note 6) and states exercising sovereign powers, which allow a state to freely determine its behavior. See René-Jean Dupuy, "Humanity and the Environment" *Colorado Journal of International Environmental Law and Policy* 2 (1991), p. 203.

often cautiously, emphasizing community interests, considerations of equity and the interests of individuals and groups; the latter introduce a discretionary role for the World Bank and related institutions vis-à-vis developing states and the individuals and groups in these states. Finally, the mismatch between the substantive and institutional and decision-making aspects of global environmental law will be addressed.

An interactional understanding of justice

Justice in this essay is understood as involving both distributive justice and procedural fairness. The distinct quality of law, however, is understood to be its potential to further "good process," including procedural fairness. This understanding is informed by the interactional theory of international law, developed by Jutta Brunnée and Stephen Toope.[9] The interactional theory of international law links constructivist theories developed by international relations scholars[10] and the work of Lon Fuller.[11]

The interactional theory of international law is based on the understanding that law, that is individual principles, policies, and rules and systems of principles, policies, and rules that merit qualification as law or a system of law for its realization, is not dependent on the exercise of power or force. Instead, law is authoritative and legitimate when mutually constructed and reciprocal.[12] By involving those affected and addressed by law in decision-making, it ensures that law is regarded as legitimate and complied with.[13] Such a mutually constructed system of law enables self-directed human action in which individuals are guided by law in making their own choices.[14]

Mutual construction of an interactive system of law takes place through processes that distinguish law from other forms of social normativity and involve "reasoned argument, references to past practices

9 See references in note 5.

10 Especially the work of Nicolas Greenwood Onuf and Friederich Kratochwil, see Brunnée and Toope, "International Law and Constructivism," p. 38.

11 Lon Fuller, *The Morality of Law* ed. (New Haven and London: Yale University Press, 1969).

12 Paraphrased from Brunnée and Toope, "International Law and Constructivism," pp. 51–52, see also pp. 48–50.

13 *Ibid.*, p. 53.

14 *Ibid.*, p. 56. Also see Gerald J. Postema, "Implicit Law," in *Rediscovering Fuller. Essays on Implicit Law and Institutional Design*, ed. Willem J. Witteveen and Wibren van der Burg (Amsterdam: Amsterdam University Press, 1999), p. 254.

and contemporary social aspirations, and the deployment of analogy," what Brunnée and Toope refer to as "the specific type of rationality apparent in the internal processes that make law possible."[15] It is this rationality that is the basis of the internal morality of law, which entails that principle, policies and rules, and legal systems as a whole in order to be regarded as legitimate, in addition to the participation of relevant actors,[16] must meet eight "tests of legality." These tests involve generality, promulgation, non-retroactivity, clarity, non-contradiction, not requiring the impossible, constancy over time, and congruence of official action with rules.[17] While these tests are to a large extent process-oriented, their focus is on attaining "good process," they are also genuinely moral in that they enable law to fulfill its moral task: supporting individual autonomy and facilitating social interaction, thus providing a moral framework for public interaction.[18] The latter concerns what has been referred to by van der Burg as the communicative function of law connected to what Fuller coined as the morality of aspiration.[19] Fuller identified two inter-connected dimensions of law: the morality of duty and the morality of aspiration. As van der Burg points out, the morality of duty relates in particular to areas of law which are socially relatively uncontroversial and where it makes sense to adopt specific rules governing human conduct, such as traffic rules.[20] In those situations law has a regulatory role. On the other hand, where law seeks to address ideals, such as the attainment of a democratic society, it operates in the dimension the morality of inspiration and the communicative function of law becomes particularly important.[21] This insight is particularly relevant to global environmental law where the practical implications of agreed principles and their substantive translation into policies and rules, is contested.

An understanding of law as set out above, I suggest, requires, among other things, that a legal system meet standards of procedural fairness, that it incorporate procedures that enable the discourse of law and thus its communicative function to unfold. Requirements regarding

[15] Brunnée and Toope, "International Law and Constructivism," p. 56.

[16] *Ibid.*, pp. 52–53. [17] *Ibid.*, pp. 54.

[18] Discussions with Jutta Brunnée; also see David Dyzenhaus, "Fuller's Novelty," in *Rediscovering Fuller. Essays on Implicit Law and Institutional Design*, ed. Willem J. Witteveen and Wibren van der Burg (Amsterdam: Amsterdam University Press, 1999), p. 97 and Colleen Murphy, "Lon Fuller and the Moral Value of the Rule of Law," *Law and Philosophy* 24 (2005), p. 239.

[19] Van der Burg, "The Morality of Aspiration," p. 185 ff.

[20] *Ibid.* at 187 [21] *Ibid.* at 187–89.

transparency, inclusive participatory entitlements, and inclusive accountability mechanism, associated with public law and the rule of law (in the sense of the *rechtstaat*), can provide such processes, thereby providing means through which "good process" and ultimately the internal morality of law can be realized. The nature of global environmental law, formally addressing states but crucially affecting states and individuals and groups in society,[22] entails that procedural fairness is important at both the inter-state level and the level of individuals and groups. This essay illustrates that procedural fairness, and thus the communicative function of law, is underdeveloped in global environmental law, at both levels.

Substantive elements of global environmental law: from a discretionary to a functional role of states

Substantive elements in global environmental law reflect concerns associated with the well-being of individuals and groups and seek to further distributive justice. Principle 1 of the 1992 Rio Declaration on Environment and Development (Rio Declaration), for example, provides that:

> Human beings are at the centre of concerns for sustainable development. They are entitled to a healthy and productive life in harmony with nature.

Moreover, Judge Weeramantry in his separate opinion in *Gabčikovo-Nagymaros*, contemplated "[w]e have entered an era of international law in which international law subserves not only the interests of individual States, but looks beyond them and their parochial concerns to the greater interests of humanity and planetary welfare."[23]

These quotes illustrate two concerns that are increasingly reflected in global environmental law: the interests of human beings and the interests of humanity as a whole. Global environmental law conceptualizes states as the protectors of these concerns by focusing on their functional role. It defines this functional role by formulating the responsibilities of

[22] Also see Daniel Bodansky, Jutta Brunnée, and Ellen Hey, "International Environmental Law, Mapping the Field," *Oxford Handbook of International Environmental Law* ed. Daniel Bodansky, Jutta Brunnée, and Ellen Hey (Oxford: Oxford University Press, 2007) p. 6 and pp. 16–21.

[23] *Case Concerning the Gabčikovo-Nagymaros Project (Hungary/Slovakia)*, 1997 ICJ Rep. 7, separate opinion of Vice-President Weeramantry, at para. C(c).

states in terms of common interests, considerations of equity, and the substantive interests and rights of individuals and groups in society.

Common interests

Common interests are reflected in global environmental law by the concept of "common concern." This concept does not address the thorny issue of state sovereignty, or lack thereof, over a certain space or resource. Instead, it qualifies a certain issue or problem as being of concern to humankind.[24] The 1992 Convention on Biological Diversity (Biodiversity Convention) in its preamble provides "that the conservation of biological diversity is a common concern of humankind" and the 1992 United Nations Framework Convention on Climate Change (Climate Change Convention), also in its preamble, provides "that change in the Earth's climate and its adverse effects are a common concern of humankind." While other multilateral environmental agreements (MEAs) do not explicitly declare an issue or problem to be of common concern, they reflect an approach similar to that employed in the Biodiversity and Climate Change conventions. This approach is characterized by state parties to an MEA sharing responsibility for addressing the detrimental consequences of environmental deterioration for developing states, for the well-being of individuals in general and certain groups in particular and for areas beyond national jurisdiction, and by identifying the need for common but differentiated action by states and action by the private sector.[25]

The concept of common concern is distinct from concepts such as "common area" and "common heritage of mankind," which treat certain areas and their resources as common property resources subject, respectively, to formal equal access (Antarctica, the high seas, and outer space) and material equal access (the Area). The concept of common concern instead leaves existing jurisdictional regimes intact, be it sovereignty over territory and the territorial sea, sovereign rights in the exclusive economic zone, or flag state or state of registry jurisdiction in the global commons. It requires that states within their territory and over activities subject to their jurisdiction adopt measures to curtail

[24] Also see Jutta Brunnée, "Common Areas, Common Heritage, and Common Concern," in *Oxford Handbook of International Environmental Law* ed. Daniel Bodansky, Jutta Brunnée, and Ellen Hey (Oxford: Oxford University Press, 2007) p. 550.

[25] See e.g. the 2001 Stockholm Convention on Persistent Organic Pollutants (Stockholm Convention), which in its preamble clearly reflects these various concerns.

environmental degradation and that states assist each other in addressing such degradation.

Considerations of equity

Considerations of equity are reflected in global environmental law most pertinently in the concepts of inter- and intra-generational equity.[26] Inter-generational equity concerns equity between generations while intra-generational equity concerns equity within a generation. Both concepts are intimately related to the concept of sustainable development as conceptualized by the Brundtland Commission. I reproduce the oft-quoted words:

> Sustainable development is development that meets the needs of the present without compromising the ability of future generations to meet their own needs.[27]

The Commission emphasizes that "the concept of needs" refers to "in particular the essential needs of the world's poor, to which overriding priority should be given."[28]

Noteworthy is the fact that the International Court of Justice (ICJ) in its advisory opinion in the *Legality of the Threat or Use of Nuclear Weapons*[29] and again in *Gabčikovo-Nagymaros*[30] determined that "the environment is not an abstraction but represents the living space, the quality of life and the very health of human beings, including generations unborn." The court thereby clarified who are to be the beneficiaries of the activities of states: individuals and groups, including those belonging to future generations.

Protection of the interests of future generations is among the explicit goals of most MEAs. Inter-generational equity, furthermore, is reflected in global environmental law through the obligations to prevent and redress environmental damage, to use natural resources sustainably, and to adopt a precautionary approach in the development and implementation of environmental policy and law.

[26] Also see Dinah Shelton, "Equity," in *Oxford Handbook of International Environmental Law* ed. Daniel Bodansky, Jutta Brunnée, and Ellen Hey (Oxford: Oxford University Press, 2007) p. 639.

[27] The World Commission on Environment and Development, *Our Common Future* (Oxford: Oxford University Press, 1987), p. 43.

[28] *Ibid.* [29] *ICJ Reports* 1999, para.29.

[30] *Case Concerning the Gabčikovo-Nagymaros Project*, judgment, para. 112.

Intra-generational equity is intimately related to the South–North, or developing–developed state, controversy. This controversy concerns issues of distributive justice and echoes the legacies of colonialism and the continued unequal relations of power between developing and developed states.[31] Intra-generational equity finds its clearest expression, at the level of principles, in the principle of "common but differentiated responsibilities."[32] This principle entails that developed states, given their past contribution to the deterioration of the environment, their concomitant accumulation of wealth, and their present financial and technological capabilities, have an obligation to take on larger burdens when it comes to protecting the environment and to transfer financial resources and technology to developing states, which are obliged to take steps to protect the environment that are within their means. The principle of common but differentiated responsibilities manifests itself through grace periods for developing states,[33] instruments that impose obligations only on developed states,[34] and provisions that make the implementation of the obligations resting upon developing states conditional on the transfer of funds, know-how, and technology from developed states.[35]

While sustainable development as conceptualized by the Brundtland Commission addresses the interests of generations,[36] arguably individuals and groups belonging to those generations, and the ICJ refers to "human beings, including generations unborn,"[37] the principle of common but differentiated responsibilities as incorporated in MEAs addresses the duties of states vis-à-vis each other. These treaties, then, might be understood as

[31] See Anghie, "Colonialism and the Birth of International Institutions"; Pogge, "The Influence of the Global Order on the Prospects for Genuine Democracy in Developing Countries."

[32] See Simon Caney, "Cosmopolitan Justice, Responsibility and Global Climate Change," *Leiden Journal of International Law* 18, (2005), p. 747; "Human Rights and Global Climate Change," this volume. Also see Ellen Hey, "Common but Differentiated Responsibility," ed. Rüdiger Wolfrum, *Max Planck Encyclopedia of Public International Law* (Oxford: Oxford University Press, 2009), available at www.mpepil.com/ (accessed 14 February 2010). For a critical analysis see Christopher D. Stone, "Common but Differentiated Responsibilities in International Law," *American Journal of International Law* 98 (2004), p. 276.

[33] Art. 5, 1990 Montreal Protocol on the Depletion of the Ozone Layer (Montreal Protocol).

[34] Art. 3, 1997 Kyoto Protocol only imposes emission reduction obligations on developed and economy in transition states.

[35] E.g. art. 4(7), Climate Change Convention; art. 20(4), Biodiversity Convention.

[36] See text at *supra* note 27. [37] See text at *supra* note 30.

emphasizing the functional role of states in attaining sustainable development for individuals and groups belonging to present and future generations, including those located in other states. While individuals and groups thus are identified as the beneficiaries of state action, they are not, as such, the addressees of the treaty provisions concerned.

Substantive rights and interests

Individual and group substantive interests and, even if sparsely, rights are addressed in global environmental instruments, either indirectly as interests that are to be the object of the policies pursued by states or as rights per se. Admittedly legally binding instruments generally do not refer to environmental rights, while legally non-binding instruments do express such rights. Moreover, human rights bodies have interpreted civil and political rights so as to include environmental considerations in their scope of application.

The right to an adequate environment has been incorporated into binding legal instruments at the regional level only.[38] It forms part of both the 1981 African Charter on Human and Peoples' Rights, which provides that "[a]ll peoples shall have the right to a generally satisfactory environment favorable to their development"[39] and the 1988 Additional Protocol to the American Convention on Human Rights in the Area of Economic, Social, and Cultural Rights (Protocol of San Salvador) which provides that "everyone shall have the right to live in a healthy environment and to have access to public services."[40] The African Charter thus conceptualizes the right to a healthy environment as a peoples right, while the Protocol of San Salvador conceptualizes it in terms of a social, and economic right. Albeit indirectly, the Committee on Economic, Social, and Cultural Rights (Committee on ESCR) in 2000 also addressed the right to adequate environmental conditions as part of the right to health as expressed in article 12(1) of the Covenant on Economic, Social, and Cultural Rights.[41] In addition, human rights

[38] See John G. Merrills, "Environmental Rights" in *Oxford Handbook of International Environmental Law* ed. Daniel Bodansky, Jutta Brunnée, and Ellen Hey (Oxford: Oxford University Press, 2007) p. 661.

[39] Art. 24, African Charter on Human and Peoples' Rights.

[40] Art. 11(1), Protocol of San Salvador.

[41] Paragraphs 4, 11, 15, 16, 22 and 36, General Comment 14(2000), Doc. E/C.12/2000/4, 11 August 2000, for the text of general comments by the Committee on ECSR, available at: http://www2.ohchr.org/english/bodies/cescr/comments.htm (accessed 14 February 2010).

courts and human rights bodies have interpreted various civil and political rights, such as the right to life, the right to physical integrity, the right to private life as well as procedural rights such as the right to fair trail, to be relevant in an environmental context.[42]

Many legally non-binding instruments, such as Agenda 21,[43] the Rio Declaration,[44] the 2002 Millennium Development Goals,[45] the 2002 Johannesburg Declaration[46] and the 2005 World Summit Outcome[47] address the interest of individuals and of particular groups in a healthy environment and emphasize the functional role of states and also the private sector in attaining these interests. These documents and especially the more recent ones, however, remain far from formulating such concerns in terms of human rights.

Some MEAs in their preambles incorporate public health concerns, including those of special groups such as women, among the *raison d'etre* of the regime.[48] Such provisions in some cases are developed further in the body of the instrument by way of provisions on public information, awareness, and education.[49]

An example of a treaty that addresses the interests of individuals and groups and the functional role of states somewhat more elaborately, but in a very specific context and in an instrumental manner, is the Biodiversity Convention. It, for example, requires states to promote the wide application of the knowledge of indigenous and local communities "with the approval and involvement of the holders of such knowledge ... and encourage the equitable sharing of the benefits arising from the utilization of such knowledge,"[50] to "[p]rotect and encourage customary

[42] See the contributions by Dinah Shelton on "Human Rights and the Environment" in the successive editions of the *Yearbook of International Environmental Law* (Oxford: Oxford University Press, 1995 etc) and Daniel García San José, *Environmental Protection and the European Convention on Human Rights*, Human Rights Files, No.21 (Strasbourg: Council of Europe, 2005).

[43] In particular its section 3.

[44] Principle 1, quoted above, as well as principles 20 through 22.

[45] See www.un.org/millenniumgoals/ (accessed 14 February 2010).

[46] Report of the World Summit on Sustainable Development, Johannesburg, South Africa, 26 August–4 September 2002, Doc. A/CONF.199/20, at 1, available at: www.un.org/jsummit/html/documents/documents.html (accessed 14 February 2010).

[47] General Assembly Resolution, 2005 World Summit Outcome, A/Res/60/1, 24 October 2005, paragraph 48 for commitments related to the environment.

[48] Second paragraph, preambles of the Stockholm Convention and the Montreal Protocol; 2nd, 3rd and 15th paragraphs, preamble, 1989 Basel Convention on the Control of Transboundary Movements of Hazardous Wastes and their Disposal.

[49] Art. 10, Stockholm Convention.

[50] Art. 8(j), Biodiversity Convention.

use of biological resources in accordance with traditional cultural practices compatible with conservation or sustainable use requirements,"[51] and to "[s]upport local populations to develop and implement remedial action in degraded areas where biological diversity has been reduced."[52] In evaluating these provisions one must take into account the fact that they are imbedded in an instrument that generally addresses the rights and duties of states, seeks to secure access to the benefits that derive from the use of biological resources, and conditions the interests of individuals and groups with provisos that emphasize the discretion of states.[53]

A pertinent example of an environmental right included in both legally binding and legally non-binding instruments is the right to water, which concerns a fundamental aspect of both the human right to life and the human right to a healthy environment.[54] The right to water is part of the right to enjoy adequate living conditions for women living in rural areas under article 14(2) of the 1979 Convention on the Elimination of All Forms of Discrimination Against Women and of the right to health under article 24(2) of the 1989 Convention on the Rights of the Child, it, however, has not been included in a binding legal instrument as a free standing right.

The right to water is addressed comprehensively in a legally non-binding document, General Comment 15, adopted by the Committee on ESCR in 2002.[55] Other instruments, albeit in terms of interests, address the need to secure access to water in adequate amounts and of adequate quality to cover basic human needs, including drinking water and water for sanitation. An example of such an instrument is the 1999 Protocol on Water and Health to the 1992 Convention on the Protection and Use of Transboundary Watercourses and International Lakes (Helsinki Convention). While the protocol does not in a geographical sense have global coverage, it, as the Helsinki Convention, harbors traits of global environmental law.[56] The most prominent among these traits

[51] Art. 10(c), Biodiversity Convention. [52] Art. 10(d), Biodiversity Convention.

[53] E.g. art. 8(j) of the Biodiversity Convention stipulates that the obligation expressed is "[S]ubject to its [a state's] national legislation," while art. 10 contains the proviso "as far as possible and as appropriate."

[54] Also see Ellen Hey, "Distributive Justice and Procedural Fairness in Global Water Law," in *Environmental Law and Justice* ed. Jonas Ebbesson, and Phoebe Okowa (Cambridge: Cambridge University Press, 2009), p. 351.

[55] General Comment 15, UN Doc. E/C.12/2002/11, 20 January 2003.

[56] Both the Helsinki Convention and the Protocol on Water and Health were adopted within the United Nations Economic Commission for Europe (UNECE) and in principle

is that states are to undertake specified actions both individually and in cooperation in order to secure proper access to water for drinking and sanitation purposes with the aim of protecting human health, and, for sanitation, also the environment. Thus, while remaining short of formulating a right to water, the Protocol on Water and Health clearly indicates that the object of state action is to be the interests of individual human beings living within the parties to the protocol, including individuals living in other states parties.

Water related instruments, thus, to various degrees illustrate a move away from the discretionary role that classical international law attributes to states towards emphasizing a functional role of states. That is, states are to undertake action to protect the environment, and water in particular, in the interest of individuals and groups. General Comment 15, moreover, also addresses the role of non-state actors and global institutions in securing the right to water. Non-state actors are addressed indirectly by requiring that states take steps, both legal and political, "to prevent their own citizens and companies from violating the right to water of individuals and communities in other countries."[57] Global institutions are addressed indirectly, by requiring that states in their activities within such institutions cooperate to realize the right to water,[58] and directly, by requiring that such institutions themselves incorporate the right to water in their policies.[59]

From discretionary to a functional role of states

The notion that states are to act in the interest of individuals and groups in society and in the common interest thus has been explicitly incorporated into global environmental law. Also included in these instruments is the notion that states, in particular developed states, are to assist developing states in protecting the interests of the individuals and groups living in the latter. States, however, remain wary of formulating environmental rights in legally binding instruments and such rights have been included in legally non-binding instruments only sparingly

apply within the UNECE region. The parties to the Helsinki Convention in 2003, however, adopted a decision that, when it enters into force, will open the convention (not the protocol) to participation by states outside the UNECE region, upon approval of the Meeting of the Parties (Decision III/1, Amendment to the Water Convention, 28 November 2003, Doc.ECE/MP.WAT/14, 12 January 2004).

[57] Para. 33, General Comment 15.

[58] Para. 36, General Comment 15.

[59] Para. 60, General Comment 15.

and in case of the right to water in a document, General Comment 15, developed by a committee of experts, rather then state representatives. Moreover, the strong manifestation of the functional role of states, even if not expressed in terms of individual rights, contained in the Protocol on Water and Health to the Helsinki Convention, adopted within the framework of the United Nations Economic Commission for Europe (UNECE), lacks worldwide coverage.[60]

Universal principles such as the principle of common concern, the principle of sustainable development, and the principles of inter- and intra-generational equity provide the basis for conceptualizing the functional role of states in terms of law, both vis-à-vis each other and individuals and groups. The functional role of states vis-à-vis each other becomes concrete in particular in the South–North context where it has been translated into more demanding obligations for developed, as opposed to developing, states and obligations that require developed states to assist developing states. The functional role of states vis-à-vis individuals and groups in society manifests itself in the obligations that limit the discretion of states to treat the environment within their territory or jurisdiction as they see fit. These developments mark a departure from the classical international legal system in which law is conceptualized as inter-state law that is reciprocal and contractual in nature. Instead, global environmental law harbors traits of national public law, in which entities, in case of national public law the state, are constructed that, through the exercise of public powers, are meant to act in the common interest while protecting the rights and interests of individuals and groups. These substantive aspects of global environmental law, then, reflect the ideals of moral cosmopolitanism in which the equal moral worth of all persons is translated into obligations binding on all. They, in other words, harbor the promise of justice by translating the ideals of moral cosmopolitanism into positive law.

As will be illustrated in the next section of this essay, global environmental law allocates public powers to global institutions, the World Bank in particular, but it does so in a manner that is incomplete, at least in terms of public law and the rule of law. It, as it were, transfers public powers that in classical international law are attributed to states to global institutions, but does not transfer or incompletely transfers to the global level of decision-making the checks and balances associated with the exercise of public powers. This development, moreover,

[60] See *supra* note 56.

is particularly noteworthy in the South–North context, because it is in this context that the World Bank exercises powers that can be conceptualized as of a public nature.

Institutional and decision-making patterns in global environmental law: from the discretion of states to the discretion of global institutions

Besides states, a variety of global institutions participate in decision-making in global environmental law. These institutions both engage in normative development and in decision-making in individual situations. The former takes place especially through the development of policies and rules that seek to implement the provisions of MEAs. Relevant institutions are the conferences of the parties to MEAs, but also specialized agencies, such as the World Bank,[61] other institutions that are part of the United Nations system, such as the United Nations Environment Programme (UNEP) and the United Nations Development Programme (UNDP), and cooperative endeavors among these institutions, such as the Global Environment Facility (GEF). Decision-making in individual situations takes place especially, but not only, by way of institutions, such as the World Bank and the GEF, deciding on the allocation of funds to projects that seek to implement MEAs in developing states and economy in transition states. Two elements are noteworthy in these processes. First, most of the decisions taken in the case of normative development are of a legally non-binding character, in terms of classical international law. Secondly, most of the decisions taken in individual situations relate to developing states.[62]

The structure of decision-making

At the basis of most of contemporary global environmental law are various MEAs. Most of these agreements, such as the Biodiversity Convention and Climate Change Convention, are concluded in the form of a framework agreement, which provides the basic principles

[61] The term World Bank refers to the International Bank for Reconstruction and Development (IBRD) and the International Development Agency (IDA), when reference is to one of these specific institutions their acronym will be used. Other institutions such as the International Financial Corporation (IFC) are affiliated to the World Bank.

[62] Also see Ellen Hey, "International Institutions" in *Oxford Handbook of International Environmental Law* ed. Daniel Bodansky, Jutta Brunnée, and Ellen Hey (Oxford: Oxford University Press, 2007) p. 749.

and institutions that form the basis for the further development of the regime. Protocols, such as the 1997 Kyoto Protocol and the 2000 Cartagena Protocol on Biosafety,[63] and decisions adopted by the conference of the parties to the framework agreement further develop the regime.[64] All MEAs contain provisions committing developed states to transfer funds and technology to developing states.[65] Within MEAs each state has one vote and while most decisions within MEAs are taken by consensus, some decisions may be taken by qualified majority vote.[66] Particularly noteworthy from a classical legal point of view, however, is the fact that most of the decisions taken within the framework of MEAs are legally non-binding even if they may affect the rights of states and of individuals and groups within the contours of the regime in question. A relevant example is the body of rules adopted within the framework of the Kyoto Protocol that determine whether a state party and its nationals are entitled to participate in the flexible mechanisms of the Kyoto Protocol, including trade in emission reduction units.[67] This development entails a significant departure from classical international law, in which a state is assumed to be bound by a rule or set of rules in the form of a treaty only if that state formally has consented to that rule or treaty or if a constituent treaty expressly attributes the competence to adopt legally binding rules to a global institution, such as the United Nations Charter to the Security Council.[68] It is this manner of decision-making, in particular, that has given rise to questions regarding the legitimacy of global environmental law.[69] However, if law, including global environmental law, is regarded as the product of interactional processes, lack of formal state consent and lack of legally binding status need not result

[63] Protocols respectively to the Climate Change Convention and the Biodiversity Convention.

[64] E.g. *The CBD Handbook*, available at: www.cbd.int/convention/refrhandbook.shtml (accessed 14 February 2010), which contains all decisions taken by the parties to implement the Biodiversity Convention and Cartagena Protocol. Similar handbooks are available for other MEAs.

[65] See *supra* note 35.

[66] E.g. art. 9(2) of the Montreal Protocol allows parties to amend certain aspects of the annexes to the protocol by a two-thirds majority vote.

[67] E.g. Decision 2/CMP.1 on the Principles, Nature, and Scope of the Mechanisms Pursuant to arts. 16, 12 and 17, adopted by the parties to the Kyoto Protocol in 2005.

[68] Also see Ellen Hey, *Teaching International Law. State-Consent as Consent to a Process of Normative Development and Ensuing Problems*, inaugural lecture (The Hague etc.: Kluwer Law International, 2003).

[69] Also see Daniel Bodansky, "Legitimacy," in *Oxford Handbook of International Environmental Law* ed. Daniel Bodansky, Jutta Brunnée, and Ellen Hey (Oxford: Oxford University Press, 2007), p. 712.

in a legitimacy deficit.[70] Lack of procedural fairness, however, is likely to give rise to such a deficit.

In global environmental law the relationship between developed states and global institutions, on the one hand, and developing states, on the other hand, suffers from lack of procedural fairness, and ultimately "good process." Why? Because an important element of MEA-based regimes, the transfer of funds and technology from developed to developing states, is implemented via institutions located outside the MEA-regime as such. In this institutional relocation a shift in the decision-making patterns takes place to the detriment of developing states: the one state, one vote system of MEAs is replaced by system of weighted voting used in the World Bank and related institutions and by the public powers exercised by the bank.

The World Bank and the GEF, administered by the World Bank, even if established jointly by the World Bank, UNEP, and UNDP, and other funds administered by the bank are particularly relevant in this context. The World Bank, for example, is the largest financier of biodiversity projects that serve, among other things, to implement the Biodiversity Convention in developing states.[71] The GEF functions as the financial mechanism of most MEAs and is subject to the guidance of the conferences of the parties of MEAs and the guidelines adopted by the GEF itself. However, the GEF in its pilot phase was subject solely to the decision-making processes and procedures of the World Bank, in which developed states have a major say. It was during this phase that some of the basic rules of the game governing the operation of the GEF were fleshed out. Due to political pressure from developing states in the early 1990s, the GEF has been restructured, with developing and developed states now sharing decision-making power more equally.[72]

Similar to the GEF, the Prototype Carbon Fund (PCF), established by the World Bank in 1999, to a large extent fleshed out the rules of the game for the implementation of the Kyoto Protocol and in particular the clean development mechanism (CDM) and joint implementation (JI), two of the flexible mechanisms of the Kyoto Protocol. The CDM seeks to implement the Kyoto Protocol through projects financed by developed states in developing states; JI seeks to implement the

[70] See Brunnée and Toope "International Law and Constructivism," p. 55.

[71] See http://web.worldbank.org (topics, environment, topics) (accessed 14 February 2010).

[72] See Nele Matz, "Financial Institutions between Effectiveness and Legitimacy – A Legal Analysis of the World Bank, Global Environmental Facility and the Prototype Carbon Fund" *International Environmental Agreements* 5 (2005), p. 265.

protocol through projects amongst developed and economy-in-transition states, but in the context of the World Bank it is relevant in particular for projects financed by developed states in economy-in-transition states. In the PCF, both developed states and private companies from developed states participate in decision-making relative to their financial input into the fund.[73] The PCF, and similar funds,[74] has played a decisive role in developing the global carbon market. However, developing states, the providers of the raw product (greenhouse gas emissions), only have a marginal say in the decision-making processes of the PCF, while developed states and private companies from developed states, the providers of the financial means to realize the reductions, hold decision-making power and obtain valuable emission reductions that they can use to satisfy their commitments under the Kyoto Protocol or trade on the global carbon market, established on the basis of the protocol. Moreover, the reductions in greenhouse gasses achieved through these funds besides benefiting the states in which the projects are executed also benefit the wider global community, including developed states.

The World Bank as such and through the various funds that it administers, thus, has become a central player in global environmental law and exercises public powers vis-à-vis developing states and the manner in which they implement their MEA-based commitments.[75] Such powers, if conceived in terms of the substantive principles discussed in the previous section, serve to protect common interests, e.g. in the conservation of biodiversity and the protection of the climate system, and implement considerations of equity, i.e. the principle of common but differentiated responsibilities, and thus merit the qualification 'public powers'. Public powers, when conceptualized in terms of public law and the rule of law, however, require that a set of checks and balances accompany those powers in order avoid their abuse.[76] Such checks and balances involve participatory rights for those that may be affected by the powers exercised. While the World Bank has not been oblivious to demands for the introduction of accountability mechanisms, its safeguard policies and other internal rules and regulations, and the World

[73] *Ibid.* [74] See http://carbonfinance.org/ (accessed 14 February 2010).

[75] Also see Anthony Anghie, "International Financial Institutions," in *The Politics of International Law* ed. Christian Reus-Smit (Cambridge: Cambridge University Press, 2004), p. 217.

[76] Also see Allot, *Eunomia, New Order for a New World*; "The Concept of International Law," p. 31.

Bank Inspection Panel (Inspection Panel), discussed below, only partly serve to address the concerns expressed here.

The position of the World Bank as an entity that exercises public powers in global environmental law challenges the inter-state paradigm. So do the mechanisms employed by the bank also due to the manner in which they involve the private sector. The private sector not only executes World Bank projects, but participates directly in institutions such as the PCF in which it exercises decision-making powers on a par with states, as investors in the fund.

Participatory rights

Participatory rights involve transparency of decision-making, participation in decision-making, and access to accountability mechanisms.[77] While many environmental instruments attest to the importance of such participatory rights, few actually include the duty to establish such rights at the national level and the examples of instruments that refer to the realization of such rights in a transboundary context or within global institutions are few and far between.

Principle 10 of the Rio Declaration provides an example of a provision stressing the importance of participatory rights at the national level. The declaration, however, does not address such rights in a transboundary context or with respect to global institutions. The United Nations Convention on the Law of the Non-Navigational Uses of International Watercourses (Watercourses Convention) provides an example of the manner in which classical international law addresses participatory rights in a transboundary context. It provides for inter-state consultation,[78] leaving it up to the states concerned whether they involve individuals and groups, and non-discriminatory access (instead of minimum standards of access) for individuals and groups to judicial and other procedures in case of transboundary harm or serious threat thereof.[79] The Watercourse Convention, then, does not establish minimum standards regarding participatory rights of individuals and groups, either in a national or in a transboundary context. Other instruments refer to the importance of involving the public in general or

[77] Also see Jonas Ebbeson, "Public Participation," in *Oxford Handbook of International Environmental Law* ed. Daniel Bodansky, Jutta Brunnée, and Ellen Hey (Oxford: Oxford University Press, 2007) p. 681.

[78] Art. 11–19, Watercourses Convention. [79] Art. 32, *Ibid.*

particular groups, such as indigenous peoples or women, in the development of policies regarding the environment, but they remain short of establishing participatory rights for individuals and groups.[80]

Relevant in this context are the World Bank's safeguard policies. These policies consist of Bank Operational Policies and Bank Procedures (OP/BP) and are internally binding on bank personnel in the execution of projects, entailing that bank personnel have to ensure that states implement these policies. Relevant examples are the bank's safeguard policies on environmental assessment, indigenous peoples, and international waterways. The bank's safeguard policy on environmental assessment requires the state concerned to consult with project-affected groups and local NGOs and requires that relevant information be made available in a timely manner and in a form and language relevant to those consulted.[81] The safeguard policy on indigenous peoples formulates the duty of the borrower state to engage in "a process of free, prior and informed consultation with the affected Indigenous Peoples' communities"[82] and determines that the bank shall only engage in projects where such consultations "result in broad community support to the project by the affected Indigenous Peoples."[83] The bank's safeguard policy on international waterways provides for interstate consultation by way of a process similar to that contained in the Watercourses Convention.[84]

World Bank safeguard policies as well as other OP/BPs constitute the policies against which the World Bank Inspection Panel, a quasi-judicial procedure,[85] assesses complaints submitted to it by two or more

[80] E.g. art. 6(a)(ii) and (iii), Climate Change Convention; paras. 12 and 13, preamble, and art. 8(j), Convention on Biodiversity; art. 10, Stockholm Convention.

[81] Paras. 14–18, Operational Policy 4.01: Environmental Assessment, 1999. All World Bank safeguard policies, available at: www.worldbank.org (projects and operations, safeguard policies) (accessed 14 February 2010).

[82] Para. 6, Operational Policies 4.10. World Bank Safeguard polices are contained in Bank Procedures/Bank Operational Policies, so called OP/BP, OP/BP 4.10, July 2005, contains the safeguard policy on Indigenous Peoples. OB/BP 4.10 replaced OP/BP 4.20 on the same topic, adopted in September 1991.

[83] Para. 1, Operational Policy 4.10: Indigenous Peoples, 2005. Also see Bank Procedure 4:10: Indigenous Peoples, para. 2 further specifies the notion of "free, prior and informed consultation."

[84] Operational Policy 7.50; Projects on International Waterways, 2001. Also see Bank Procedure 7.50, Projects on International Waterways, 2001.

[85] See Laurence Boisson de Chazournes, "The World Bank Inspection Panel: about Public Participation and Dispute Settlement," in *Civil Society, International Courts and Compliance Bodies* ed. Tullio Treves, Marco Frigessi di Rattalma, Attila Tanzi,

individuals alleging that they have or are likely to suffer harm due to failure of the bank to meet its own internal rules in the execution of projects supported by the bank. The Inspection Panel, established in 1993, considers complaints submitted in regard of projects executed by the IBRD and IDA, thus not all projects financed through the GEF since these are not necessarily executed by these institutions,[86] nor does it consider complaints regarding projects financed by the International Financial Corporation (IFC) or the PCF and similar funds.

The most comprehensive approach to participatory rights is contained in instruments adopted within the ambit of the UNECE.[87] These instruments incorporate participatory rights, also in a transboundary context, both in treaties dealing with specific topics, such as water management[88] and environmental impact assessment,[89] and provide a comprehensive regime in the Aarhus Convention.[90] The Aarhus Convention provides minimum standards on access to information,[91] participation in decision-making,[92] and access to justice[93] and also requires that these be applied without discrimination in a transboundary context.[94] The Arhus Convention moreover requires its parties to promote the application of the principles contained in the convention "in international environmental decision-making processes and within the framework of international organizations in matters related to the environment."[95] This provision was further elaborated in the 2005 Almaty Guidelines, which sets out standards on how access to information and public participation can be improved in international forums.[96] A further salient

Alessandro Fodella, Cesare Pitea, Chiara Ragni (The Hague: T.M.C. Asser Press, 2005), p. 187.

86 The GEF has adopted its own set of guidelines on participation, available at: www.gefweb.org/Operational_Policies/Public_Involvement/public_involvement.html.

87 For environmental instruments adopted within the UNECE see www.unece.org/env (accessed 14 February 2010).

88 Art. 16 Helsinki Convention; Artt. 5(1), 6(2), 8(1)(a)(iii), 9 and 10, Protocol on Water and Health.

89 Art. 2(6), 1991 Convention on Environmental Impact Assessment in a Transboundary Context.

90 1998 Convention on Access to Information, Public Participation in Decision-Making and Access to Justice in Environmental Matters (Aarhus Convention).

91 Arts. 4 and 5, Aarhus Convention.

92 Arts. 6–8, Aarhus Convention.

93 Art. 9, Aarhus Convention.

94 Art. 3(9), Aarhus Convention.

95 Art. 3(7), Aarhus Convention.

96 Almaty Guidelines in Promoting the Application of the Principles of the Aarhus Convention in International Forums, Annex to Decision II/4, *Report of the Second Meeting of the Parties*, Doc. ECE/MP.PP/2005/2/Add.5 (20 June 2005).

element of the Aarhus Convention is its compliance committee, which is entitled to hear claims of non-compliance submitted by individuals against a party.[97] The Aarhus Convention, moreover, is open to states outside the UNECE-region, subject to the approval of the meeting of the parties.[98]

The discretion of global institutions

What the analysis in this section illustrates is that while global institutions, especially the World Bank and associated institutions, exercise considerable decision-making, or public, powers in global environmental law, the availability of instruments to check and balance those powers is extremely limited. In other words, the institutional and decision-making patterns of global environmental law constitute the reality of global environmental law in which the cosmopolitan promise reflected in substantive law is taken away from and not realized. In order to start to address that situation, I suggest, procedural fairness, and in particular participatory rights, needs to be introduced in the decision-making processes of relevant institutions

First, I suggest that a much more balanced approach to the participation in decision-making by developing states needs to be adopted. I see no valid reason why those who "pay taxes" should be fully represented in an institution, such as the World Bank and the PCF, that deals with common interest problems and why those who provide the other part of the solution, "the raw product," should be under-represented. This is even more so if the returns obtained by those who pay taxes are valuable assets (greenhouse gas emission reductions) on the global carbon market. The result seems to be that the substantive principle of common but differentiated obligations incorporated in the Climate Change Convention is being used to facilitate lucrative trade, with developed states and their companies reaping the financial benefits. Such a system is unlikely to be regarded as legitimate.

Formal procedures alone, however, may not suffice to generate the mutual understanding required for the development of interactional law, especially not in situations, as in the international community,

[97] Decision I/7, Doc ECE/MP.PP/2/Add.8, 1 April 2004.

[98] Art. 19(3), Aarhus Convention. The parties to the Espoo Convention, as those to the Helsinki Convention (see *supra* note 56), adopted a decision opening the convention to states outside the UNECE-region, subject to the approval of the meeting of the parties (Decision II/4, 27 February 2001, not yet in force).

where disagreement often is about values.[99] Less formal processes may serve to generate mutual understanding, not about the "good life" but about the contours of the issues at stake, and pave the way for the development of interactional law.[100] Consideration might, for example, be given to the processes involving the Organization for Security and Co-operation in Europe (OSCE), and its predecessor, the Conference in Security and Co-operation in Europe (CSCE), together with UNECE. Starting during the Cold War, these processes served to build mutual understanding between Eastern European states, on the one hand, and Western European states and the United States and Canada, on the other hand. They led first to the adoption of non-legally binding and eventually legally binding texts, including the UNECE conventions referred to in this essay.[101] The World Commission on Dams, established by the World Bank and the World Conservation Union (IUCN) in 1998 in response to the widely criticized policy of the bank regarding large dams, provides another example of such a process.[102] The commission, consisting of twelve persons in their individual capacity, from various backgrounds and coming from both developing and developed states, developed a number of recommendations, most of which significantly influenced the World Bank's policy on large dams.[103] However, when the outcome of such an informal process is undone through formal decision-making processes that lack procedural fairness, informal processes are unlikely to generate sufficient mutual understanding for the development of interactional law. This was the fate of the recommendations of the World Commission on Dams regarding the decisive effect that the outcome of consultation processes should have in its view.[104] Regardless

[99] Also see Bronwen Morgan, "Technocratic v. Convivial Accountability," in *Public Accountability Designs, Dilemmas and Experiences* ed. Michael W. Dowdle (Cambridge: Cambridge University Press, 2006), p. 243.

[100] Also see Jutta Brunnée and Stephen J. Toope, "Environmental Security and Freshwater Resources: Ecosystem Regime Building" *American Journal of International Law* 91 (1997), p. 26.

[101] See Alexandre Kiss and Jean-Pierre Beurier, *Droit International de L'Environnement* 3rd edn. (Paris: Pedone, 2004), pp. 88–89; Patricia Birnie and Alan Boyle, *International Environmental Law & the Environment* 2nd edn. (Oxford: Oxford University Press, 2002), pp. 62–64.

[102] See www.unep.org/dams/WCD/ (accessed 14 February 2010).

[103] See 'A Set of Guidelines for Good Practice', World Commission on Dams, *Dams and Development, A New Framework for Decision-Making*, Report of the World Commission on Dams (London, 2000), pp. 278–307. For the World Bank's reaction see its *Water Resources Strategy* (Washington DC, 2004), p. 75.

[104] See the World Bank's reaction to the Report of the World Commission on Dams, *Ibid.*

of the merits of these recommendations, such a manner of proceeding emphasizes the discretionary role of the World Bank.

Increased participation by developing states, however, is unlikely to be sufficient to commit institutions, such as the World Bank, to a functional role. In order to enhance that role, I suggest, the participatory rights of individuals and groups vis-à-vis the bank also need to be enhanced. Ideally, such solutions should be provided in the context of the localities where projects are being implemented and where their effects are most likely to be experienced. While this is relatively easier where transparency and participation in decision-making are concerned, as evidenced by World Bank safeguard policies,[105] international law poses a formidable obstacle to the realization of accountability mechanisms vis-à-vis global institutions at that level due to the immunity that global institutions enjoy under national law for activities related to their policies.[106] This doctrine, I suggest, should be revisited. If global institutions exercise public powers as outlined in this essay, powers that are not commensurate with the manner in which international institutions are regarded in classical international law, which assumes they act at the inter-state level only, then it would seem appropriate to limit those powers in accordance with legal concepts associated with public law and the rule of law.

Given that global institutions are unlikely to relinquish the immunities that they enjoy under national law, it is at present most likely that any accountability mechanisms that may be established will be launched by these institutions. In the case of the World Bank this could be done, for example, through the further development of the operational and bank policies and the expansion of the mandate of the Inspection Panel. Other institutions might take similar steps[107] or introduce an ombudsperson, as the IFC has done[108] and was proposed for the GEF,[109] but not implemented to date.

[105] See text following *supra* note 80.

[106] See generally, Henry G. Schermers and Niels Blokker, *International Institutional Law* (Boston/Leiden: Martinus Nijhoff Publishers, 2003) paras. 1591–1616. Note, moreover, that the project documents governing projects executed by the World Bank and agreed to by the state where the project is executed generally provide for the immunity of the bank under the national legal system of the developing state in question.

[107] See Daniel Bradlow, "Private Complaints and International Organizations: a Comparative Study of the Independent Inspection Mechanisms in International Financial Institutions," *Georgetown Journal of International Law* 36 (2005), p. 403.

[108] See www.cao-ombudsman.org/ (accessed 14 February 2010).

[109] Speech delivered by Monique Barbut, CEO and Chairperson of the GEF, delivered at the GEF Council Meeting, Washington DC, December 5, 2006, http://www.gefweb.org/uploadedFiles/Council_speech_in_booklet_form_dec06%20web.pdf (accessed 14 February 2010).

This manner of proceeding, however, requires critical consideration as it does not take into account the multi-faceted nature (diversity of loci of decision-making and of actors) of decision-making in global environmental law. Instead, it reproduces at the global level, albeit incompletely, elements of governmental structures familiar from the national level in states governed by the rule of law.[110] Perhaps most importantly, such procedures, in tandem with any procedures that may be available within a state where the project is executed, do not allow for a comprehensive consideration of the decision-making involved. Instead, they compartmentalize decision-making into separate processes – the national and the international – and force complainants to present their claims in a piecemeal approach – hampering them from presenting the harm suffered or likely to be suffered as the result of a complex of but intimately interrelated decision-making processes linked to the project. The World Bank Inspection Panel exemplifies this manner of proceeding, given that the state concerned does not play a role in the complaint procedure, at least not in a formal sense. I suggest, that we need to consider how participatory rights might be realized closer to the individuals and groups that may be affected by relevant projects so that problems can be considered in their local context, perhaps in the form of ombudspersons located in developing states appointed especially to consider complaints involving projects in which global institutions exercise public powers vis-à-vis individuals and groups in those states.[111] More in general, we need to depart from the notion that participatory rights and in particular accountability mechanisms cannot have a hybrid character, involving global, national, and local elements: hence the suggestion to revisit the doctrine regarding the immunities of global institutions under national law. This suggestion is related to the multi-faceted, as opposed to multi-layered, manner in which decision-making takes place in global law. We are not confronted with neatly distinguished layers, but rather with a host of inter-linked decision-making processes and actors whose decisions ultimately culminate at the "localest" of levels, that of individuals and groups.

[110] But see Simon Caney, *Justice Beyond Borders, A Global Political Theory* (Oxford: Oxford University Press, 2005), pp. 148–88, arguing for the establishment of strong supra-state authorities within 'a multi-level system of governance, in which power is removed from states to both supra-state and sub-state authorities' (at 188).

[111] See Simon Chester, *Justice under International Administration: Kosovo, East Timor and Afghanistan* (New York: International Peace Academy, 2002), available at: http://www.ipacademy.org/publication/policy-papers/detail/149-justice-under-international-kosovo-east-timor-and-afganistan.html (accessed 14 February 2010).

Conclusion: the mismatch between substantive elements and institutional and decision-making patterns in global environmental law

While substantive global environmental law holds the promise of a more just global environmental legal order, the institutional and decision-making patterns employed take away from that promise, especially in the relationship between the World Bank and related institutions and developing states. Developing states and individuals and groups in those states do not have, or have insufficient, access to processes that enable the discourse of law to unfold. Ultimately, global environmental law, then, does not provide a moral framework for public interaction and does not provide a framework in which the communicative function of law can be realized.

How might this mismatch be explained? Moral theories of cosmopolitanism provide at least two parts of the answer. First, that global environmental law does not treat human beings as equal even though it should, while its substantive provisions harbor the promise that it will. Second, that the emphasis of the international legal system on the discretionary role of states is problematic. This essay illustrates that the substantive aspects of global environmental law to some extent address this latter concern by emphasizing the functional role of states. The discretionary role of global institutions vis-à-vis developing states, backed-up by legal doctrine, however, seems to be at least equally problematic. I name but two examples: the aforementioned doctrine that entitles global institutions to considerable immunities under national law regardless of the role they perform at that level and the doctrine that global institutions, just as private actors, are not bound by international, i.e. inter-state, law. These doctrines together enable global institutions to function outside of any system of law and to create their own system of rules, as illustrated by developments in the World Bank and related institutions.

I suggest we need to rethink the above mentioned doctrines and others, not primarily in terms of universal substantive principles of law, as moral cosmopolitan theories propose. Instead, I suggest, we rethink these doctrines in terms of the functions of law distinguished by van der Burg and, in particular, law's communicative function. Instituting procedural fairness in global environmental law thus should be a primary focus of attention. Installing procedural fairness in decision-making, I suggest, is a first step in enabling interactional global environmental law to develop. It is through interactional decision-making processes, and not the intellectually sound drawing-board of political theorists, that universal substantive principles of law may develop to influence the practice of global environmental law. Moreover, having in place universal substantive principles, as this essay illustrates, does not necessarily result in a system of law that meets considerations of justice.

The procedural fairness deficit in global environmental law, I suggest, needs to be addressed in a manner that takes into account the multi-faceted nature of decision-making within this body of law. This approach requires new ways of thinking, by both legal scholars and political philosophers. Whether moral theories of cosmopolitanism, grounded in inter-individual moral responsibilities are the answer, I am not sure. Much, I suggest, depends on how we relate that view to global law. First, the inter-individual moral responsibilities central to moral theories of cosmopolitanism can provide an external morality against which to asses the need for change in global environmental law,[112] which can inspire negotiators and commentators alike. However, only if such responsibilities are engendered through interactional processes are they likely to be regarded as legitimate and can the communicative function of law play its role and the aspirational morality of law be realized.

Secondly, I doubt whether a global environmental legal system in which global institutions are regarded as the institutions par excellence for realizing the aspirations of individuals is morally justifiable. States provide vital functions for their populations and as part of our identities are especially relevant when it comes to realizing societies governed by the rule of law.[113] They probably provide the better context in which to realize interactional systems of law and for providing us with a moral framework for public interaction, both at the national and international levels of decision making. As questions to ponder I offer the following. How would the discussion regarding access to medicine for the poor be framed without states? Would pharmaceutical companies be our only focus of critique and hope? And, if states are replaced by global institutions, why should we expect these institutions to do a better and more just job than states vis-à-vis those dependent on those

[112] Brunnée and Toope, "International Law and Constructivism," pp. 56–59, esp. p. 59.

[113] See Kwame Anthony Appiah, *The Ethics of Identity* (Princeton: Princeton University Press, 2005), pp. 245–46 and *Cosmopolitanism* (New York/London: W.W. Norton & Company, 2006), p. 163.

companies for their health? Pondering the answers to these questions, I suggest that the present multi-faceted global legal system has more to say for it than a legal system based on moral cosmopolitan ideals of world government, even if the current system can be subjected to significant critique, based on those ideals. However, I suggest that an interactional understanding of law offers a more fruitful source of critique and inspiration, because it enables us to include in our considerations the communicative function of law, and thus the relevance of the institutional and decision-making patterns of law, including global environmental law.

But, allow me, at the end of this essay to briefly return to my own discipline and what I believe merits the attention of legal scholars. Their research, I suggest, should focus, amongst other things, on how existing patterns of decision-making and dominant paradigms in legal doctrine foster a system of law which institutionalizes the inequalities between the South and the North and on the implications of a multi-faceted system of decision-making for enhancing procedural fairness. The former requires a critical stance towards our own discipline; the latter a creative approach to that same discipline. While the language of national public law can help us conceptualize the problems at stake – be critical – I am not sure that the answers found at the national level should be replicated in the institutional or decision-making patterns of global environmental law – we need to be more creative.

PART II

World Trade Organization

4

The WTO/GATS Mode 4, international labor migration regimes and global justice

TOMER BROUDE

1. Introduction: labour migration and global justice

The WTO's General Agreement on Trade in Services (GATS)[1] "Mode 4" is currently the only internationally-agreed legal instrument with the potential to become a functioning multilateral regime regulating temporary labor migration.[2] It is an international mechanism aimed at liberalizing service-related labor mobility[3] on the basis of qualified negotiated commitments by states to accept non-permanent foreign

The paper was presented at a conference on "Global Justice and International Law" VU University Amsterdam, March, 2007, at the Annual Meeting of the American Society of International Law, Washington, DC, March, 2007, and at the Law Faculty Workshop, Hebrew University of Jerusalem, May, 2007. The author thanks the participants at these presentations for their helpful comments, and in particular David Enoch, Roland Pierik, and Wouter Werner, as well as M arcia Harpaz and Lior Herman. The research for this paper was made possible by a Faculty Research Award from the Israel Association for Canadian Studies and the Department of Foreign Affairs and International Trade of the Government of Canada (2005–2006).

[1] General Agreement on Trade in Services, April 15, 1994, Marrakesh Agreement Establishing the World Trade Organization, Annex 1B, Legal Instruments – Results of the Uruguay Round, I.L.M. 33 (1994), 1125.

[2] Regional labor mobility arrangements do exist, though their scope is usually limited. See Julia Nielson, "Labour Mobility in Regional Trade Agreements," in *Moving People to Deliver Services*, ed. Aaditya Mattoo and Antonia Carzaniga (Washington, DC: World Bank and Oxford: Oxford University Press, 2003), pp. 93–111. The exception is the freedom of movement of workers in the European Union, that while not free of any of the problems discussed here, is geographically restricted to the European regional space and more importantly, is deeply embedded within an advanced system of economic and political integration. For a comprehensive, if not up to date, monograph on the subject, see Friedl Weiss and Frank Woolridge, *Free Movement of Persons within the European Community* (The Hague: Kluwer, 2002).

[3] The GATS aims to achieve higher levels of liberalization in international trade in services towards "the growth and development of the world economy" (see GATS Preamble). Within this context, Mode 4 regulates the "temporary presence of natural persons" for the purpose of service provision. Thus, the GATS does not deal with

labor migrants, subject to substantive rules that regulate and constrain states' unilateral temporary labor migration policies.

International trade and migration specialists query whether Mode 4 is effective as a global economic regime, and what may be done to make it work better.[4] In this chapter I ask, rather, if GATS Mode 4 is *just*: does the model of international labor migration regulation that it represents conform to principles of global justice? This question is closely related to evaluations of the morality of autonomous national migration policies, but is independent of them, going one step beyond and considering an international legal and institutional migration arrangement from a global justice perspective.[5] The exercise clearly holds lessons for the design of any future labor migration regime, but it is also important in the more general WTO context. To the extent that the WTO purportedly represents a global economic "constitution" for globalization, as is sometimes suggested,[6] it must be sensitive to conflicting political and philosophical visions of global justice and the way that they relate to international economic disparity.[7] This is especially poignant with respect to GATS Mode 4, because labor migration is strongly associated with transnational differentials in wages, social benefits, and skills, and because the more general area of immigration policy constitutes a major a fault line between cosmopolitan and communitarian liberal theories of global justice.

"migration" or "immigration" in explicit terms. Moreover, it is important to note that in the present article, the terms "migration" and "immigration" are used primarily with respect to temporary labor migration, to which the GATS is relevant, as opposed to permanent immigration and related issues such as naturalization, citizenship, or political rights of immigrants, which are in fact explicitly excluded from the GATS, as explained below.

[4] *Trade and Migration: Building Bridges for Global Mobility*, (Paris: OECD, 2004).

[5] This will be accomplished from the viewpoint of a number of approaches, namely: cosmopolitanism, realism, "society of states/peoples" approaches, and nationalism. For a description of these different approaches, see section 4 *infra*. For a series of critiques of global institutions, primarily from a cosmopolitan point of view, see Christian Barry and Thomas Pogge, *Global Institutions and Responsibilities: Achieving Global Justice*, (Oxford: Blackwell, 2005).

[6] "Constitutionalism" in the WTO is multi-faceted. For a thorough critique, see Jeffrey L. Dunoff, "Constitutional Conceits: The WTO's 'Constitution' and the Discipline of International Law," *European Journal of International Law* 17, no. 3 (2006), pp. 647–75, and the sources cited there.

[7] For a general egalitarian critique of the WTO, see Darrel Moellendorf, "The World Trade Organization and Egalitarian Justice," in Barry and Pogge, *Global Institutions and Responsibilities*, pp. 141–58.

2. GATS Mode 4 and labor mobility

How does a trade agreement relate to labor mobility?[8] The GATS applies to labor as an internationally tradable service. Under article I:2 GATS, the agreement covers four "Modes" of international service provision.[9] Among these, "Mode 4" is the provision of a service "by a service supplier of one Member, through presence of natural persons of a Member in the territory of another WTO Member." This entails movement of labor for the purpose of supplying a service on site in a foreign, service-importing country, and may include either self-employed suppliers remunerated directly by consumers or employees of service suppliers.[10] Such labor mobility may in principle occur in any of the service sectors covered by the GATS (e.g. health professionals, construction workers, tour guides, accountants, or software developers).[11] However, the GATS applies only to labor-migration that is service-related and does not establish free movement of yet unemployed labor. The GATS *Annex on Movement of Natural Persons Supplying Services under the Agreement* expressly provides that the GATS "shall not apply to measures affecting natural persons seeking access to the employment market of a Member, nor shall it apply to measures regarding citizenship, residence, or employment on a permanent basis." This caveat has regulatory implications that technically (if not artificially) differentiate GATS commitments from immigration laws, and service-provision from labor. Mode 4 may facilitate the mobility of workers, but these enter a foreign country under GATS as service suppliers for the purpose of supplying a service in a specific sector. They cannot enter for the purpose of seeking employment, and their entry is for a limited period of time, as may be necessary for the provision of a service under contract.

[8] The well-worn disclaimer apologizing for the brevity of the background discussion is especially apt here. For a good introduction to the GATS see *A Handbook on the GATS Agreement*, (Cambridge: Cambridge University Press, 2005).

[9] The four Modes are (1) *Cross Border Supply* (supply of a service "from the territory of one Member to the territory of any other Member"); (2) *Consumption Abroad* (supply of a service "in the territory of one Member to the service consumer of any other Member"); (3) *Commercial Presence* (supply of a service "by a service supplier of one Member, through commercial presence in the territory of any other Member"); and (4) *Temporary Presence of Natural Persons*.

[10] Antonia Carzaniga, "The GATS, Mode 4, and Pattern of Commitments," p. 23.

[11] The GATS covers twelve general service sectors (Business, Communication, Construction and Engineering, Distribution, Education, Environment, Financial, Health, Tourism and Travel, Recreation, Culture and Sporting, Transport, and the catch-all "Other") that are further divided into sub-sectors.

The GATS does, however, cover significant labor-intensive service sectors, and there is substantial overlap between the Mode 4 definitional concept of the supply of a service through presence of natural persons and what would more regularly be considered temporary movement of labor. For example, a foreign company providing services in the sub-sector "General construction work for buildings" (CPC 512), which includes "construction work (including new work, additions, alterations and renovation work) for all types of buildings, residential or non-residential, whether privately or publicly owned"[12] in a service-importing country, could do so either through Mode 3 commercial presence, contracting local labour or (if so allowed by local laws and regulations that may or may be not anchored in a GATS Mode 4 specific commitment) through the temporary presence of construction workers from its home country or from other WTO Members. From the GATS legal perspective these laborers would be service providers; they would not necessarily have a labor contract in the host country, nor have any right to seek further employment there, let alone a right to pursue permanent residence and citizenship. However, in direct economic terms they would be fully equivalent to temporary labor.

The GATS attempts to adapt the classical legal principles of trade in goods under the General Agreement on Tariffs and Trade (GATT)[13] to the more complex areas of trade in services. Thus, as a general obligation, the most-favoured nation (MFN) principle applies to all measures covered by the agreement, in any service sector, preventing discrimination between foreign service suppliers from different WTO Members (article II).[14] However, a Member is only obligated to allow service suppliers access to its market in those sectors and in those modes of supply in which it has entered specific commitments in its GATS schedule, subject to any terms and conditions specified therein (article XVI). The national treatment principle that prevents discrimination between domestic and foreign service suppliers similarly applies only to sectors in which a Member has elected to make specific market access commitments (article XVII).

[12] For discussion, see WTO, *Council for Trade in Services – Construction and Related Engineering Services – Background Note by the Secretariat*, S/C/W/38, June 8, 1998.

[13] General Agreement on Tariffs and Trade, Oct. 30, 1947, 61 Stat. A-11, T.I.A.S. 1700, 55 U.N.T.S. 194.

[14] MFN is subject to regional services agreements (article V), labor market integration agreements (article V *bis*) and valid MFN exemptions, some of which relate to Mode 4. *OECD*, p.148.

Taken together (and at face value), these principles mean that if a WTO Member commits to opening its services market in a certain sector under Mode 4, it must provide market access, MFN, and national treatment to foreign labor, significantly constraining the autonomy of its temporary foreign labor introduction policy in that sector. It is therefore not surprising that specific commitments under Mode 4 have so far been very modest and subject to significant reservations; for example, a major portion of commitments that have been made are restricted to "intra-corporate transferees," whose presence is related to Mode 3, investment-related commitments; executives; and business visitors.[15]

Mode 4's small impact in practice enhances rather than diminishes the unique opportunity that it provides us to examine the global justice implications of a multilateral labor migration regime, as applied. Indeed, a pragmatic view holds the concepts of justice and effectiveness as mutually reinforcing. Mode 4's practical weaknesses hint at the existence of both political impossibilities and moral deficiencies. In contemplating the ethics of global labor migration regimes in general, and the GATS Mode 4 in particular, this article considers that neither pure consequentialist analysis nor untainted deontological thinking will prove satisfactory. When applied to problems of international labor migration, ideal theories of global justice lead to prescriptions that are either politically impractical (e.g. utopianly advocating fully "open borders") or practically unhelpful (e.g. merely upholding the right of states to regulate the entry of labor migrants to their territory).[16] Nonetheless, the opportunity costs and real injustices of the current virtually unregulated international environment are too high to ignore. The question of international labor migration regulation thus lies deep in the realm of "non-ideal theory," in which we must search for "policies and courses of action that are morally permissible and politically possible as well as likely to be effective."[17] Making the gradual shift from ideal to non-ideal

[15] Carzaniga, "The GATS, Mode 4, and Pattern of Commitments," p.25.

[16] A similar problem has been noted with respect to the ethics of refugee policy (an area whose guiding justifications are distinct from those of labor migration; see note 38): "Political philosophy appears to present us with a rather polarized choice between a communitarian, or nationalist, ethics of closure and an expansive, universalist ethics of inclusion that appears to impose unfeasible demands." Christina Boswell, "The Liberal Dilemma in the Ethics of Refugee Policy," in *The Migration Reader: Exploring Polities and Policies* ed. Anthony M. Messina and Gallya Lahav (London: Lynne Reiner, 2006), p. 664.

[17] This reference to Rawls does not imply that I adhere to Rawls's distinction between ideal theory and non-ideal theory as dependent on the (non-)existence of a world in

even more difficult, the field is bogged with empirical uncertainty and scientific controversy. If "any defensible global political theory must rely on factual statements about the world,"[18] a global theory of labor migration regulation must, at least for the time being, rely on incomplete facts, and so maintain a degree of flexibility in accommodating competing political and philosophical perspectives.

This article ultimately argues that Mode 4 fails to meet even these elastic benchmarks, and is in at least this sense inappropriate as a prototypical labor migration regime. The next section provides an overview of the different dimensions of the global labor migration debate, as context for the global justice analysis of GATS Mode 4. The third section applies principal theories of global justice to the idea of a multilateral global labor migration regime, drawing the outer policy bounds of what might be considered as common, morally-acceptable ground. The fourth section then returns to the GATS Mode 4, critiquing it as a labor migration regime from the perspectives of these limits of global justice, followed by brief conclusions.

3. The three dimensions of the global labor migration debate

(a) *The 'international development' debate*

The first dimension of the migration debate revolves around the effects of international labor migration on the reduction of global economic inequality and the development of poor countries, many of which are labor-abundant. International migration is a distinctly North–South phenomenon (though not exclusively so). In 2000, about three per cent

which "all peoples accept and follow the (ideal of the) Law of Peoples" considered as "well-ordered peoples." John Rawls, *The Law of Peoples with "the Idea of Public Reason Revisited,"* (Cambridge, Mass.: Harvard University Press, 1999), pp. 4, 89. More generally, the gap between ideal and non-ideal theory depends on political realities. If ideal theory suggests that states should maintain full control over immigration, non-ideal theory would acknowledge that in practice borders are highly permeable to migration that the state might not be interested in; and if ideal theory conversely indicates that the world should be borderless, non-ideal theory would acknowledge that in practice states impose strict barriers to migration. On the differences between ideal and non-ideal theory, See Michael Phillips, "Reflections on the Transition from Ideal to non-Ideal Theory," *Noûs 19*, no, 4 (1985), pp. 551–70; and with specific reference to migration, see Joseph H. Carens, "Realistic and Idealistic Approaches to the Ethics of Migration," *International Migration Review* 30, no. 1 (1996), pp. 156–70.

[18] Simon Caney, *Justice Beyond Borders: A Global Political Theory,* (Oxford: Oxford University Press, 2005), p. 2.

of the world's population lived in a country other than that in which they were born, approximately 175 million people.[19] At the same time, the US alone was home to 28.4 million foreign born-people, or 10.4 per cent of the total US population.[20] Europe, as a region, contained 56 million people of migrant stock,[21] roughly equivalent to the entire population of France at the time. Clearly, most migrants move from low-income to high-income countries, and stay there, if they can. Most labor migrants are relatively poor in global terms, even if they do not come from the poorest segments of their source societies.

The constituent questions in this debate are many:[22] what are the effects of "brain drain," highly-skilled migration from developing countries, on their development? Who in developing countries benefits from labor emigration? How useful are financial labor remittances to developing economies and under which conditions? What are the differences between temporary and permanent labor migration in these respects? Do migrant diasporas contribute to development in their source countries, and if so, how? Which immigration policies of developed countries are most conducive to development? How can developing countries influence emigration patterns to their benefit? International labor migration is now in the cutting edge (or *bon-ton*) of

[19] "International Migration: Who, Where and Why" in *Current Issues: Demography Special*, (Frankfurt: Deutsche Bank Research, August 1, 2003), reproduced in *The Migration Reader*, ed. Messina and Lahav, p. 15; Or less: compare Roger Zegers de Beijl, "Combating Discrimination against Migrant Workers: International Standards, National Legislation and Voluntary Measures – The Need for Multi-Pronged Strategy," ILO Paper prepared for the Seminar on Immigration, Racism, and Racial Discrimination, (Geneva: Centre for Human Rights, May 5–9 1997), available at: www.ilo.org/public/english/protection/migrant/papers/disstrat. According to whom "the global stock of migrant workers, defined as persons who are economically active in a country of which they are not nationals and excluding asylum-seekers and refugees, is estimated by the International Labour Organization to be between 36 and 42 million. Accompanied by a slightly higher number of dependents, the total population of migrants is in the range of 80–97 million ... The economically active persons amount to a mere 1.4 to 1.6 per cent of the world's labour force of 2.6 billion."

[20] Lisa Lollock, "The Foreign-Born Population in the United States: Population Characteristics," (*US Census Bureau*, 2001), p. 1.

[21] *International Migration Report, 2002*, UN Doc. ST/ESA/SER.A/ 220, (New York: UN, Department of Economic and Social Affairs, Population Division, 2002).

[22] Devesh Kapur and John McHale, *Give Us Your Best and Brightest: The Global Hunt for Talent and its Impact on the Developing World*, (Washington, DC: Center for Global Development, 2005); Robert E.B. Lucas, *International Migration and Economic Development: Lessons from Low-Income Countries*, (Cheltenham: Edward Elgar, 2005); Lant Pritchett, *Let Their People Come: Breaking the Gridlock on Global Labor Mobility*, (Washington, DC: Center for Global Development, 2006).

international development policy, with the historical record of development aid provision so dismal[23] and the prospects of international trade effects on development appearing so moribund within the WTO's Doha "Development" Round.[24]

A common point of departure in this debate is the assessment of net global welfare gain from labor migration, as well as potential benefits for both developed and developing countries. Estimates of the overall economic gains from the elimination of all restrictions on labor mobility are as high as a net doubling of worldwide annual Gross National Product, leading to a fairer international distribution of income as well.[25]

More conservative estimates also indicate very significant welfare gains from freer movement of people.[26] The potential benefits of increased international labor mobility are strongly linked to economic differentials between developed countries and developing countries (or as one economist has bluntly put it, "[I]f people were goods, the solution to different wage and employment levels would be obvious: encourage the transfer of 'surplus' people from poorer to richer nation states."[27] Much of the growing interest in labor-migration regulation relates, therefore, to the different anticipated economic effects of liberalized migration in low- and high-income states. A recent World Bank study calculated that the continuation of increased migration from developing to developed countries at the same rate as was observed during the period 1970–2000 would raise the labor force of developed countries by three per cent over the period 2001–2025, leading to a small decline in wages in developed countries that would be offset by a rise in income, on average, from increased returns to capital. At the same time, new migrants' wages would rise as would wages in developing countries, in addition to direct economic effects of financial remittances. Overall net

[23] See William Easterly, *The White Man's Burden: Why the West's Efforts to Aid the Rest Have Done So Much Ill and So Little Good*, (New York: Penguin Press, 2006).

[24] Tomer Broude, "The Rule(s) of Trade and the Rhetos of Development: Reflections on the Functional and Aspirational Legitimacy of the World Trade Organization," *Columbia Journal of Transnational Law* 27, no. 4 (2006), pp. 221–61.

[25] Bob Hamilton and John Whalley, "Efficiency and Distributional Implications of Global Restrictions on Labour Mobility: Calculations and Policy Implications," *Journal of Development Economics* 14 (1984), pp. 61–75.

[26] Alan L. Winters, "The Economic Implications of Liberalizing Mode 4 Trade," in *Moving People to Deliver Services*, ed. Mattoo and Carzaniga, pp. 59–91.

[27] Philip Martin, "Migration," in *Global Crises, Global Solutions* ed. Bjorn Lomborg (Cambridge: Cambridge University Press, 2004), p. 443.

welfare gains would therefore be positive in both developed and developing countries.[28]

Beyond the aggregate global economic considerations, labor migration is regarded as an extremely important generator of economic benefits for developing countries and for the weaker segments of their societies. Empirical research has found that international migration has a strong impact on the reduction of poverty in developing countries.[29] In the rosiest scenario, labor migration can achieve a "win–win–win" outcome: the migrating individuals receive higher income and improved benefits, the country of origin gains from financial remittances, poverty reduction, and "networking" effects with its diaspora; and the receiving country gains a workforce that addresses pressing economic and demographic needs.[30]

Along these lines of analysis, the October 2005 Report of the Global Commission on International Migration (GCIM), an expert group appointed by the previous United Nations (UN) Secretary-General, expounded on the importance of migration to development calling for concrete international steps that would realize "the potential of human mobility."[31] Senior economists such as Joseph Stiglitz, a Nobel Prize laureate in economics, have also suggested that the liberalization of labor migration from developing countries to developed countries should be prioritized in multilateral negotiations in the WTO's Doha Round, and that the development dividends in this area, if taken seriously by all involved, would be no less important, if not greater, than the effects of reduced subsidies and increased liberalization in agricultural trade.[32]

(b) The 'national interest' debate

The second dimension of labor migration discourse is the national interest debate, a politically-charged argument that recurs in many

[28] *Global Economic Prospects: Overview and Global Outlook*, (Washington, DC: The World Bank, 2006). Note that these figures relate primarily to permanent immigration.

[29] Richard H. Adams and John Page, "International Migration, Remittances, and Poverty in Developing Countries," World Bank Policy Research Working Paper No. 3179, (December, 2003).

[30] Arno Tanner, *Emigration, Brain Drain and Development*, (Helsinki: East–West Books, 2005), pp. 23–24.

[31] UN (2006), Global Commission on International Migration, *Migration in an Interconnected World: New Directions for Action* (October 2005), ch. 2.

[32] Andrew Charlton and Joseph Stiglitz, *The Development Round of Trade Negotiations in the Aftermath of Cancun*, (London: Commonwealth Secretariat/Initiative for Policy Dialogue, 2004).

jurisdictions. It focuses on the effects of immigration on the well-being of the nation and its citizens in the face of the socio-economic changes that labor migration brings. The debate in each state may have its own special characteristics and idiosyncrasies, but in general the parameters are quite similar. In each case, the state is considered as the most relevant unit of policy analysis, relying on the authority[33] of the national government to regulate the entry of labor migrants according to the national interest, as perceived by politicians and their constituencies. Dilemmas that rise in this context include, among others, questions such as whether labor migrants are beneficial to the nation and its economy? Which immigrants should the state accept and how should it screen them? How many immigrants should the state allow, and under which conditions? Which domestic groups gain most from the influx of labor migration and which are most hurt by it? Is labor migration a sustainable solution to the problems posed by an aging population in developed states? How may labor migration impinge on the social rights that the state grants its nationals? How can the social costs of immigrant reception be reduced? What is the impact of immigration on social cohesion? How may unwanted immigration to the state be deterred and nationally desirable immigration promoted? These are the questions that dominate the national-interest immigration policy debate in rich, labor-importing countries: "who gets in" to "heaven's door."[34]

Thus, the US debates its policy towards "illegal" immigrants and the construction of a wall-like barrier on the Mexican border. Europeans ponder the costs and benefits of allowing the "Polish plumber" in, under equitable terms or otherwise. Israelis argue how temporary labor migrants impact upon the preservation of national agrarian ideals, how the treatment of temporary laborers can conform to the national civil rights regime, and how "demography" will be affected by the continued

[33] If not power – even once a national immigration policy is formulated, it is often very difficult to enforce, causing much of the migration debate to deal with the management of "illegal" immigration. For a provocative discussion of the distinction between national immigration policy targets ("first-order" immigration rules) and the different national rules and institutions used to implement them, *ex ante* and *ex post* ("second-order" immigration rules), see Adam B. Cox and Eric A. Posner, "The Second Order Structure of Immigration Law," *Stanford Law Review* 59, no. 4 (2006), p. 809.

[34] Daniel Stoffman, *Who Gets In: What's Wrong with Canada's Immigration Program – and How to Fix It* (Toronto: Macfarlane, Walter and Ross, 2002); George J. Borjas, *Heaven's Door: Immigration Policy and the American Economy* (Princeton: Princeton University Press, 1999).

reception of laborers from Eastern Europe, China, and South East Asia, themselves substitutes for cheap Palestinian labour now excluded for political conflict-related reasons.[35]

The national interest debate can be broken down into a political–economic aspect and a social–communitarian aspect. In the first, what is on the line are the general and distributive economic effects of increased labor immigration, including their impact on the incumbent skilled and unskilled workforce, on industry, and on labor unions. Because of the implications for sensitive interest groups and the intuitive fear of losing jobs, research in this area is susceptible to political capture. However, among economists there is an emerging dominant view that in most scenarios only the least-skilled native workers suffer adverse effects from increased labor migration and that these effects are small and countervailable by domestic social policy measures rather than immigration restrictions.[36] The social–communitarian dimension of the debate relates to the impact of increased immigration on the character and definition of the national community (more salient in the case of permanent immigration, but worrying also when temporary migration is significant). Academically, this is primarily a philosophical and sociological debate, but in practice it is highly politicized, as natural chauvinistic tendencies merge with job-loss fear to form electoral platforms.

The national interest debate clearly involves ideal moral deliberation and serves as a focal point for differences between cosmopolitan and communitarian liberal approaches. One might rightly ask, what is the moral justification for determining access to labor markets on the basis of concepts such as "borders," "citizenship," and "nationality," the fundamental terms upon which the national interest debate depends in both its economic and social–communitarian aspects. However, from a lawyer's pragmatic perspective, these questions are scholastic. What is more important is that international law *de lege lata* accepts that states have the authority, if not the obligation, to regulate labor immigration.[37] In terms of non-ideal theory, it would appear useless to

[35] Zeev Rosenhek, "Migration Regimes, Intra-State Conflicts and the Politics of Inclusion and Exclusion: Migrant Workers in the Israeli Welfare State," *Social Problems* 47, no. 1 (2000), p. 49.

[36] Howard F. Chang, "The Economic Impact of International Labor Migration: Recent Estimates and Policy Implications," *Temple Political & Civil Rights Review* 16, no. 2 (2007).

[37] Alexander T. Aleinikoff, "International Legal Norms and Migration: A Report," in *Migration and International Legal Norms*, ed. Alexander T. Aleinikoff and Vincent Chetail (The Hague: T.M.C. Asser, 2003), p. 3.

argue that states do not have the moral right to regulate the influx of labor migrants, by measures taken either at the border (e.g. in the form of admittance criteria, licensing procedures, and the like) or "behind the border" (e.g. by prescribing equal or differential employment conditions and social rights for migrant workers). This is an authority that states exercise in practice (albeit with varying degrees of success), and so it must be taken well into account when evaluating the justness of global migration regimes.

(c) The 'migrant welfare/rights' debate

The last, though not least important, dimension of the labor migration debate relates to the rights and welfare of labor migrants themselves, as individuals. Although labor may be commoditized as a "factor of production," labor migrants do not act like commodities; rather, they are non-passive human actors (and beings), driven by aspirations that transcend simple economic logic. International migration is a clear expression of people's aspirations to improve their lot,[38] as practiced by a significant chunk of humanity.[39] These observations may be obvious but they have significant policy implications for international labor migration regimes, relating to both effectiveness and justness. Migrants that are highly motivated and determined to participate in a foreign labor market in the face of immigration restrictions will take

[38] Among migrants, the "vast majority [...] move in search of better economic opportunities" while only ten per cent are considered "refugees"; World Migration 2005: Costs and Benefits of International Migration, *IOM* (2005), p. 379–81. A "Refugee" is a person who "owing to a well-founded fear of being persecuted for reasons of race, religion, nationality, membership of a particular social group, or political opinion, is outside the country of his nationality, and is unable to or, owing to such fear, is unwilling to avail himself of the protection of that country"; see art. 1(a)(2) of the 1951 United Nations ("UN") *Convention Relating to the Status of Refugees*, 189 UNTS 150; and art. 1(2) of the 1967 UN *Protocol Relating to the Status of Refugees*, 606 UNTS 267. These definitions clearly exclude migrants who simply migrate in pursuit of better lives. In practice, however, there are obvious gaps and overlaps between such economic migrants and refugees – people counted as political refugees even though they have sufficient cause to seek economic migration, or economic migrants who are also politically persecuted, or people whose economic deprivation is the result of political persecution – these may all be counted as both economic migrants and refugees.

[39] The 175 million figure mentioned above reflects only the number of those people who have actually managed to realize their migratory hopes under the current international regulatory conditions, which are not conducive to labor migration, to say the least. A more liberal labor migration regime would likely multiply the number of migrants manifold, for better or for worse.

great risks, even life threatening ones, and endure great hardships to do so: braving shark-infested waters in rickety, overcrowded boats, walking for weeks through inhospitable deserts (and many times, dying there),[40] paying excessive premiums to people-smugglers and labor contractors, subsequently living invisible, undocumented lives, treated "like rustlers, like thieves."[41] For "illegal" or "irregular" immigrants, it matters little whether the immigration restrictions that they are circumventing are unilaterally imposed by the target country's government, or the result of an internationally agreed migration regime. It cannot be assumed willy-nilly that a global labor migration regime will be any easier to enforce than national migration policy. Thus, in order to be effective, its design must take into account migrants' willingness to adjust to the regime, increasing incentives to comply with it. Furthermore, as a matter of legal context, migrants have been granted several specific rights under international law, including protection from racism and racial discrimination, procedural rights in case of expulsion, and, in some cases, national treatment in work conditions,[42] although often these rights are not enjoyed by them in practice. For the sake of legal consistency, a labor migration regime must take account of these rights.

The area of migrant rights is of independent importance, and many might consider that it is the core of the moral problems relating to immigration. Moreover, the debate becomes particularly important for present purposes when it raises questions that may contradict goals and interests that emerge at the global development or national interest levels. For example, enhanced migrant rights may agitate towards granting temporary labor migrants social protection at the level granted to domestic laborers. However, in welfare states this would impose significant fiscal burdens that reduce the willingness of governments to allow labor immigration, thus foregoing the national and global benefits of labor mobility altogether. This is what has been called the "immigration paradox": the liberal commitment to grant migrant workers equal rights once admitted to the labor market agitates against their admission, in which case migrants may end up worse off than they would have

[40] Wayne A. Cornelius, "Death at the Border: Efficacy and Unintended Consequences of US Immigration Control Policy," *Population and Development Review* 27, no. 4 (2001), pp. 661–85.

[41] Woody Guthrie, *Deportees (Plane Wreck at Los Gatos)*.

[42] For an overview, see Joan Fitzpatrick, "The Human Rights of Migrants?" in *Migration and International Legal Norms*, ed. Aleinikoff and Chetail, pp.169–84.

been if they had been admitted yet granted lesser rights.[43] Furthermore, the entire concept of "temporary" labor migration, which in theory is attractive to both national interests (e.g. by reducing social disruption) and global development (e.g. by reducing brain drain and increasing remittances) is problematic from a migrant rights perspective, to the extent that enforcement of the temporariness of migrants' stay may involve infringement of their human rights and dignity (such as detention although they have committed no offense, or labor licensing arrangements that bind migrants to a single employer in a manner tantamount to enslavement).

These are the main dimensions of labor migration that pose any would-be international labor migration regime with a policy justice "trilemma": how to encourage welfare-enhancing and poverty reducing labor migration while accommodating and/or overcoming national-interest based resistance, and preserving the rights of migrants? Is there a coherent moral approach to global justice that might be able to take all factors of this equation into account?

4. Political–philosophical approaches to international labor migration regimes

(a) From national immigration policy to international migration regulation

The critique of national immigration policy is an obvious battleground for international political philosophers, serving as a watershed distinguishing between schools of thought about global society, the state, the community, the individual, and their interrelationships.

Modern states reserve the authority to prevent non-nationals from crossing their borders, no matter how well-intentioned or industrious these people may be, through national immigration policies that distinguish among people primarily on the basis of the place where they were born. Is this a morally-relevant criterion, or merely an arbitrary one? By segregating different social environments in which people may act, on a national basis, immigration restrictions produce inequalities of opportunity among individuals who should otherwise be considered equal. Are these restrictions morally defensible? To enforce immigration policy, states at least project the willingness to use force against innocent

[43] Howard F. Chang, "The Immigration Paradox: Poverty, Distributive Justice, and Liberal Egalitarianism," *DePaul Law Review* 52 (2003), p. 759.

and harmless people ("Borders have guards and the guards have guns," as Carens so plainly notes.[44] How could this violence, actual or threatened, be justified?

The reflexive responses to these queries rest on "sovereignty" and "community" (at times mutually compatible, but not always so). States are mainly defined by their territory, population, and government. Their sovereign governors are charged with the maintenance of order in their territory, the well-being of their nationals, and the national interest. Their first order of duty is therefore accepted as owed to their own "people." It might then be argued that states and their nationals have no obligations towards non-compatriots, and that national immigration control is legitimately self-interested, with openness towards migrants at most a display of charity or hospitality, not moral obligation.[45] Most reasons advanced for limitations on immigration fall well within the bounds of the "national interest" debate discussed above: nationals pay taxes, non-nationals do not; immigrants harm the economic well-being of (some) nationals; immigration increases inequality among incumbents within the state; immigration compromises national culture; immigration erodes the capacity of national institutions to provide the just entitlements of nationals.[46]

In response to these national/communitarian defenses of restrictions on immigration, universalist or cosmopolitan critiques argue, on the basis of the shared humanity of nationals and non-nationals, that international borders should generally be open, and that the only justifiable immigration restrictions are those that would apply in equal force towards nationals at home (*mutatis mutandis*).[47] While these "open-border" arguments focus on the (im)morality of restrictions on

[44] Joseph H. Carens, "Aliens and Citizens: The Case for Open Borders," *Review of Politics* 49, no. 2 (1987), p. 251.

[45] For an interesting case study of Australian employment visa requirements on the backdrop of Derrida's reading of Kant's right to hospitality, see Amir Kordvani, "Hospitality, Politics of Mobility, and the Movement of Service Suppliers under the GATS," *Melbourne Journal of International Law* 7 (2006), pp. 74–103; referring to Jacques Derrida, *On Cosmopolitanism and Forgiveness*, Mark Dooley, and Michael Hughes, trans., (London: Routledge, 2000).

[46] For a survey and rebuttal of such arguments supporting immigration restrictions, see: Darrel Moellendorf, *Cosmopolitan Justice*, (Boulder, CO: Westview, 2002), pp. 61–67; Robert E. Goodin, "If People Were Money ...," in Brian Barry and Robert E. Goodin, *Free Movement: Ethical Issues in the Transnational Migration of People and of Money*, (Pennsylvania, University Park: The Pennsylvania State University Press, 1992), pp. 6–11.

[47] Carens, "Aliens and Citizens: The Case for Open Borders."

international free movement because of the injustice they cause individuals (raising arguments related to the "migrant welfare/rights" debate), they muster additional force by pointing out that national immigration restrictions impair global distributive justice, serving as barriers to movement from poorer countries to more affluent and developed ones (thus engaging in the "global development" debate).[48]

Moreover, this article is not directly concerned with the general justification (or undermining) of the existing practice of nationally-imposed immigration restrictions. Neither does it aim to determine what might independently be considered as just national immigration policy, particularly not as far as permanent immigration and naturalization is concerned. Rather, the question is whether GATS Mode 4, a seminal *international* temporary labor migration *regime*, satisfies principles of global justice. The fact that states exercise their own independent immigration policies may be judged separately, but when examining international labor migration policy regimes from a pragmatic moral perspective, this fact should rather be taken as a given, a worst-/best-case expression of political reality. The intellectual task in the present case is not to critique national immigration policies as such, but to identify the contours of morally defensible and practically effective global structures of international labor migration regulation.

The next sections examine migration regimes from different perspectives, referring to Caney's useful classification of theories of global justice, consisting of cosmpolitanism; realism; 'society-of-states' approaches (including Rawls's 'society-of-peoples'); and nationalism.[49] Each theory naturally gravitates towards a certain ideal-type of international labor migration regime. However, when the real multi-dimensional complexities of the global labor migration debate are grafted on to ideal theory, each approach proves capable of adjustment and compromise, suggesting a number of general policy prescriptions. These provide us with a common, pragmatic basis for evaluating international labor migration regimes, the outer bounds of what is considered morally acceptable, if not ideally so, by each theory.

[48] See, e.g. Caney's reference to a "standard economics textbook," David Begg, Stanley Fischer, and Rudiger Dornbusch, *Economics*, 3rd edn. (London: McGraw-Hill, 1991), p. 644, maintaining that "[t]he quickest way to equalize world income distribution would be to permit free migration between countries." Caney, *Justice Beyond Borders*, p. 106.

[49] Caney, *ibid.*, p. 3.

(b) Cosmopolitanism

Cosmopolitan approaches emphasize the equal moral worth of all human beings, independent of group membership, from which derive universally-applicable mutual obligations among all persons.[50] Important expressions of moral cosmopolitanism are extensions of the basic principles of Rawls's liberal *A Theory of Justice*[51] to the international sphere,[52] although Rawls himself rejected this project.[53]

Applied to questions of international labor migration, cosmopolitanism, as a form of liberal egalitarianism, generally agitates against national immigration control.[54] "Open borders" are preferred, as these would best conform to the global equality of opportunity among human beings that can be understood as cosmopolitanism's underlying system of distributive justice.[55] "National interest" is pushed aside, the focus being on international development and migrant rights. This might be somewhat qualified to the extent that entirely free movement of people might induce chaotic outcomes that would cause excessive harm to incumbents and also undermine the achievement of the rights it was intended to promote,[56] or might otherwise be tempered by attempts to resolve gaps between national immigration restrictions and the liberal cosmopolitan paradigm.[57] There is however no intention here to reopen this aspect of the debate, i.e. are national immigration restrictions themselves morally justified? Rather, the question is, given that states retain the authority to restrict labor immigration to their territory, what would be the attributes of an international global temporary labor

[50] Thomas Pogge, "Cosmopolitanism and Sovereignty," in *Political Restructuring in Europe: Ethical Perspectives*, ed. Chris Brown (London: Routledge, 1994), pp. 89–122; Kok-Chor Tan, *Justice Without Borders: Cosmopolitanism, Nationalism and Patriotism*, (Cambridge: Cambridge University Press, 2004), p .2.

[51] John Rawls, *A Theory of Justice*, (Cambridge, MA: Harvard University Press, 1971).

[52] Charles R. Beitz, *Political Theory and International Relations*, with a new afterword by the author, (Princeton, NJ: Princeton University Press, 1999 [1979]), pp. 127–36; Thomas Pogge, *Realizing Rawls*, (Ithaca, NY: Cornell University Press, 1989).

[53] Rawls, *The Law of Peoples*.

[54] See Joseph H. Carens, "Migration and Morality: A Liberal Egalitarian Perspective," in Barry and Goodin, *Free Movement*, p. 43: "liberal egalitarianism entails a deep commitment to freedom of movement which can be overridden at the level of principle only with great difficulty."

[55] Caney, *Justice Beyond Borders*, pp. 122–23.

[56] Carens, "Aliens and Citizens: The Case for Open Borders" p. 259.

[57] See Joel P. Trachtman, "Welcome to Cosmopolis, World of Boundless Opportunity," *Cornell International Law Journal* 39 (2006), pp. 477–501.

migration regime that would be morally acceptable from a cosmopolitan perspective? In answering this question two general parameters emerge.

First, a (non-ideal) cosmopolitan approach would evaluate the extent to which an international migration regime encourages states to liberalize immigration in patterns that promote global distributive justice in cosmopolitan terms. This is not merely to say that the more migration restrictions are removed or reduced, the better, but that the regime should obligate and motivate well-off states to allow labor migration (a) from those locations whose residents would most benefit from increased migration (these may not necessarily be states, but rather regions and locales, although in practice it would be very difficult to apply this logic otherwise); and (b) of those migrant workers who would most benefit from migration (themselves, as well as their families). This formulation is a practical interpretation of the cosmopolitan's global application of Rawls's "difference principle," whereby social and economic inequalities should be arranged to the greatest advantage of the least advantaged to be acceptable.

Second, a cosmopolitan approach would assess the way the regime applies to the individual migrant and his or her dependants. The reality of state-imposed immigration control cannot justify any other infringements of universal human rights. An international labor regime that allows violations of the basic human rights of migrants, in the process of immigration, while working as labor migrants, or in their repatriation, would be unacceptable from a cosmopolitan moral perspective.

(c) Realism

Realists are statist communitarians who assert that to the extent international relations include a moral component, states have an obligation to pursue their own interest, not utopian ideals such as universal equity.[58] Yet as we have seen, the "national interest" debate in the labor

[58] Hans J. Morgenthau, *In Defense of National Interest: A Critical Examination of American Foreign Policy*, (New York, NY: Alfred Knopf, 1951); Kenneth Waltz, *Theory of International Politics*, (Reading, Mass.: Addison Wesley, 1979). For a survey of nuanced versions of realism, see Caney, *Justice Beyond Borders*, pp. 7–10. Political theoreticians of international relations who have advanced beyond the basic realist paradigm to explore strategic interactions between states (sometimes known as "neo-liberalism") should also be considered, in terms of moral justification, as realists, in that their assumptions retain the statist–communitarian understanding, generally considering the state as a rational, self-interested, and utility-maximizing unit of analysis.

migration context is fraught with definitional and empirical problems, presenting the realist with difficult policy choices. However, this uncertainty may ossify realist perspectives of international migration regimes, in both principle and practice, rather than loosen them. For the realist, a legally-binding migration regime would at first blush not seem to accomplish anything that a state might not achieve through unilateral policy. Long-term commitments would constrain the state from adjusting its immigration policy to changing needs and interests over time. The first choice of the realist would therefore likely be to remain with the current "regime," i.e. the condition in which states have overall and essentially absolute authority to determine their labor migration policy.

This rigid realist approach would, however, ignore the real, non-moral, constraints on the ability of the state to unilaterally pursue its interests, however defined. These constraints include, at minimum, the difficulties faced by states in preventing the entry of immigrants that their self-interested policy has defined as "unwanted"; and the problem of enforcing the temporariness of "wanted" temporary immigration. These are problems that might be mitigated through international cooperation, increasing the attractiveness of an international migration regime even in realist eyes. A (non-ideal) realist approach might therefore accept an international labor regime that would conform to the following parameters:

First, an international labor regime should provide significant payoffs to migration-attracting states in areas in which unilateral policy has proven ineffective, to the detriment of national-interest-based policy. Specifically, an international regime would be morally acceptable to the realist only if it included mechanisms that increase rather than reduce the state's capacity to enforce immigration policy and its ability to repatriate labor migrants once their presence is no longer in the "national interest" (even at the price of binding or at least restricting national immigration policy and accepting additional terms that the state would not otherwise consider necessary).

Second, the realist would be wary of any international regime that does not provide the state with some sort of trump card in the case of unexpected developments that are seriously detrimental to the state's interest, such as economic disruption due to unbridled labor immigration, or large social welfare expenditures that are not covered by the benefits of immigration. Contingent and temporary state safeguard measures are therefore an essential component of any international labor migration regime that a realist approach might subscribe to, although the depth and breadth of such safeguard measures would need to be carefully considered.

(d) *'Society-of-states/peoples' approaches*

In contrast to cosmopolitanism, society-of-states approaches to international political philosophy acknowledge that states have independent value as bearers of moral rights. Although these approaches are also statist–communitarian, they differ from realism in that they recognize that states have moral duties beyond the state itself, that is, towards other states, though not individuals. Taken in conjunction, these elements of a society-of-states approach would maintain that "a just global order is one in which there are states and the states accept that they have moral duties to other states."[59]

Society-of-states theories are highly attuned to current international legal structural realities. Indeed, if one supplants the "moral" with the "legal," society-of-states approaches are formally similar to traditional Westphalian doctrines of international law as reflected in contemporary international relations. How would these approaches apply to the idea of an international labor migration regime? Taken narrowly, a society-of-states approach would merely uphold the independence of states' policy-making as constrained by the principle of non-intervention.[60] In actual terms, this would be far less of an obstacle to an international migration regime than a realist approach, merely granting states unconstrained authority (and hence, the discretion to cooperate) in the area of immigration control, but not linking migration policy to a particular policy guideline, such as the "national interest."

However, we must also address the implications of a more complex (if controversial) "society-of-states" theory, that is, Rawls's "society-of-peoples."[61] Rawls considered global society to constitute five types of "peoples": liberal peoples, committed to individual rights; non-liberal but "decent" peoples[62]; aggressive and despotic "outlaw states"; societies

[59] Caney, *Justice Beyond Borders*, p. 10.

[60] Hedley Bull, *The Anarchical Society: A Study of Order in World Politics*, (London: Macmillan, 1977).

[61] Rawls, *The Law of Peoples*; For a critique of the distinction between "'states' and "peoples," see Caney, *Justice Beyond Borders*, pp. 11–12.

[62] These are both, to Rawls, "well-ordered" peoples; "Decent" peoples are "nonliberal societies whose basic institutions meet certain specified conditions of political right and

burdened by unfavorable conditions; and benevolent absolutisms.[63] To Rawls, principles of international justice are those principles that are acceptable to both liberal and decent peoples – this is a partial or selective social contract, from which the other forms of peoples are all but excluded.

Rawls assumes that most migration is caused by the effects of bad governance in the source country.[64] Free movement would therefore cause the costs of the bad governance of non-liberal, non-decent peoples to be borne by liberal and decent peoples. For this reason, according to Rawls, well-ordered peoples have "at least a qualified right to limit immigration."[65] Moreover, Rawls did not directly address the issue of migration between liberal peoples and non-liberal, decent peoples (i.e. among well-ordered peoples); presumably, if the cause of migration is the lack of respect for human rights, there is no reason to prevent such migration. If, however, the cause of migration is the denial of public participation, then Rawls's justification for migration restrictions would apply in his model. Moreover, none of these questions would be problematic once the deficiencies of non-liberal and non-decent societies were solved, because Rawls surmises that in these conditions the demand for migration would disappear of itself. This approach is clearly a justification of the unilateral and restrictive immigration policies of the affluent states who define the meaning of liberalism and 'decency'.

Does this mean that an international labor migration regime comprising agreements between well-ordered peoples and other peoples on the regulation of labor migration could never be justified under Rawls's terms? This would be a difficult position to defend. While to Rawls well-ordered states (and indeed, any state) may bear no *duty* to allow immigration, they do have a *right* to do so (or put otherwise, they have no duty to refrain from accepting immigrants). At the very least, the choice to either accept or reject labor migrants as the externalities of poorly-ordered peoples, so to speak, and of their bad governance, even

justice," including public participation in political decisions. Rawls, *The Law of Peoples*, p. 3.

[63] "Benevolent absolutisms" honor human rights but deny participatory politics and so "are not well-ordered," Rawls, *ibid.*, p. 4.

[64] *Ibid.*, pp. 8–9.

[65] This seems unpersuasive, in that it allocates the consequences of bad governance to the governed, not to the governors, in peoples whose non-liberal political systems prevent participatory governance, and so should not be faulted for their leaders' conduct. The people are punished twice – first, by suffering from poor governance; second, by not being able to migrate to more liberal pastures. *Ibid.*, p. 39, fn. 48.

if it is temporary, is the prerogative of well-ordered societies. Surely the acceptance of labor immigrants has important benefits to liberal and decent societies – Rawls simply emphasizes (one of) the "push" factors of emigration (bad governance) but ignores the "pull" factors or demand for immigrants in developed countries. Nothing in Rawls's theory suggests that agreements to bind immigration policy are improper as such.

With respect to "burdened societies," while the duty to assist may not include migration as a method of assistance,[66] it ought to be the case that the immigration policy of well-ordered peoples should not be allowed to *contradict* the aims of the duty of assistance. Thus, immigration policy should not impair the prospects of burdened societies to gain the independent capacity to manage their affairs reasonably. Surely this implies that immigration policies should avoid enhancing "brain drain" problems in developing countries, and encourage the return of labor income to their economies. These are goals that might better be achieved through international cooperative arrangements on temporary migration, and so an international labor migration regime that promotes the goal of the duty of assistance should be accepted as reasonable by liberal and decent societies. This would be the case even if the labor migration regime established obligations on well-ordered societies to accept temporary labor migrants.

One qualification to this is Rawls's concern that egalitarian ideals should not be foisted on non-liberal societies. Rawls rejects cosmopolitan principles of distributive justice because they would be "intolerant" to non-liberal societies.[67] This does not appear to be a concern because a labor migration regime that did not intervene in the political systems of source countries by imposing political or economic policy conditionality would be considered "tolerant" in this sense.

In addition, Rawls agrees that peoples have a duty to honor human rights. Thus, a regime that promoted respect for migrants' rights (to be distinguished from the right to migrate) would be morally acceptable and even desirable. Furthermore, although Rawls rejects equality of opportunity as a moral principle at the global level, he does include the right to means of subsistence among the rights to be respected.[68] To be sure, this cannot form the basis for a right to migrate, but if an

[66] Rawls implies that allowing migration from burdened societies is *not* part of the duty of assistance, particularly because the aim of the duty is "to help burdened societies to be able to manage their own affairs reasonably and eventually to become members of the Society of well-ordered peoples," Rawls, *The Law of Peoples*, p. 111, fn. 17. Other positions on this issue may be defensible, but there is no need to pursue them here.

[67] Rawls, *ibid.*, p. 59 ff. [68] *Ibid.*, p. 65.

international labor migration regime had as one of its objectives the promotion of this right, this would not be objectionable, even if it applied to non-decent peoples.

In sum, an international labor migration regime would be morally consistent with Rawls's theory if it increased the capacity of burdened societies to become well-ordered, respected human rights, and promoted the right to subsistence, while avoiding the imposition of egalitarian ideals upon non-liberal societies. Rawls's "society-of-peoples" accepts global inequality but does not mandate it; thus, while it may not demand an international labor migration regime, such a regime could be considered morally attractive, under these conditions.

(e) Nationalism

Communitarian nationalism attaches moral significance to nationality, bearing on rights and duties.[69] This is distinct from a realist approach, because a "nation" is a community with a shared ethnic or cultural identity, as opposed to the state conceived of as a political entity. I will not linger on the merits of these distinctions or their implications – indeed, even "nationalist" philosophers blur them at times.[70] For present purposes, what is important is that a nationalist perspective would require an international labor regime to strengthen the nation's capacity to enforce its immigration policy, even at the cost of making prior commitments to accept migrants; and would also, like the realist approach, expect a migration regime to provide effective safeguards should increased immigration pose a threat to the nation.

5. GATS Mode 4: a global justice critique

(a) Synthesis: principles for a just labor migration regime

The following principles may be distilled from the discussion, delineating the bounds of international migration regimes that might be morally acceptable to all approaches:

1. *Global distributive justice*: The regime should address global inequality by liberalizing international labor migration and causing well-off

[69] Caney, *Justice Beyond Borders*, p. 13.

[70] See for example Miller, referring to the justification of immigration policies of "nation-states": David Miller, "Immigration: The Case for Limits," in *Contemporary Debates in Applied Ethic*, ed. Andrew L. Cohen and Christopher Heath Wellman (Oxford: Blackwell, 2004).

states to accept immigration (a) from those states/locations whose residents would most benefit from increased migration; and (b) of those migrant workers who would themselves most benefit from migration, while avoiding the establishment of migration patterns that are detrimental to the social, economic, and political development of developing countries.

2. *Human rights protection*: The regime must protect labor migrants from violations of their basic human rights, in the process of migration, while working as labor migrants in the host country, and in their repatriation.
3. *Migration policy effectiveness*: The regime should increase the capacity of the international system and of states to control and enforce agreed immigration policy effectively and their ability to repatriate temporary labor migrants whose legal term of stay under the regime has ended.
4. *Emergency safeguards*: In the backdrop of increased labor mobility liberalization, contingent and temporary emergency safeguard measures should be allowed in situations where labor migration patterns seriously threaten economic and social interests of migration-receiving states.

Of course, this would not be the set of legal principles advocated by any single global justice paradigm taken on its own. As we have seen, the initial assumptions of cosmopolitan and communitarian approaches are at times far removed from each other, and their ideal prescriptions seem mutually incompatible. Nonetheless, a shift to non-ideal formulations and conceptual bargaining allows a general compromise to be struck, opening a broad range of complementarities. For example, a realist or nationalist would not consider human rights protection as a necessary component of a labor migration regime, but would not consider it offensive or burdensome if it were coupled with increased effectiveness of enforcement. Conversely, a cosmopolitan might consider mechanisms aimed at ensuring the temporariness of labor migration as unnecessary; but if they allowed greater global equality and were subjected to effective human rights protection, the cosmopolitan would accept them as superior to the current situation in which neither global distributive justice nor human rights are well-served. To be sure, these principles remain general, and the ensuing challenge is their translation into concrete legal prescriptions that would preserve the viability of the conceptual bargain. Moreover, these principles furnish us with tools for assessing the justness of GATS Mode 4 as an international labor migration regime given the backdrop of the dimensions of the international migration debate previously described. As argued below, Mode 4 runs afoul of these principles on many counts.

(b) Global distributive justice

The most damning indication of Mode 4's weakness in addressing global disparities is its *de facto* negligible impact on global migration and development to date. Historically, the inclusion of Mode 4 in the GATS was the result of developing-country demands during the Uruguay Round. Yet in practice, specific commitments remain few, and most of them do not address developing-country interests. The actual economic effects of temporary labor migration are generally very difficult to assess,[71] but it seems well nigh impossible to establish any causality between any such effects and Mode 4 liberalization, given its paucity. In addition, in many cases national labor migration policies are more liberal than GATS' specific commitments would require (though still selective and self-serving), so that any existing development dividend cannot be attributed to the GATS.

The failure of GATS to encourage developed countries to reduce labour migration restrictions stems from multiple causes, but the clearest is the asymmetrical North–South structure of labor migration combined with the traditionally reciprocal nature of concessions in the WTO.[72] Developing countries have little or nothing to offer in return within Mode 4 itself, and cross-linkages with liberalization in other Modes that would be of interest to developed countries, or indeed in other areas of WTO law and policy, have failed to materialize.[73] Article

[71] *World Trade Report 2004: Exploring the Linkage between the Domestic Policy Environment and International Trade*, (Geneva: WTO, 2004); Marion Jansen and Roberta Piermartini, "The Impact of Mode 4 Liberalization on Bilateral Trade Flows," *WTO, Economic Research and Statistics Division*, Staff Working Paper ERSD, 2005–2006.

[72] On reciprocity and development, see Broude, "The Rule(s) of Trade …," pp. 259–61. Indeed, the logic of reciprocity explains why developing states have also refrained from making Mode 4 commitments: they would have little value at the bargaining table vis-à-vis developed countries.

[73] A full analysis of the political economy of the weakness of Mode 4 is beyond the scope of this article. For one study, explaining that the GATS' effort to encourage labor-receiving countries to allow entry will have little migration liberalization impact, see Mohammad Amin and Aaditya Mattoo, "Does Temporary Migration have to be Permanent?," *World Bank Policy Research Working Paper No. 3582*, (2005).

IV GATS recognizes the link between development and trade in services, including through the presence of natural persons.[74] This sentiment is also echoed in the WTO's Council for Trade in Services "Guidelines and Procedures for the Negotiations on Trade in Services"[75] and in subsequent proposals and declarations produced during the ongoing Doha Round. Yet the language remains aspirational, and does not establish any concrete criteria that must be met for development and global distributive justice, such as quotas of commitments of interest to developing countries, or preferences for service-providing labor migrants from developing countries.

Not only are there no justice-oriented criteria for specific commitments in Mode 4, but some of the legal principles of GATS may actually prevent an applied consideration of development needs. As analyzed above, global distributive justice would require labor-receiving countries to discriminate in favor of labor migrants from developing countries, and even among those, in favour of those migrants who would most benefit from liberalization. Yet MFN applies as a general commitment to all service-related labor migration, even in sectors in which no market-access commitments have been made, legally precluding such preferences, as a rule (indeed this is sometimes mentioned as a source of reluctance to liberalize labor migration under Mode 4). Notably, the "Enabling Clause" that permits developing countries to grant preferential market access to developing countries on a non-reciprocal basis,[76] applies to goods, but not to services. Under article V:1 GATS, preferential treatment may be granted through regional services' trade agreements, provided there is substantial sectoral coverage and national treatment among the parties. This could allow for increased North–South liberalization in the services trade, but on a reciprocal basis, and only if significant levels of overall service market integration were agreed upon.[77] Article V *bis* specifically permits the establishment

[74] "The increasing participation of developing country Members in world trade shall be facilitated through negotiated specific commitments [...] relating to: [...] (c) the liberalisation of market access in sectors and modes of supply of export interest to them."

[75] WTO, *Council for Trade in Services – Guidelines and Procedures for the Negotiations on Trade in Services*, S/L/93, March 29, 2001.

[76] Waiver Decision on the Generalized System of Preferences, June 25, 1971, GATT B.I.S.D. (18th Supp.) at 24 (1972), *superseded by* Decision on Differential and More Favorable Treatment, Reciprocity, and Fuller Participation of Developing Countries, November 28, 1979, GATT B.I.S.D. (26th Supp.) at 203 (1980).

[77] Article V:2 allows a degree of flexibility to developing countries who are party to such regional services' trade agreements in the application of national treatment, but this

of bilateral or regional labor market integration agreements, but these would have to be fully integrative. Thus, the GATS does not include provisions that could be the basis for limited preferences for developing countries in Mode 4. Moreover, when the services provisions of existing North–South regional trade agreements are examined,[78] the Article V GATS consistency of many of them is questionable, because they provide for only limited or controlled GATS-style "positive list" sectoral liberalization, and some do not at all liberalize the movement of labor beyond GATS commitments.

As for discrimination in favor of particularly deserving migrants, technically this is possible (e.g. by restricting market access in a given sector to labor migrants with an annual source-country income below a certain threshold), but no schedules of specific commitments do so in practice. Indeed, at a more fundamental level, the GATS' somewhat euphemistic treatment of labor migration as services-provision, and its exclusion of employment seeking migrants[79] significantly impair the capacity of Mode 4 to promote global equality of opportunity among potential migrant workers.

Another deficiency in Mode 4's potential to facilitate labor migration promotive of distributive justice is Article XVII GATS national treatment. In areas in which market access has been granted under Mode 4, labor migrants cum service suppliers must receive treatment no less favourable than the treatment accorded to domestic laborers, by any measure affecting the supply of services. Although Article XVII has its roots in international trade theory and Article III GATT 1947, not in international human rights law, it exemplifies the liberal immigration paradox. On the basis of Article XVII GATS, one might argue that foreign labor migrants must receive national minimum wage and social benefits. In some cases, this would deter the introduction of labor from low-wage countries, having been robbed of its competitive advantage, and hence trapped in its domestic setting. National treatment, originally designed to overcome non-tariff barriers to international trade, is in these cases a barrier to both trade and development. Beyond formal equality as such, human rights infringements do not necessarily arise

would appear to merely permit developing countries to retain some discrimination in favor of local service-suppliers, and could not sanction an agreement whose main function was to grant market access to service-providers from a developing country.

[78] Nielson, "Labour Mobility in Regional Trade Agreements."

[79] As per the GATS *Annex*, *supra* section 1.

in this scenario, as I will discuss presently, but distributive outcomes are thwarted.

Last but not least, the GATS simply does not include any language that might prevent labor migration policies of developed countries that are potentially detrimental to the social, economic, and political development of developing countries. Brain drain and remittance-dependence concerns are not incorporated into the GATS in any way.

(c) Human rights protection

The relationship between WTO disciplines and international human rights norms is a complex one.[80] Moreover, the specific nexus between GATS Mode 4 and human rights is ostensibly far simpler in the sense that the rights in question are the rights of the actual workers whose migration is to be enabled by commitments under the GATS itself, not of indirectly affected persons (such as laborers manufacturing traded goods), and as we have seen, even a non-ideal global justice analysis would sincerely expect a labor migration regime to provide basic human rights protection.

Moreover, the GATS does not require Members to protect labor migrants from violations of basic human rights or to make international commitments in this respect. In GATS, reference is made to several non-WTO, international corpora of law,[81] but international human rights and labor rights obligations are not among them. Absent direct incorporation, the status of non-WTO human rights commitments in the WTO is academically controversial but effectively unenforceable in WTO law.[82] Thus, a labor-providing WTO Member could not complain

[80] See Ernst-Ulrich Petersmann, "The WTO Constitution and Human Rights," *Journal of International Economic Law* 3, no. 1 (2000), pp. 19–25; Robert Howse, "Human Rights in the WTO: Whose Rights, What Humanity? Comment on Petersmann," *European Journal of International Law* 13, no. 3 (2002), pp. 651–60; ed. Thomas Cottier, Joost Pauwelyn, and Elisabeth Burgi *Human Rights and International Trade* (Oxford: Oxford University Press, 2005).

[81] Article VII:5 refers to relevant international and non-governmental standardization organizations; Article XII:2(b) refers to the Articles of Agreement of the International Monetary Fund (IMF), and Article XII:5(e) grants IMF findings an elevated factual status; and Article XIV(e) bases a general exception to GATS obligations on international agreements on avoidance of double taxation.

[82] See most recently, the Panel Report in *EC-Measures Affecting the Approval and Marketing of Biotech Products*, WT/DS291, 292, 293/R (29 September, 2006), in which the Panel denied applicability of the 1992 Convention on Biological Diversity and the 2000 Cartagena Protocol on Biosafety even for interpretative purposes under Article

against another Member for not protecting the basic rights of service providing labor-migrants. This stands in stark contrast to the situation in international intellectual property rights protection, where WTO Members may complain against lax protection of intellectual property rights of their nationals.[83]

Again demonstrating the liberal immigration paradox, human rights or labor rights might nevertheless become relevant to Mode 4 in the reverse – if they were raised by labor-receiving states as justifications for preventing or restricting labor migration and its positive distributive effects through the discourse of rights. This could be done, for example, through the article XVII GATS national treatment principle,[84] augmented as the case may be by the International Labour Organization's (ILO) non-discrimination rules.[85] Moreover, where local labor conditions are high, non-discrimination establishes a higher standard of treatment than basic human rights do. Thus, labor migration may be excluded on this basis even when human rights are not truly at risk, while in other contexts human rights violations relating to labor migration may proceed unhindered by the GATS. For example, a Member may restrict labor migration by interpreting national treatment and non-discrimination norms as requiring full social benefits for labor migrants at the level of the host country, while at the same

31.3(c) of the Vienna Convention on the Law of Treaties because not all WTO parties were states party to these conventions.

[83] See art. 41 of the TRIPS (Agreement on Trade-Related Aspects of Intellectual Property Rights, April 15, 1994, Marrakesh Agreement Establishing the World Trade Organization, Annex 1C, Legal Instruments – Results of the Uruguay Round, 33 I.L.M. 1125) and the request for consultations in *China – Measures Affecting the Protection and Enforcement of Intellectual Property Rights – Request for Consultations by the United States*, WTO Doc. WT/DS362/1 (April 16, 2007).

[84] Another channel would be the public morals exception in Article XIV(a), but this would presumably enter into action only when genuine violations of human rights were involved, such as human trafficking, and would in any case also need to satisfy the "necessity" test and the terms of the Article XIV GATS *chapeau*. For a discussion of these elements of Article XIV(a) in the light of the WTO Appellate Body Report, *US – Measures Affecting the Cross-Border Supply of Gambling and Betting Services*, WTO Doc. WT/DS285/AB/R (April 7, 2005), see Tomer Broude, "Taking Trade and Culture Seriously: Geographical Indications and Cultural Protection in WTO Law," *University of Pennsylvania Journal of International Economic Law* 26, no. 4 (2005), pp. 623–92.

[85] See Zegers de Beijl, "Combating Discrimination against Migrant Workers." Notably, ILO conventions entailing non-discrimination against migrant workers are sparsely subscribed to by labor-receiving states, but economic non-discrimination would in many cases achieve the same affect, except that the complaining party would not necessarily be the migrants or their source country.

time violating basic human rights through aggressive repatriation policies for temporary labor migrants. Taking this to absurd heights, GATS and ILO national treatment norms have (unsuccessfully) been cited by labor-importing contractors in order to simply lower the cost of foreign labor, while the basic human rights of labor migrants remain exposed to abuse both nationally and internationally.[86]

(d) Migration policy effectiveness

Quite simply, the GATS does not provide Members receiving temporary labor migration under Mode 4 with any legal or other mechanism that would make migration policy any more effectively enforceable. Labor-attracting states interested in an international regime that might assist them in making their immigration patterns more predictable and controllable will not find any comfort in the GATS. This is noted here from a global justice perspective, but as in other cases, it is supported by political and economic considerations: World Bank economists have pointed out that the GATS is an ineffective mechanism for liberalizing international labor migration, because it does not include or even allow commitments from labor-providing states to repatriate labor migrants.[87] Such commitments would of course need to conform to international human rights norms that limit a state's ability to prevent people from leaving their territory, while establishing obligations to receive prodigal nationals. The GATS, however, is quite oblivious to these issues.

(e) Emergency safeguards

The GATS does not currently include any general emergency safeguard mechanisms, let alone in the specific contexts of GATS Mode 4 labor migration. Article X GATS calls for negotiations on the topic, but deadlines for the completion of these talks have been repeatedly missed and the default is that such safeguards do not exist. As an alternative, Article XXI GATS could permit a labor-receiving Member to modify or withdraw a GATS commitment, at any time after three years have elapsed from the date on which that commitment entered into force, subject to compensatory adjustments made towards Members whose

[86] See H.C.J. *Bukhris et al.* v. *Hedera Tax Office et al.*, Israeli Supreme Court, unpublished, June 23, 2005.

[87] Amin and Mattoo, "Does Temporary Migration have to be Permanent?"

GATS benefits have been affected by the modification or withdrawal. However, such a change in commitments would not be temporary *ex ante*, nor contingent on emergency conditions.

6. Conclusion

In this chapter I have attempted to tease out the basic principles of an international labor migration regime that could conform to competing theories of global justice on a pragmatic, non-ideal basis, and address the multitude of problems associated with the international labor migration debate. I have shown that these principles should include elements of global distributive justice, human rights protection, immigration policy enforcement, and contingent emergency safeguards or "escape clauses." These principles reflect a pragmatic common ground based on a conceptual bargain between cosmopolitan and communitarian approaches to this difficult area, that itself reflects a compromise among different political views.

However, the GATS Mode 4 spectacularly fails to meet any of these criteria. It is as ineffective in the promotion of global distributive justice as it is in the strengthening of migration policy enforcement, and as inadequate in the protection of human rights as it is in the prevention of the seriously detrimental effects of labor migration. The establishment of a global labor migration regime that is morally permissible, politically possible, and likely to be effective[88] will no doubt require careful consideration, negotiation, and time; but the GATS Mode 4 does not appear to be the appropriate model, in too many senses.

[88] Rawls, *The Law of Peoples*, p. 89.

5

Incentives for pharmaceutical research: must they exclude the poor from advanced medicines?

THOMAS POGGE

Introduction

During the last 15 years, the United States and other affluent countries have worked hard and successfully to incorporate substantial and uniform protections of intellectual property rights (IPRs) into the fabric of the global trading system. This initiative included the *Trade-Related Aspects of Intellectual Property Rights* (TRIPS) Agreement formulated in the so-called Uruguay Round that led up to the formation of the World Trade Organization (WTO). It was continued through a series of bilateral free-trade agreements including additional ("TRIPS-plus") provisions that enable patent holders to extend (or "evergreen") their market exclusivity beyond the twenty years enshrined in the TRIPS Agreement[1] and also discourage, impede, and delay the manufacture of generic medicines in many other ways, e.g. through provisions on data exclusivity[2] and through restrictions on the effective use of compulsory licences.

Intellectual Property Rights (IPRs) can help ensure that creative productions are protected from unauthorized modification and that their authors receive royalties or licensing income from the reproduction

Many thanks to Aidan Hollis and Matt Peterson for their helpful comments and suggestions.

1 During the life of its primary patent, the patent holder can take out additional patents on a wide range of often trivial or irrelevant aspects of a successful drug, such as its packaging or dosing regimen. Having been applied for later, these additional patents outlast the primary patent. In some countries, such as the US and Canada, these supplementary patents ensure that, even after the primary patent expires, the patent holder retains the right to be notified by any firm planning to commence generic production of the drug. Once notified, the patent holder can then threaten or initiate legal action that, though it has no chance of ultimate success, can delay commencement of generic production by several years or even deter generic production altogether. See NIHCM Foundation, Changing Pattern of Pharmaceutical Innovation, 2002, available at: www.nihcm.org.

2 See www.accessmed-msf.org/documents/Data%20exclusivity%20May%2004.pdf.

of their work. Much more consequential than such copyrights, however, are patents, which prohibit the unauthorized reproduction of a vast range of products and productive processes. Such patent protections are more problematic, morally, than copyrights, especially when they confer property rights in biological organisms (such as seeds used in food production), in molecules that make medicines effective, or in pharmaceutical research tools needed to develop new pharmaceuticals.[3] The present essay analyses the severe moral problems the current regime engenders in the domain of pharmaceuticals. It also proposes a complement to the existing rules – the Health Impact Fund – that would substantially mitigate these problems.

Essential medicines and patents

Medical progress has traditionally been fuelled from two main sources: government funding and sales revenues. The former – given to universities, corporations, other research centres and governmental research facilities such as the US National Institutes of Health – has typically been *push* funding focused on basic research. Sales revenues, usually earned by corporations, have mostly funded more applied research resulting in the development of specific medicines. Sales revenues, by their nature, constitute *pull* funding: an innovation has to be developed to the point of marketability before any sales revenues can be realized from it.

With medicines, the fixed cost of developing a new product is extremely high for two reasons. It is very expensive to research and fine-tune a new medicine and then to take it through elaborate clinical trials and national approval processes. Moreover, most promising research ideas fail somewhere along the way and thus never lead to a marketable product. Both reasons combine to raise the research and development cost per new marketable medicine to somewhere around half a billion dollars or more. Commencing manufacture of a new medicine once it has been invented and approved is cheap by comparison. Because of this fixed-cost imbalance, pharmaceutical innovation is not sustainable in a

[3] Among the pharmaceutical research tools for which patents have been granted are expressed sequence tags (ESTs), restriction enzymes, screening systems, techniques related to DNA sequencing, and single nucleotide polymorphisms (SNPs). For details, see Arti K. Rai and Rebecca S. Eisenberg "Bayh–Dole Reform and the Progress of Biomedicine," *Law & Contemporary Problems* 66, 1 (2003), pp. 289–314 (also available at: www.law.duke.edu/journals/66LCPRai).

free market system: competition among manufacturers would quickly drive down the price of a new medicine to near its long-term marginal cost of production, and the innovator would get nowhere near recovering its investment.

The conventional way of correcting this market failure of undersupply is to reward innovators with patents that entitle them to forbid others to produce or distribute the innovative product and to waive this entitlement in exchange for a licensing fee. The result of such market exclusivity is an artificially elevated sales price that, on average, enables innovators to recoup their initial investment through selling products that, even at prices far above marginal cost, are in high demand.

Monopolies are widely denounced by economists as inefficient and by ethicists as an immoral interference in people's freedom to produce and exchange. In regard to patents, however, many believe that the curtailment of individual freedom can be justified by the benefit, provided patents are carefully designed. One important design feature is that patents confer only temporary market exclusivity. Once the patent expires, competitors can freely enter the market with copies of the original innovation and consumers need thus no longer pay a large mark-up over the competitive market price. Temporal limits make sense, because additional years of patent life barely strengthen innovation incentives: At a typical industry discount rate of eleven per cent per annum,[4] a ten-year effective patent life generates sixty-eight per cent, and a fifteen-year effective patent life eighty-two per cent, of the profit (discounted to present value) that a permanent patent would generate.[5] It makes no sense to impose monopoly prices on all future generations for the sake of so slight a gain in innovation incentives.

During the life of the patent, everyone is legally deprived of the freedom to produce, sell, and buy a patented medicine without permission from the patent holder. This restraint hurts generic producers and it

[4] Joseph A. DiMasi, Ronald W. Hansen, and Henry G. Grabowski, "The Price of Innovation: New Estimates of Drug Development Costs," *Journal of Health Economics* 22 (2003), pp. 151–85.

[5] Patent life is counted from the time the patent application is filed. Effective patent life is the time from receiving market clearance to the time the patent expires. My calculation in the text assumes constant nominal profit each year. In reality, annual profit may rise (due to increasing market penetration or population growth) or fall (through reduced incidence of the disease or through competition from "me-too drugs" developed by competing firms). For most drugs, sales decline after they have been on the market for six years or so, and this strengthens the reasons for limiting patent life. My reasoning assumes that future health benefits are not to be discounted.

also hurts consumers by depriving them of the chance to buy such medicines at competitive market prices. But consumers also benefit from the impressive arsenal of useful medicines whose development is motivated by the prospect of patent-protected mark-ups.

IPRs and essential medicines for the world's poor

Patents are morally problematic insofar as they directly or indirectly impede access by the global poor to basic foodstuffs and essential medicines. The urgency of this concern can be gauged by examining the present condition of the global poor. Today, one-third of all human deaths are from poverty-related causes: 50,000 each day or 18 million every year,[6] including 9.2 million children under the age of five.[7] Hundreds of millions more suffer grievously from treatable medical conditions; and the lives of even more people are shattered by severe illnesses or premature deaths in their family. Living with such severe deprivations, poor people are bound to be susceptible and vulnerable to infectious diseases and often unable to overcome them. Health problems of epidemic proportions weigh down the economies of poor countries and regions, thereby perpetuating their poverty which in turn contributes to the ill health of their populations.

Severe deprivation has always been the fate of a large segment of humankind – in slaveholding societies, under feudalism, and in the colonial period. These past deprivations were associated with what we now understand to have been grievous injustices. We must suspect that existing massive deprivations are also associated with similarly grievous social injustices today, when humankind has become so affluent in aggregate that such massive deprivations are clearly avoidable. With 15.7 per cent of the world population, the high-income OECD countries control 79 per cent of the global product, while the aggregate income of the poorer half of humankind is well below 2 per cent. While many of these poor live on somewhere around $100 or $200 per person per year, the annual *per capita* social product is $7,958 for the world at large and $37,566 for the high-income countries.[8]

6 World Health Organization, *The Global Burden of Disease: 2004 Update* (Geneva: WHO Publications, 2008 and available at: www.who.int/healthinfo/global_burden_disease/2004_report_update/en/index.html).

7 Roshni Karwal, "Policy advocacy and partnerships for children's rights" (2008), available at: www.unicef.org/policyanalysis/index_45740.html.

8 World Bank, *World Development Report 2009* (Washington, DC: The World Bank, 2009), p. 353.

The existing intellectual property regime for pharmaceuticals is morally deeply problematic. Long recognized among international health experts, this fact has come to be more widely understood in the wake of the AIDS crisis which pits the vital needs of poor patients against the need of pharmaceutical companies to recoup their investments in research and development.[9] Still, this wider recognition does not easily translate into political reform. Some believe, like Winston Churchill about democracy, that the present regime is the lesser evil in comparison to its alternatives that have any chance of implementation. Others, more friendly to reform, disagree about what the flaws of the present system are exactly and have put forward a wide array of alternative reform ideas.

My assessment of the intellectual property regime and its possible modifications is guided by the cosmopolitan principle that the health, well-being, and longevity of each human being is of equal value.[10] It is a wonderful thing about the products of thought that they are, as economists say, non-rivalros: the intellectual labors of composing a novel are exactly the same, regardless of whether it has millions of readers or none at all. Likewise for the labors of producing music, composing software, developing a new breed of plant or animal, and discovering a new medically effective type of molecule. Millions can benefit from such intellectual efforts without adding at all to their cost. To be sure, to benefit many, the intellectual achievement must typically be physically encoded in multiple copies: in books, CDs, seeds, DNA molecule tokens, pills, or vaccines. Such physical instantiations of intellectual achievements do have a cost that rises – typically at a decreasing rate – as additional copies are made. But such physical reproduction begins only after the creative intellectual labors are complete. Physical reproduction adds nothing to these intellectual labors; and these intellectual labors add nothing to the marginal cost of physical reproduction. The creative intellectual ingredient to physical reproduction is entirely cost-free. Yet, the driving idea of the grand IPR initiative of recent years is that any benefit derived from any such intellectual achievement, by any person, anywhere, must be paid for, and that any unpaid-for benefit

[9] David Barnard, "In the High Court of South Africa, Case No. 4138: The Global Politics of Access to Low-Cost AIDS Drugs in Poor Countries," *Kennedy Institute of Ethics Journal* 12 (2002), pp. 159–74.

[10] Thomas Pogge, "Cosmopolitanism" in *A Companion to Contemporary Political Philosophy*, ed. Robert E. Goodin, Philip Pettit, and Thomas Pogge (Oxford: Blackwell, 2007), pp. 316–31.

constitutes theft, piracy, counterfeiting, or worse. Even though the additional ride is entirely cost-free, none are to have a free ride – no matter how desperately poor they may be and no matter how desperately they may need it.

The argument from natural rights

Before 2005, Indian law allowed only patents on processes, none on products. As a result, India had a thriving generic pharmaceuticals industry that cheaply supplied copies of patented medicines for poor patients throughout the world's poor regions.

> But when India signed the TRIPS agreement in 1994, it was required to institute patents on products by Jan. 1, 2005. These rules have little to do with free trade and more to do with the lobbying power of the American and European pharmaceutical industries. India's government has issued rules that will effectively end the copycat industry for newer drugs. For the world's poor, this will be a double hit – cutting off the supply of affordable medicines and removing the generic competition that drives down the cost of brand-name drugs.[11]

What could possibly justify blocking the supply of life-saving medicines from Indian manufacturers to the world's poorest populations? In response, one might invoke a natural right of any inventor to control the use of her invention. But this response faces four grave difficulties.[12] First, even on the most property-friendly accounts of rights — such as those of Locke and Nozick — it is puzzling why the innovative creation of a physical object should earn one property rights not merely in this object token but in all objects of its type. Why should the fact that you produced a certain molecule out of ingredients you legitimately own give you veto power of my producing a like molecule later out of ingredients that I legitimately own? Second, it is hard to see why pharmaceutical firms should qualify for such exclusive inventors' rights when so much of the basic research used in their medicines is conducted at universities and public institutions with funds supplied by governments and tax-advantaged foundations.[13] Third, it is very hard to explain why

[11] Editorial, "India's Choice," *The New York Times*, January 18, 2005.

[12] See also Aidan Hollis and Thomas Pogge, *The Health Impact Fund: Making New Medicines Accessible for All* (Incentives for Global Health, 2008), pp. 62–68. The book is freely available at: www.healthimpactfund.org.

[13] This pattern emerged in the US after Congress, in 1980, passed the Bayh–Dole Act which allows pharmaceutical companies, professors, and clinicians to cash in on patented

such a natural right of inventors should have precisely the contours enshrined in the TRIPS and TRIPS-plus agreements: why should this natural right cover all and only the intellectual achievements that can now be protected by patents (or copyrights or trademarks)? Why should this natural right entitle inventors to market exclusivity for precisely twenty years? And, most perplexing, why should this natural right prohibit unauthorized use of the idea by someone who invents it independently? Fourth, it must also be shown that this natural right of inventors is so weighty that even the right to life of poor patients must be curtailed to accommodate it, rather than the other way around.

The argument from social utility

The difficulties of defending IPRs as natural rights are so overwhelming that most defenders of the ongoing IPR initiative appeal instead to the social utility of protecting property rights in intellectual achievements: such rights incentivize intellectual innovation, or so we are told. The experience of recent years suggests that IPRs in seeds and medicines inspire a great deal of copy-cat efforts and innovative gamesmanship – attempts to influence the formulation of the rules and attempts abusively to take advantage of the rules.[14] Yet, IPRs also encourage research efforts that result in genuinely new seeds and pharmaceuticals. So the argument from social utility cannot be dismissed.

To assess this argument, we need to ask: how does the global IPR regime now taking shape affect social utility by raising or reducing the well-being of diverse human populations? We can formulate a number of drawbacks of this regime.

High prices. While a medicine is under patent, it will be sold near the profit-maximizing monopoly price which is largely determined by

applications of basic research done at universities or at the National Institutes of Health. For a brief account with further references, see note 3, Rai and Eisenberg 2003. See also Marcia Angell, "The Truth about the Drug Companies," *The New York Review of Books* 51, 12 (2004), pp. 52–58 (also available at: www.nybooks.com/articles/17244); Donald Light, "Basic Research Funds to Discover New Drugs: Who Contributes How Much?" in *Monitoring Financial Flows for Health Research 2005: Behind the Global Numbers* ed. Mary Anne Burke and Andrés de Francisco, (Geneva: Global Forum for Health Research, 2006), pp. 29–46.

[14] Merrill Goozner *The $800 Million Pill: The Truth Behind the Cost of New Drugs.* (Berkeley and Los Angeles: University of California Press, 2004), ch. 8; Marcia Angell *The Truth about the Drug Companies: How They Deceive us and What to Do about It* (New York: Random House, 2004), ch. 10.

the demand curve of the affluent. When wealthy people really want a drug, then its price can be raised very high above the cost of production before increased gains from enlarging the mark-up are outweighed by losses from reduced sales volume. With patented medicines, mark-ups in excess of 1000 per cent are not exceptional.[15] When such exorbitant mark-ups are charged, only a few of the poor can have access through the charity of others.

Neglect of diseases concentrated among the poor. When innovators are rewarded with patent-protected mark-ups, diseases concentrated among the poor – no matter how widespread and severe – are not attractive targets for pharmaceutical research. This is so because the demand for such a medicine drops off very steeply as the patent holder enlarges the mark-up. There is no prospect, then, of achieving high sales volume *and* a large mark-up. Moreover, there is the further risk that a successful research effort will be greeted with loud demands to make the medicine available at marginal cost or even for free, which would force the innovator to write off its initial investment as a loss. In view of such prospects, biotechnology and pharmaceutical companies predictably prefer even the trivial ailments of the affluent, such as hair loss and acne, over tuberculosis and sleeping sickness. This problem of neglected diseases is also known as the 10/90 gap, alluding to only ten per cent of all pharmaceutical research being focused on diseases that account for ninety per cent of the global burden of disease.[16] Malaria, pneumonia, diarrhoea, and tuberculosis, which together account for twenty-one per cent of the global burden of disease, receive 0.31 per cent of all public and private funds devoted to health research.[17] And diseases confined to the tropics tend to be the most neglected: of the 1393 new medicines approved between 1975 and 1999, only thirteen were specifically indicated for tropical diseases and, of these thirteen, five were by-products of veterinary research and two had been commissioned by the military.[18] An additional three drugs were indicated

[15] In Thailand, Sanofi-Aventis sold its cardiovascular disease medicine Plavix for 70 baht ($2.20) per pill, some 6000 per cent above the price at which the Indian generic firm Emcure agreed to deliver the same medicine (Clopidogrel). See Oxfam, *Investing for Life*, Oxfam Briefing Paper, November 2007: 20, available at: www.oxfam.org/en/policy/bp109_investing_for_life_0711 (accessed 10 January 2009).

[16] Global Forum for Health Research, *The 10/90 Report on Health Research 2003–2004* (Geneva: GFHR, 2004) (also available at: www.globalforumhealth.org).

[17] *Ibid.*, p. 122.

[18] Patrice Trouiller, Els Torreele, Piero Olliaro, *et al.* "Drugs for Neglected Diseases: A Failure of the Market and a Public Health Failure?," *Tropical Medicine and International*

for tuberculosis. The next five years brought 163 new drugs of which five were for tropical diseases and none for tuberculosis which together account for twelve per cent of the total disease burden.[19]

Bias toward maintenance drugs. Medicines can be sorted into three categories: curative medicines remove the disease from the patient's body; maintenance drugs improve well-being and functioning without removing the disease; preventative medicines reduce the likelihood of contracting the disease in the first place. Under the existing patent regime, maintenance drugs are by far the most profitable, with the most desirable patients being ones who are not cured and do not die (until after patent expiration). Such patients buy the medicine week after week, year after year, delivering vastly more profit than would be the case if they derived the same health benefit from a cure or vaccine. Vaccines are least lucrative because they are typically bought by governments, which can command large volume discounts. This is highly regrettable because the health benefits of vaccines tend to be exceptionally great as vaccines protect from infection or contagion not merely each vaccinated person but also their contacts. Once more, then, the present regime guides pharmaceutical research in the wrong direction – and here to the detriment of poor and affluent alike.

Wastefulness. Under the present regime, innovators must bear the cost of filing for patents in dozens of national jurisdictions and then also the cost of monitoring these jurisdictions for possible infringements of their patents. Huge amounts are spent in many jurisdictions on costly litigation that pits generic companies, with strong incentives to challenge any patent on a profitable medicine, against patent holders, whose earnings depend on their ability to defend, extend, and prolong their patent-protected mark-ups. Even greater costs are due to the deadweight loss "on the order of $200bn" that arises from blocked sales to buyers who are willing and able to pay some price between marginal cost and the much higher monopoly price.[20]

Health 6, 11 (2001), pp. 945–51; Drugs for Neglected Diseases Working Group, *Fatal Imbalance: The Crisis in Research and Development for Drugs for Neglected Diseases* (Geneva: MSF and DNDWG, 2001) (also available at: www.msf.org/source/access/2001/fatal/fatal.pdf), p. 11.

19 Pierre Chirac and Els Toreelle, "Global Framework on Essential Health R&D," *The Lancet* 367, (2006), pp. 1560–61, also available at: www.cptech.org/ip/health/who/59wha/lancet05132006.pdf.

20 Personal communication from Aidan Hollis, based on his rough calculation. See also Aidan Hollis, "An Efficient Reward System for Pharmaceutical Innovation" (2005:8) at http://econ.ucalgary.ca/fac-files/ah/drugprizes.pdf, where he quantifies the deadweight

Counterfeiting. Large mark-ups also encourage the illegal manufacture of fake products that are diluted, adulterated, inert, or even toxic. Such counterfeits often endanger patient health. They also contribute to the emergence of drug-specific resistance, when patients ingest too little of the active ingredient of a diluted drug to kill off the more resilient pathogenic agents. The emergence of highly drug resistant disease strains – of tuberculosis, for instance – poses dangers to us all.

Excessive marketing. When pharmaceutical companies maintain a very large mark-up, they find it rational to make extensive efforts to increase sales volume, often by scaring patients or by rewarding doctors. This produces pointless battles over market share among similar ("me-too") drugs as well as perks that induce doctors to prescribe medicines even when these are not indicated or when competing medicines are likely to do better. With a large mark-up it also pays to fund massive direct-to-consumer advertising that persuades people to take medicines they don't really need for diseases they don't really have (and sometimes for invented pseudo diseases).[21]

The last-mile problem. While the present regime provides strong incentives to sell even unneeded patented medicines to those who can pay or have insurance, it provides no incentives to ensure that poor people benefit from medicines they urgently need. Even in affluent countries, pharmaceutical companies have incentives only to sell products, not to ensure that these are actually used, properly, by patients whom they can benefit. This problem is compounded in poor countries, which often lack the infrastructure to distribute medicines as well as the medical personnel to prescribe them and to ensure their proper use. In fact, the present regime even gives pharmaceutical companies incentives to disregard the medical needs of the poor. To profit under this regime, a company needs not merely a patent on a medicine that is effective in protecting paying patients from a disease or its detrimental symptoms. It also needs this target disease to thrive and spread because, as a disease waxes or wanes, so does market demand for the remedy. A pharmaceutical company helping poor patients to benefit from its patented medicine would be undermining its own profitability in three ways: by paying for the effort to make its drug competently available to them, by

loss in the region "of $5 bn–20 bn annually for the US. Globally the deadweight loss is certain to be many times this figure, because in many markets drug insurance is unavailable and so consumers are more price-sensitive."

21 See the special issue on disease mongering, ed. Ray Moynihan and David Henry, *PLoS Medicine* 3 (2006), pp. 425–65.

curtailing a disease on which its profits depend, and by losing affluent customers who find ways of buying, on the cheap, medicines meant for the poor.

In assessing the emerging global IPR regime it is crucial to avoid the false dichotomy that asks us either to accept this regime or else to renounce all hope for innovation. An additional possibility was exemplified in the recent past, when IPRs were legally recognized in most affluent countries but not (or not to anything like the same extent) in most of the poorer ones. The existence of this third possibility has two implications. First, the social-utility argument for the emerging global IPR regime cannot succeed by showing merely that this regime is preferable to the complete absence of IPRs anywhere. Second, the social-utility argument for the ongoing IPR initiative fails if the decline in social utility it brings for poor populations (by reducing their access to patented seeds and pharmaceuticals) is greater than the increase in social utility it brings to rich populations (by enhancing corporate income from patents and by expanding the innovation flow of new seeds and pharmaceuticals). On any cosmopolitan understanding of social utility, which gives equal weight to the well-being of rich and poor human beings alike, the new global IPR regime is greatly inferior to its more differentiated predecessor.

Responsibility for the IPR regime

But if the new regime is so much worse for the global poor, then why did they agree to it? Membership in the WTO is voluntary, after all, and the poor countries chose to sign up. And surely they are more reliable and more legitimate judges of their own interests than we outsiders are?

To understand why this objection fails, one must bear three points in mind. First, in the negotiations that preceded the WTO Agreement and its subsequent modifications, the representatives of the poor countries were "hobbled by a lack of know-how. Many had little understanding of what they signed up to in the Uruguay Round."[22] Even back then, poor-country representatives were facing some 28,000 pages of treaty text drafted in exclusive ("Green Room") consultations among the most powerful countries and trading blocks.

Second, most poor countries lacked the bargaining power needed to resist the imposition. All the Western free-trade rhetoric

[22] "White Man's Shame." *The Economist*. 1999, September 25, p. 89.

notwithstanding, the poor countries are required to pay for access to the huge markets of the rich. Any poor country is required to open its own markets widely to the corporations and banks of the rich countries and required also to commit itself to the costly enforcement of their IPRs. The World Intellectual Property Organization (WIPO), a specialized agency of the United Nations, has the task of "helping" poor countries enforce IPRs. The cost of such enforcement efforts cut into government expenditures on basic social services: "implementing commitments to improve trade procedures and establish technical and intellectual-property standards can cost more than a year's development budget for the poorest countries."[23] And the extraction of monopoly rents for foreign corporations also raises prices in the poor countries, including prices charged for seeds and essential medicines. Poor countries deemed insufficiently aggressive in the enforcement of foreign IPRs are singled out in the "301 reports" of the US Trade Representative, held up for reprimand and exposed to actual or possible trade sanctions (www.ustr.gov).[24]

The third point we need to bear in mind is that the poor countries are heavily stratified. Even if an international treaty is disastrous for a country's poor, signing up to this treaty as proposed by the rich states may nonetheless be advantageous for this country's political and economic elite. It may be advantageous to them by affording them export opportunities, by winning them diplomatic recognition and political support, by enabling them to buy arms, by protecting their ability discreetly to transfer and maintain wealth abroad, and in many other ways. Consent by the ruling elite is not then a valid indicator of advantage to the general population. This point is made vivid when we look through the list of rulers who actually signed up their countries to the WTO Agreement. Among them we find Nigeria's military dictator Sani Abacha, Myanmar's SLORC junta (State Law and Order Restoration Council), Indonesia's kleptocrat Suharto, Zimbabwe's Robert Mugabe, Zaire's Mobutu Sese Seko, and a host of less well-known tyrants of comparable brutality and corruptness. Even if the consent of these rulers was rational in reference to their own interests, it hardly follows that this consent was in the best interest of their oppressed subjects.

[23] *Ibid.*

[24] This kind of relentless pressure goes a long way toward explaining why poor countries have rarely issued compulsory licences for patented medicines, even though they are legally entitled to do so pursuant to para. 6 of the 2001 Doha Declaration.

Volenti non fit iniuria

These reflections on the third point also speak to another popular defence of the new rules of the world economy. This defence points out that it is not unfair to hold people to rules that are disadvantageous to them if these people themselves have agreed to the rules beforehand. *Volenti non fit iniuria* – no injustice is being done to the willing. The problem with this defence is that it justifies the *status quo* only insofar as the consent of national populations can be inferred from the signatures of their rulers. But in countries like those just listed we cannot plausibly consider the population to have consented through its rulers. How can a tyrant's success in subjecting a population to his rule by force of arms give him the right to consent on behalf of those he is oppressing? Does this success entitle *us* to count the ruler's signature as the population's consent? On any credible account of consent, the answer is no. We cannot invalidate the complaint of those now excluded from essential medicines by appealing to the prior consent of their ruler when this ruler himself lacks any moral standing to consent on their behalf. And even in cases where this ruler has some moral standing, it is still doubtful whether his consent can waive supposedly inalienable human rights of his subjects whom the rich countries' IPR initiative is depriving of secure access to essential medicines – including the human rights of children under five, who constitute about half of those killed by such deprivation.

But is it not an accepted principle that those exercising effective power in a country are entitled to act on behalf of its people? Yes, indeed, it is current international practice to recognize any person or group holding effective power in a country – regardless of how they acquired or exercise it – as entitled to sell the country's resources and to dispose of the proceeds of such sales, to borrow in the country's name and thereby to impose debt service obligations upon it, to sign treaties on the country's behalf and thus to bind its present and future population, and to use state revenues to buy the means of internal repression. This practice of recognition is of great importance to us – mainly because we can gain legal title to the natural resources we need from anyone who happens to possess effective power. This practice is also well-liked among rulers, elites, and military officers in the poor countries.

Yet the effects of this accepted international practice on the world's poor are devastating: the practice enables even the most hated, brutal, oppressive, corrupt, undemocratic, and unconstitutional juntas or dictators to entrench themselves. Such rulers can violently repress the people's efforts toward good governance with weapons they buy from abroad and pay for by selling the people's resources to foreigners and by mortgaging the people's future to foreign banks and governments. Greatly enhancing the rewards of *de facto* power, the practice also encourages coup attempts and civil wars, both of which often provoke opportunistic military interventions from neighbouring countries. And in many (especially resource-rich) countries, these privileges make it all but impossible, even for democratically elected and well-intentioned leaders, to rein in the embezzlement of state revenues: any attempt to hold military officers to the law is fraught with danger, because these officers know well that a coup can restore and enhance their access to state funds which, after such a coup, would still be replenished through resource sales and still be exchangeable for the means of domestic repression. Far from being a defence against the charge that the newly globalized IPR regime is harming the global poor, the present practice of international recognition is a further example of such harming.

What if we really cared about social utility?

We have seen that, on any plausible conception of social utility, the rich countries' IPR initiative goes in the wrong direction, foreseeably causing many additional premature deaths among the global poor by cutting them off from life-saving patented medicines. Although generic producers in poor countries could manufacture such medicines very cheaply for use throughout the world's poor regions, they are no longer permitted to do so; and these medicines are now available only at the monopolist's chosen price, typically vastly higher than the marginal cost of production.[25]

Imagine for a moment that we really cared about social utility understood in the cosmopolitan way that gives equal weight to the well-being of rich and poor alike. If we did, we would certainly want the intellectual achievements embedded in life-saving seeds and medicines to be freely available in poor countries. But such free availability, which was standard before TRIPS, leaves two big problems unaddressed. One problem is that the health systems of many poor countries are so undeveloped that they fail to afford poor people effective access even to essential medicines that are available very cheaply or (by donation) cost-free. The

[25] Second-line AIDS and TB medicines are prominent examples.

other problem arises from the fact that poor populations face many serious health problems that are very rare among the affluent and therefore predictably ignored under a regime that forces pharmaceutical inventor firms to recoup their research and development costs from paying patients. These special health problems are due to a variety of poverty-related factors: the global poor often lack access to minimally adequate nutrition, to clean water, to sanitation, to minimally adequate clothing and shelter, to adequate sleep and rest, and to minimal health-related knowledge and advice. And little is spent on controlling environmental hazards (such as malaria-carrying mosquitoes, parasites, dangerous pollution, etc.) in regions inhabited by poor populations – even while such hazards have been successfully eradicated from affluent regions (e.g. South Florida) with similar climate and geography.

To make progress, we must understand the political obstacles. An intellectual property reform plan must not merely be *feasible*, such that, once implemented, it generates its own support from governments, pharmaceutical companies, and the general public (taking these three key constituencies as they would be under the reformed regime). A reform plan must also be *realistic*: it must possess moral and prudential appeal for governments, pharmaceutical companies, and the general public (taking these three constituencies as they are now, under the existing regime). A reform plan that fails these tests is destined to remain an idealistic dream. We will reach our common and imperative goal of universal access to essential medicines either in collaboration with the pharmaceutical industry or not at all.

A cosmopolitan proposal: The Health Impact Fund

With generous funding from the Australian Research Council, the BUPA Foundation, and the European Union, an international team of researchers has been developing just such a politically realistic reform plan: proposing the creation of the Health Impact Fund (HIF), designed to stimulate pharmaceutical innovation while also reducing allocative inefficiencies.

Financed primarily by governments, this pay-for-performance scheme would give pharmaceutical innovators the option to register any new product. They would guarantee to make it available, wherever it is needed, at the lowest feasible cost of production and distribution. In exchange, each registered product would, during its first ten years on the market, participate in the HIF's annual reward pools, receiving a share equal to its share of the assessed global health impact of all HIF-registered products.[26] The HIF would not require substantial additional taxation since government savings from lower-priced products would offset the cost of funding the reward pools.

The HIF achieves three key advances. It directs some pharmaceutical innovation toward the most serious diseases, including those concentrated among the poor. It makes all HIF-registered medicines cheaply available to all. And it incentivizes innovators to promote the optimal use of their HIF-registered medicines. Magnifying one another's effects, these advances would engender large health gains.

Because registration is optional, the HIF would be fully consistent with the TRIPS Agreement. Offering an additional arena where companies can compete, it would attract high-impact medicines some of which would not have been developed otherwise. Even for medicines that would have come on the market anyway, the HIF multiplies their global health impact by making them immediately accessible to poor people and by engendering their more careful deployment (avoiding drug-specific resistance, for instance). If it were found to work well, the HIF could be scaled up to attract an increasing share of new medicines.

To provide stable incentives, the HIF would need guaranteed financing some fifteen years into the future to assure pharmaceutical innovators that, if they fund expensive clinical trials now, they can claim a full decade of health-impact rewards upon market approval. Such a solid guarantee is also in the interests of the funders who would not want the incentive power of their contributions to be diluted through skeptical discounting by potential innovators. The guarantee might take the form of a treaty under which each participating country commits to the HIF a fixed fraction of its future gross national income (GNI). Backed by such a treaty, the HIF would automatically adjust the contributions of the various partner countries to their variable economic fortunes, would avoid protracted struggles over contribution proportions, and would assure each country that any extra cost it agreed to bear through an increase in the contribution schedule would be matched by

[26] Ten years corresponds roughly to the profitable period of a patent: under TRIPS, WTO members must offer patents lasting at least twenty years from the patent filing date which is typically many years before the medicine receives market clearance after clinical trials. Because some patents may outlast the reward period, HIF registration requires the registrant to offer a royalty-free open license for generic versions of the product following the end of the reward period.

a corresponding increase in the contributions of all other partner countries. Any country providing 1/n of the HIF's core funding will understand that each additional dollar it agrees to contribute will raise HIF rewards by n dollars – or by even more thanks to economies of scale achievable in the HIF's administration and health impact assessments. (If contribution increases were left to ad hoc negotiations, by contrast, then each additional dollar a country agreed to contribute would add only this one dollar to the HIF budget.) Tying contributions to GNIs would also eliminate uncertainty related to exchange and inflation rates, as each country would pay in its own currency.

In view of the great cost ($200 to $1300 million) of bringing a new medicine to market, and to take advantage of economies of scale in health impact assessment, the annual reward pools should be at least $6 billion (which is about five per cent of current pharmaceutical R&D spending worldwide). If all countries were to join up, each would need to contribute about 0.01 per cent of its GNI. If countries representing only a third of the global product participated, each would need to contribute a still-modest 0.03 per cent of its GNI – mitigated by massive cost savings their governments, firms, and citizens would enjoy from low-cost HIF-registered medicines.

Because HIF-registered medicines would be cheaply available everywhere, there would be no cheating problems as commonly attend any differential pricing schemes aimed to make a medicine more affordable to poor patients or in poor countries. The HIF's global scope also brings huge efficiency gains by diluting the cost of innovation without diluting its benefits.[27] By including all diseases as well as all patients on equal terms, the HIF fulfills the cosmopolitan principle invoked above.

The HIF has five main advantages over conventional innovation prizes, including advance market commitments and advance purchase commitments. First, it is a structural reform, establishing an enduring source of high-impact pharmaceutical innovations. Second, it is not disease-specific and thus much less vulnerable to lobbying by firms and patient groups. Third, conventional prizes must define a precise finish line, specifying at least what disease the sought medicine must attack, how effective and convenient it must minimally be, and how bad its side effects may be. Such specificity is problematic because it presupposes the

[27] In the case of medicines targeting communicable diseases, this benefit will increase super-proportionally: Each user of such a medicine benefits from others using it as well, because wide use can decimate or even eradicate the target disease and thereby reduce the probability that this disease will adapt and rebound with a drug-resistant strain.

very knowledge whose acquisition is yet to be encouraged. Since sponsors lack this knowledge ahead of time, their specifications are likely to be seriously suboptimal: they may be too demanding, with the result that firms give up the effort even though something close to the sought medicine is within their reach, or they may be insufficiently demanding, with the result that firms, to save time and expense, deliver a medicine that is just barely good enough to win even when they could have done much better at little extra cost.[28] The HIF avoids this problem of the finish line by flexibly rewarding any new registered medicine in proportion to its global health impact. Fourth, formulated to avoid failure and in ignorance of the true cost of innovation, specific prizes are often much too large and thus overpay for innovation. The HIF solves this problem by letting its health impact reward rate adjust itself through competition: a high reward rate would correct by attracting additional registrations (producing an increase in the number of registered medicines) and an unattractively low reward rate would correct by deterring new registrations (producing a decrease in the number of registered medicines). Fifth, the HIF gives each registrant powerful incentives to promote the optimal end-use of its product: to seek its wide and effective use by any patients who can benefit from it.

The requisite global health impact assessment of HIF-registered products could be conducted in terms of quality-adjusted life years (QALYs), a metric that has been deployed for about two decades by academic researchers, insurers, NGOs, and government agencies. The assessment would rely on clinical and pragmatic trials of the product, on tracing (facilitated by serial numbers) of random samples of the product to end-users, and on statistical analysis of correlations between sales data (including time and place of sale) and target disease burden.

The HIF could use three methods (or a combination of these) to ensure the lowest feasible prices of registered products.[29] It could prescribe a maximum price determined by engineering estimates of the cost of production, which might be adjusted over time to reflect advances in manufacturing technology. Or, alternatively, the HIF could require open licensing of registered products, thus relying on competition

[28] For an excellent discussion, see Aidan Hollis, "Incentive Mechanisms for Innovation," *IAPR Technical Paper*, 2007, available at: www.iapr.ca/iapr/files/iapr/iapr-tp-07005_0.pdf, pp. 15–16.

[29] See Aidan Hollis, "The Health Impact Fund and Price Determination," *IGH Discussion Paper* no. 1 (2009), available at: www.yale.edu/macmillan/igh/files/papers/DP1_Hollis.pdf.

among generic producers to achieve a low price. Or, finally, the HIF could require each registrant to invite competitive tender bids from generic manufacturers and then to contract with the lowest bidder(s) to produce the global supply. These tender competitions, in which the registrant could also compete, might be repeated in two-year intervals, say, to take advantage of advances in manufacturing technology. The registrant would then distribute the product at the contract price plus reasonable distribution costs as determined by the HIF. These three methods might be combined in various ways, for example by allowing the registrant to choose from among two or three of them. In designing this part of the HIF scheme, the goal of low prices is paramount. A secondary objective is to simplify the global health impact assessments, which might become considerably more complex under the second method which, if it works well, would engender a large number of competing bioequivalent products.

There is no space here to discuss the design of the HIF in greater detail,[30] but what has been said should suffice to convey the basic idea. The HIF would give pharmaceutical innovators, for each of their new products, a standing option to forgo their patent-based pricing powers worldwide in exchange for a guaranteed payment stream based on this product's global health impact. Without revision of the existing patent regime, the HIF would thereby provide systemic relief for its seven drawbacks described above.

High prices would not exist for HIF-registered medicines. Innovators would typically not even want a higher price as this would reduce their health impact rewards by impeding access to their product by most of the world's population. The HIF counts health benefits to the poorest of patients equally with health benefits to the richest.

Diseases concentrated among the poor, insofar as they contribute substantially to the global burden of disease, would no longer be neglected. In fact, the more destructive ones among them would come to afford some of the most lucrative R&D opportunities for biotechnology and pharmaceutical companies. This would happen without undermining the profit opportunities such companies now enjoy by developing remedies for the ailments of the affluent.

Bias toward maintenance drugs would be absent from HIF-encouraged R&D. The HIF assesses each registered medicine's health impact in terms of how its use reduces mortality and morbidity worldwide – without

[30] See note 12, Hollis and Pogge and www.healthimpactfund.org.

regard to whether it achieves this reduction through cure, symptom relief, or prevention. This would guide firms to deliberate about potential research projects in a way that is also optimal for global public health – namely in terms of the expected global health impact of the new medicine relative to the cost of developing it. The profitability of research projects would be aligned with their cost effectiveness in terms of global public health.

Wastefulness would be dramatically lower for HIF-registered products. There would be no deadweight losses from large mark-ups. There would be little costly litigation as generic competitors would lack incentives to compete and innovators would have no incentive to suppress generic products (because they enhance the innovator's health impact reward). Innovators might therefore often not even bother to obtain, police, and defend patents in many national jurisdictions. To register a medicine with the HIF, innovators need show only once that they have an effective and innovative product.

Counterfeiting of HIF-registered products would be unattractive. With the genuine item widely available near or even below the marginal cost of production, there is little to be gained from producing and selling fakes.

Excessive marketing would also be much reduced for HIF-registered medicines. Because each innovator is rewarded for the health impact of its addition to the medical arsenal, incentives to develop me-too drugs to compete with an existing HIF-registered medicine would be weak. And innovators would have incentives to urge a HIF-registered drug upon doctors and patients only insofar as such marketing results in measurable therapeutic benefits for which the innovator would then be rewarded.

The last-mile problem would be mitigated because each HIF-registered innovator would have strong incentives to ensure that patients are fully instructed and properly provisioned so that they make optimal use (dosage, compliance, etc.) of its medicines, which will then, through wide and effective deployment, have their optimal public-health impact. Rather than ignore poor countries as unprofitable markets, pharmaceutical companies would, moreover, have incentives to work with one another and with national health ministries, international agencies, and NGOs toward improving the health systems of these countries in order to enhance the impact of their HIF-registered medicines there.

In all these ways, the HIF would align the interests of innovators with those of patients – interests that the current regime brings into sharp opposition. The HIF also harmonizes the moral and prudential interests of innovators who must now all too often choose between recouping their R&D investments and preventing avoidable suffering and deaths.

In its early years, the HIF would make the greatest difference to diseases that are widespread and concentrated among the poor. Yet the HIF's reach would increasingly extend to diseases that are widespread among poor and affluent populations alike. Even if profit per patient is substantially smaller with HIF rewards than with traditional patent-protected mark-ups, the choice of HIF registration would often enable pharmaceutical innovators to earn a larger overall profit by helping a much larger patient population. In cases of uncertainty about which option is more lucrative, pharmaceutical innovators would be inclined to choose the HIF because they want to be, and to be seen as, contributors to global health when this is economically feasible.

Citizens of the richer countries would thus increasingly benefit from the HIF through lower drug prices, insurance premiums, or national health-care outlays. They would also benefit from HIF-stimulated research into neglected poor-country diseases, which would enable more effective responses to public health emergencies by increasing medical knowledge faster and by providing a stronger and more diversified arsenal of medical interventions. In addition, better human health around the world would reduce the threat from invasive diseases. As the SARS and swine flu outbreaks illustrate, dangerous diseases can rapidly spread to affluent countries which – given the current neglect of the medical needs of poor populations – are ill-prepared to cope with such challenges. By joining the HIF, an affluent country would also build goodwill in the poor countries by demonstrating in a tangible way concern for their horrendous public-health problems.

To be sure, for many citizens of affluent countries such prudential reasons pale beside the moral imperative to end the needless pain and dying among the world's poor. Creation of the Health Impact Fund would go a long way toward easing the disparities in access to medicines, which have been aggravated by the TRIPS Agreement.

PART III

Collective security and intervention

6

Cosmopolitan legitimacy and UN collective security

NICHOLAS TSAGOURIAS

Introduction

Legitimacy is a desired property of political orders because it generates compliance by justifying and disciplining the exercise of power.[1] More specifically, legitimacy prescribes the substantive and procedural conditions to which power should ascribe in order to be accepted by those over whom it is exercised. Although legitimacy is associated with state orders, it has become increasingly important in the context of international organizations[2] (IOs) due to the expansion of their powers which nowadays reach states as well as individuals.[3] That having been said, legitimacy is a multifaceted concept whose study is even more complicated in the case of international organizations because of their idiosyncratic nature: IOs may be independent and autonomous actors but, on the other hand, they are derivative and composite entities created by states and consisting mainly of states. Furthermore, IOs exist and operate in the international society whose other subjects are the same states that constitute IOs and with whom IOs compete for the same goods, such as peace, human rights, or development. As a result, questions are

[1] Thomas M. Franck, *The Power of Legitimacy Among Nations*, (New York: Oxford University Press, 1990), p. 24; Jean-Marc Coicaud, *Legitimacy and Politics: A Contribution to the Study of Political Rights and Political Responsibility*, (Cambridge: Cambridge University Press, 2002) p. 10; Max Weber, *The Theory of Social and Economic Organization*, A. Henderson and T. Parsons trans., (New York, Oxford University Press, 1947), pp. 124–25; Thomas M. Franck, "Legitimacy in the International System" (1988) 82 *American Journal of International Law* 705; Ian Hurd, "Legitimacy and Authority in International Politics," (1999) 53 *International Organization* 379; A. Hyde, "The Concept of Legitimation in the Sociology of Law," (1983) *Wisconsin Law Review* 379; Allen Buchanan and Robert O. Keohane, "The Legitimacy of Global Governance Institutions" (2006) 20 *Ethics and International Affairs* 405.

[2] Jean-Marc Coicaud and Veijo Heiskanen (ed.), *The Legitimacy of International Organizations*, (Tokyo: United Nations University Press, 2001).

[3] Such expansion provokes fears that IOs may turn into a "new variety of tyranny, global in scope." Inis L. Claude, Jr., *Swords into Plowshares. The Problems and Progress of International Organization*, 4th edn. (New York: Random House, 1971), p. 169.

raised about the standards that inform judgments on the legitimacy of IOs as well as about the stakeholders of their legitimacy.[4] Such questions are even more intense in the case of the United Nations (UN) because of its universal membership and aims.

Any study of the legitimacy of IOs is also complicated by the fact that legitimacy is not a fixed quality but is subject to a continuous process of change and adaptation in response to external or internal changes or events. As a result, IOs often suffer from what is coined as "legitimacy crises," which refers to shifts, mainly contractions, in the legitimacy of an IO and internally or externally evolving patterns of legitimacy. Such shifts necessitate changes and reforms but in order for reforms to restore the legitimacy of an IO there must be agreement on their direction. Such agreement however is dependent on the prescriptive claims made on the IO by its constituency. If competing visions about the content of such reforms exist because conflicting claims are made upon the IO by its constituency, reforms and the sought-after legitimacy can provoke political struggles, cause disruptions, or eventually cancel each other out.

In this chapter, I propose to examine the legitimacy of the UN by focusing on the UN collective security system. First, I will examine the premises upon which the legitimacy of UN collective security has been based and discuss subsequent changes and readjustments to maintain such legitimacy. In the second part I will examine the interaction between the UN and international society. In this regard, I will focus on the UN's role as dispenser of legitimacy in the international society. In the third part, I will discuss current challenges to the legitimacy of the UN collective security system and evaluate proposals for reform. This will be followed, in the final part, by a discussion of the relationship between legitimacy, cosmopolitanism, and constitutionalism to the extent that there is a strong body of opinion that views the UN Charter as the constitution of the international society.

The UN collective security system and legitimacy

If, as was said above, legitimacy is about the justification of power, it applies to UN collective security because the latter involves the exercise of power. Power is defined as 'the capacity … to produce intended and

[4] Thomas M. Franck, *Fairness in International Law and Institutions*, (Oxford: Oxford University Press, 1995), p. 26.

foreseen effects on others'[5] and UN collective security is about the use of coercive or non-coercive power in order to maintain or restore international peace and security.[6] More specifically, the UN collective security system sets out the rules and principles that should inform state behavior in order to maintain international peace and security.[7] For example, states should refrain from the threat or use of force in their international relations[8] unless they act in self-defence,[9] whereas any violation of the norms of the system is to be dealt with by the Security Council (SC) which is established as the central decision-making and enforcement organ of the system.[10] In this regard, the SC has the power to decide whether a threat to the peace, a breach of the peace, or an act of aggression has occurred[11] and then take measures to restore or maintain international peace and security. By doing so, the SC can affect states' rights. For example, the SC can impose sanctions on states,[12] legislate for all states,[13] or even use force against states.[14] The use of force is probably the SC's ultimate power which is exercised on behalf of the whole membership and for the common good.[15] As the preamble to the UN Charter states, "by the acceptance of principles and the institution of methods ... armed force shall not be used, save in the common interest."[16]

The principles that inform the UN collective security system as well as its rules support a cosmopolitan account of its legitimacy.[17] One obvious trait of its cosmopolitan character is its universality. The UN is the only organization whose membership is universal and whose values and principles such as peace and security are also universal. Moreover, the UN strives for the common good as well as for the good of each and every one of its constituents. The difference, though, from cosmopolitan theories lies in the fact that, whereas in cosmopolitan theories

[5] Dennis H. Wrong, *Power: Its Forms, Bases and Uses*, (Oxford: Blackwell Publishing, 1979), p. 2; David Beetham, *The Legitimation of Power*, (London: Macmillan, 1991), pp. 43–45.

[6] Ch.VII of UN Charter. [7] Arts. 1 and 2 of UN Charter.

[8] Art. 2(4) of UN Charter. [9] Art. 51 of UN Charter.

[10] Ch. VII of UN Charter; Claude, Jr., *Swords into Plowshares*, pp. 244–85.

[11] Art. 39 of UN Charter. [12] Art. 41 of UN Charter.

[13] See for example SC Res 1373 (2001). [14] Art. 42 of UN Charter.

[15] Art. 24 of UN Charter. [16] Preamble to the UN Charter.

[17] Bruno Simma (ed.), *The Charter of the United Nations: A Commentary*, (Oxford: Oxford University Press, 2002), (hereinafter referred to as *The Charter*), p. vii; Bruno Simma, "From Bilateralism to Community Interest in International Law" 250 *Recueil des Cours* (1994 IV) 229ff. For a critique see Danilo Zolo, *Cosmopolis: Prospects for World Government*, (Cambridge, Polity Press, 1997) pp. 94–127.

the ultimate unit of concern is the human being, for the UN that unit is the state, that is, an inanimate entity. That said, there is a personified and anthropomorphic conception of the state in the UN as the direct unit of its concern, whereas human beings are indirect units of concern addressed through their states. The personified and anthropomorphic conception of the state within the UN reveals another trait of its cosmopolitan legitimacy, which is the principle of equality. As with individuals who in cosmopolitan theories posses equal moral status, states possess equal moral and legal status within the UN irrespective of their material differences. Their equal status is premised on the concept of sovereignty, which is treated as an undifferentiated quality attributed to each and every state. As Article 2(1) of the UN Charter states, "the Organization is based on the principle of the sovereign equality of all its Members." In collective security, this means that its principles and rules apply without distinction to all members of the UN collective security system, even if they involve the use of force.

Another trait of the cosmopolitan character of the UN collective security system is the supranational character of its decision-making process in that the SC can take decisions on behalf of all UN members and bind them all.[18] Moreover, reactions to violations of the norms of the system are not private sanctions or punishment but enforcement, that is, public and institutional action with the aim of securing compliance with the rules, norms, and interests of the system as a whole. In other words, within the UN collective security system, it is not individual states that protect their interests or the common interest of the society of states but a central authority, the SC, which protects the common interest as a whole.

This brings us to another trait of the cosmopolitan character of the UN collective security system, that of solidarity. The meaning of solidarity in a cosmopolitan setting was given by Vattel:

> The end of the natural society established among men in general is that they should mutually assist one another to advance their own perfection and that of their condition; and Nations, too, are mutually bound to advance this human society. Hence the end of the great society established by nature among all nations is likewise that of mutual assistance in order to perfect themselves and their condition.[19]

[18] Arts. 24 and 25 of UN Charter.

[19] Emmerich de Vattel, *Law of Nations or the Principles of Natural Law*, Charles G. Fenwick trans., (Washington, DC: The Carnegie Institution, 1916), Bk. I, Introduction, para.11.

Within the UN, solidarity covers a wide spectrum of issues such as development, the environment, and so on but, as far as peace and security is concerned, it means that "all member states have a stake in the management and resolution of the conflict, if only as part of the larger enterprise of establishing peace that the United Nations represents."[20] In other words, peace as a universal value concerns all states and requires common efforts; therefore, each state should not only abstain from using force against fellow member states but also contribute to common efforts to secure peace – even if its individual or immediate interests are not at stake.[21]

That having been said, the legitimacy of the UN collective security system has been erected around a cosmopolitan edifice of rules, values, organs, and processes that conceal the deep-seated normative cleavages and tensions that linger in the background. As a result, the management of the UN's legitimacy capital has proven very difficult when the UN was called upon to put the rules and values of its collective security system into operation and this was further exacerbated by subsequent changes in the international political and security environment.

UN collective security may represent a cosmopolitan project in that the principles, values, and rules that underpin the system are universal and attract in their generality universal agreement; their interpretation or implementation however gives rise to disputes because they are often vague, ambiguous, or contradictory. Such disputes are not just theoretical but are projected onto the whole spectrum of UN activities affecting thus the overall performance of the Organization. Moreover, even if supranational decision-making mechanisms exist that could in principle resolve such differences, they are, themselves, forums where the different interests, views, and expectations of UN member states are played out, not to mention any inherent structural flaws in decision-making. The above alludes to a fundamental problem besetting the UN, namely, its heterogeneous membership. The UN may be a universal organization, its member states however represent different political communities with different understandings of the values that underpin the system. This inevitably causes disagreements and disputes about the operation of the system or its direction. Its diverse membership also weakens any feelings of solidarity upon which the cosmopolitan

[20] *Report of the Panel on United Nations Peace Operations of 21 August 2000*, UN Doc. A/55/305, S/2000/809, para. 52 (hereinafter referred to as *Brahimi Report*).

[21] Arts. 42–48 of UN Charter.

legitimacy of UN collective security is based. Because UN member states have different political, legal, or social identities and membership of the UN collective security system does not necessarily make them allies, their feelings of solidarity towards their fellow members are in short supply. As Vattel long ago noted, "it is impossible for Nations to fully acquit themselves of their mutual duties if they do not love one another."[22] The same can be said about the principle of sovereign equality, one of the traits upon which UN cosmopolitan legitimacy is based. Sovereignty is an ambivalent concept that can support but also demolish the UN collective security system. Sovereignty is not adverse to a collective security system because the system protects state sovereignty. However, sovereignty accentuates state individualism and partisanship and, for this reason, it is not always comfortable with supranational decision-making processes or with institutional controls.[23] Moreover, sovereignty institutionalizes normative plurality and thus delays or frustrates the shaping of common policies required for the efficient operation of the system. As a result, sovereignty makes states' commitment to collective security ambivalent and erratic and cannot preclude extra-systemic actions. In Vattel's words, "since every Nation is free, independent, and sovereign in its acts, it is for each to decide whether it is in a position to ask or grant anything in that respect."[24]

What transpires from the above is that, whereas the UN collective security mechanisms are still there, the spirit that initially bound everything together and contributed to the legitimacy of UN collective security either departed or took different directions.[25] This has been translated into cracks or gaps in the legitimacy of the system which forced the UN to adapt and readjust its norms and mechanisms in order to manage its legitimacy capital.

For example, the UN readjusted its decision-making process in collective security in order to address instances of SC decisional paralysis. As was noted above, decision-making evolves around the SC whose operation is however dependent on agreement among its five permanent

[22] Vattel, *Law of Nations*, Bk. II, ch. 1, para. 11.

[23] "... [E]very state was the sole and sovereign judge of its own acts, owing no allegiance to any higher authority, entitled to resent criticism or even questioning by other states." Francis P. Walters, *A History of the League of Nations*, (Oxford: Oxford University Press, 1952), vol. I, pp. 1–2.

[24] Vattel, *Law of Nations*, Bk. II, ch. 1, para. 8.

[25] Alfred Zimmern, *The League of Nations and the Rule of Law 1918–1935*, (London: Macmillan, 1945), p. 289.

members. Such agreement floundered under the strain of political antagonism that erupted between the West and the Soviet block during the Cold War. The paralysis of the system posed a serious challenge to the legitimacy of the Organization because it was unable to perform the tasks for which it was created. Its response was to shift decision-making to the General Assembly (GA). According to the "Uniting for Peace" resolution, when the SC is blocked due to lack of unanimity, the GA can intervene and recommend collective measures including, where appropriate, the use of force.[26] In sum, by transferring decision-making powers to the GA, the UN was able to function in peace and security as it did in Korea and the Suez even if its main organ was blocked, but at the same time it maintained the centralized and institutional character of its decision-making process, something that, as was noted above, contributes to its legitimacy.

Another area revisited by the UN is the meaning of peace and security. At the beginning, peace and security had a rather narrow and negative meaning; they were about interstate and transborder threats and were synonymous with the absence of war. They also referred to the external, not to the internal manifestations of state sovereignty. However, in the intervening years the security environment has changed. Security threats have not only multiplied and diversified but have also deterritorialized. As the President of the SC acknowledged:

> the absence of war and of military conflicts among states does not in itself ensure peace and security. The non-military sources of instability in the economic, social, humanitarian and ecological field have become threats to peace and security.[27]

[26] GA Res 377 (V); *Certain Expenses of the United Nations (Article 17, Paragraph 2, of the Charter)*, Advisory Opinion, ICJ Rep. (1962), p. 151, pp. 163–65; *Legal Consequences of the Construction of a Wall in the Occupied Palestinian Territory Advisory Opinion of 9 July 2004*, I.C.J. Rep. (2004), p. 200, paras. 23–25.

[27] UN Doc S/23500 (31 January 1992) p. 3; *An Agenda For Peace: Preventive diplomacy, peacemaking and peace-keeping*, A/47/277 – S/24111 (1992); Thomas M. Franck, "The Security Council and 'Threat to the Peace': Some Remarks on Remarkable Recent Developments" and Pieter H. Kooijmans, "The Enlargement of the Concept 'Threat to the Peace'," in René-Jean Dupuy, *Le développement du rôle du Conseil de sécurité*, (Dordrecht: Martinus Nijhoff Publishers, 1993), pp. 83ff and 111ff respectively; Simma, *The Charter* pp. 722–26. Peter Wallensteen and Patrik Johansson, "Security Council Decisions in Perspective," in *The UN Security Council: From the Cold War to the 21st Century*, ed. David M. Malone (Boulder and London: Lynne Rienner Publishers, 2004), pp. 17ff; *A More Secure World: Our Shared Respsonsibility*, Report of the Secretary-General's High-level Panel on Threats, Challenges and Change, UN Doc. A/59/565 (2004), pp. 10–16, paras. 1–28.

The UN responded to such changes by adding a number of new phenomena onto its peace and security agenda. It was able to do so by using the SC's rather broad powers of appreciation as to whether a threat to the peace or a breach of the peace exists.[28] For example, the SC considered as "threats to the peace" human rights violations; internal conflicts;[29] violations of humanitarian law;[30] or violations of the right to self-determination.[31] After "9/11," both international terrorism[32] and the proliferation of weapons of mass destruction (WMD)[33] were declared as threats to peace.

In sum, the SC addressed military but also non-military; actual but also potential; interstate but also intrastate threats and by doing so, the UN maintained its legitimacy as a global and all-inclusive organization, a position that otherwise would have been challenged by states or other institutions. It also responded to normative changes in the international environment which saw human beings as direct units of international concern. However, the SC acted with extreme caution so as not to offend its diverse membership. Thus, it dealt with internal violations of human rights only when they were detrimental to interstate peace or when they had transborder effects, because otherwise it might have been accused of violating the principle of state sovereignty enshrined in the Charter and cherished by large sections of its membership.[34]

[28] Art. 39 of UN Charter.

[29] SC Res 1289 (2000) and SC Res 1306 (2000) on Sierra Leone; SC Res 1399 (2002) and SC Res 1484 (2002) on DRC; SC Res 1566 (2004) and SC Res 1590 (2005) on Sudan.

[30] SC Res 794 (1992) on Somalia; SC Res 940 (1993) and SC Res 1529 (2004) on Haiti; SC Res 827 (1993) on Yugoslavia; SC Res 929 (1994) on Rwanda; SC Res 1078 (1996) on Zaire; SC Res 1565 (2004) on DRC; SC Res 1556 (2004) on Sudan; SC Res 1727 (2006) on Côte d'Ivoire; SC Res 1756 (2007) on DRC.

[31] SC Res 216 (1965) and SC Res 217 (1965) on Rhodesia; SC Res 181 (1963), SC Res 417 (1977), and SC Res 418 (1977) on South Africa.

[32] SC Res 1368 (2001); SC Res 1377 (2001); SC Res 1566 (2004). Also SC Res 731 (1992) and SC Res 748 (1992) on Libya; SC Res 1267 (1999) and SC Res 1333 (2000) on Afghanistan.

[33] SC Res 1540 (2004).

[34] SC Res 688 (1991) on Iraq; SC Res 1556 (2004) on Sudan; SC Res 1565 (2005) on DRC; SC 1577 (2004). Simma, *The Charter*, p. 609. *Independent International Commission on Kosovo: The Kosovo Report* (2000), 62: "... the Charter provisions relating to human rights were left deliberately vague, and were clearly not intended when written to provide a legal rationale for any kind of enforcement, much less a free-standing mandate for military intervention without UNSC approval. Human rights were given a subordinate and marginal role in the UN system in 1945, a role that was understood to be, at most, aspirational." Susan Marks, *The Riddle of all Constitutions: International Law, Democracy and the Critique of Ideology* (Oxford: Oxford University Press, 2000), p. 107; Antonio Cassese, *Human Rights in a Changing World,* (Cambridge: Polity, 1990), p. 23.

Another area which the UN was obliged to revisit was its collective security tools. Its main tool is enforcement; but states refused to commit forces to the UN and share the burden of collective enforcement because they had different expectations from the UN, and entertained different understanding about the aims of any proposed action. Being deprived of its main operative tool, its legitimacy also suffered because the UN was unable to fulfil one of its main functions, that of enforcement. The UN responded by inventing "peacekeeping" which, since then, has become its primary collective security instrument. With peacekeeping, the UN was able to restore its legitimacy; not only because it was able to act in peace and security,[35] but also because the premises upon which peacekeeping is based make it more legitimate in the eyes of states which contribute to or host such operations.[36] More specifically, peacekeeping is predominantly a civilian tool in contrast to enforcement which is a military tool. More than that, peacekeepers are deployed with the consent of the host state, they are neutral, and use force in self-defence whereas enforcement is coercive, employs overwhelming force, and is based on value judgments about wrongdoing. Whereas the apolitical and non-threatening nature of peacekeeping boosted the legitimacy of the UN because it reflected the expectations of states about the reach of UN collective security tools, traditional peacekeeping proved inadequate when faced with the new security environment after the end of the Cold War. Thus the UN revisited its peacekeeping operations in order to meet the new challenges. First, it deployed peacekeepers, not only between states as before, but also within states and during ongoing conflicts. Then it expanded the meaning of self-defence to include the defence of the mission.[37] More than that, it expanded their mandates to include, amongst other actions, demobilization, election monitoring, policing, protection of civilians, humanitarian and human rights tasks, even territorial administration as in East Timor[38] or

[35] Jean-Marc Coicaud, "International democratic culture and its sources of legitimacy: the case of collective security and peacekeeping operations in the 1990s," in *The Legitimacy of International Organizations*, ed. Jean-Marc Coicaud and Veijo Heiskanen (Tokyo: United Nations University Press, 2001), p. 256.

[36] Nicholas Tsagourias, "Consent, neutrality/impartiality and the use of force in peacekeeping: their constitutional dimension" (2006) 11 *Journal of Conflict and Security Law* 465.

[37] Tsagourias, "Consent," 478–81.

[38] SC Res 1272 (1999), para. 8; *Report of the Secretary-General on the United Nations Transitional Administration in East Timor*, S/2000/738 (26 July 2000); *An Agenda for Democratisation*, UN Doc A/51/761 (1996).

Kosovo.[39] Yet multifunctional peacekeeping operations tested the UN's legitimacy. For example, operations with humanitarian tasks have been perceived as a challenge to state sovereignty as the many failed attempts to secure Sudan's acceptance of a peacekeeping force in Darfur show.[40] Furthermore, when the UN adopted a more robust posture to protect the mandates of its peacekeeping operations, local parties viewed it as intervention and withdrew their consent. As far as territorial administration is concerned, the UN vested itself with extensive executive, legislative, and judiciary functions but often overlooked the need to consult and cooperate with the local population.[41] As a result, its legitimacy was diminished in the eyes of local populations. Faced with such challenges to its legitimacy, the UN responded by scaling down operations and by placing more weight on the traditional principles of consent, neutrality, and self-defence.[42] It also tried to rationalize the mandates of peacekeeping operations and build up resources and capacities as, for example, with the establishment of the Peace Building Commission whose mandate is to integrate and coordinate resources and advise on peace-building strategies.

The UN as dispenser of legitimacy

As was mentioned in the introduction, the UN exists and operates in international society. Moreover, states that are members of the UN are at the same time members of the international society. However, the UN and international society are not reducible to each other. They are distinct lego-political entities which produce their own practices and legitimacies, but, whereas the UN can produce univocal judgments on legitimacy, in international society such judgments are multi-sourced and multifarious because international society is pluralistic and acentric. As a result, legitimacy judgments in international society lack *erga omnes* validity and are often contested.

[39] SC Res 1244 (1999); *Report of the Secretary-General on the United Nations Interim Administration Mission in Kosovo*, S/2006/906 (20 November 2006); *Report of the Security Council Mission on the Kosovo Issue*, S/2007/256 (4 May 2007).

[40] For example, Sudan rejected SC Res 1706 (2006). See *Report of the Secretary-General on the Sudan*, S/2006/728 (12 September 2006), para. 65.

[41] UNMIK/REG/1999/1 (25/07/99) where it is stated that "all legislative and executive authority with respect to Kosovo including the administration of the judiciary, is vested in UNMIK and is exercised by the Special Representative of the Secretary-General."

[42] *Brahimi Report* p. 78.

The area in which the UN and international society overlap is collective security. The UN collective security system is the global security system which covers the "four corners" of international society whereas its rules, principles, and values are points of reference for peace and security in international society. This does not mean that there is no room for other security providers to emerge within international society, something that has been acknowledged in Chapter VIII of the UN Charter. Indeed, a number of security organizations, such as NATO, OAS, or ECOWAS (to mention but a few), were created which, as partial security systems, cater for the particular needs of their members and enjoy the legitimacy ascribed to them by the values or objectives they pursue. These organizations are free to take action in peace and security but any action involving the use of force should be authorized by the SC.[43] In this regard, the UN acts as dispenser of legitimacy by granting its "seal of approval" to forcible actions undertaken by other security providers within the international society.[44] This is because the UN is the only institution which can legitimately use force in international society for reasons other than self-defence; hence, uses of force by other actors that go beyond the UN Charter paradigm of self-defence need UN authority in order to be legitimate. That is why such actors try to legitimize their actions by procuring SC authorizations;[45] whereas, by granting such authorizations, the SC confers global legitimacy to the action as being compatible with the rules and principles of the global collective security system.

UN authorizations to use force have in fact taken the place of the initial collective security scheme of UN-led enforcement action. As noted above, the UN defaulted on the enforcement functions of its collective security system because it was deprived of the necessary resources. In its place, the SC authorizes member states to take such action and, by doing so, it envelops the operation within the collective security system and endows it with universal legitimacy; even if, in reality, it is states

[43] Art. 53 of UN Charter.

[44] Inis L. Claude Jr., "Collective Legitimization as a Political Function of the United Nations," (1966) 20 *International Organization*, 367; Inis L. Claude Jr., *The Changing United Nations*, (New York: Random House, 1967), p. 83; Thomas M. Franck, "Legality and Legitimacy in Humanitarian Intervention," *Humanitarian Intervention*, ed. Terry Nardin and Melissa S. Williams (New York: New York University Press, 2006), p. 143. Also see Secretary-General's Address at the Truman Presidential Museum and Library, (11 December 2006), available at: www.un.org/apps/sg/sgstats.asp?nid=2357.

[45] For example, the US, UK, and Spain proposed a new resolution authorizing their action against Iraq in 2003 but were not successful.

that actually put together and manage the operation[46] with no, or limited, UN control.[47] The different reactions to the 1991 and 2003 operations against Iraq prove this point. Both operations were conceived and planned outside the UN and were executed with little or no UN involvement. However, only the 1991 action enjoyed global legitimacy because it was authorized by the UN,[48] whereas the legitimacy of the 2003 action which was launched without UN authorization was hotly contested.

In addition to authorizing enforcement actions, the UN has recently projected itself as dispenser of legitimacy with regard to humanitarian actions. Following a number of instances such as Rwanda or Kosovo where, faced with UN inaction or prevarications, states or IOs intervened without UN authorization in order to avert the evolving humanitarian catastrophe, the UN enunciated the "responsibility to protect" (R2P) doctrine.[49] The "R2P" doctrine tries to rebalance the relationship between state sovereignty and human rights by allowing, in exceptional circumstances and under certain conditions, forcible humanitarian actions. According to this doctrine, state sovereignty is qualified and is protected only if the state fulfills its responsibilities towards its population and towards the UN. When the state is unable or unwilling to do so, the responsibility towards the local population must be borne by the international community represented by the UN.[50] That said, the "R2P" doctrine does not imply an automatic right of intervention; it is only in cases of genocide, ethnic cleansing, or serious violations of humanitarian law[51] that the SC should authorize states to intervene or, when

46 *Supplement to an Agenda for Peace*, para. 80; *A More Secure World*, para. 81.

47 SC Res 929 (1994) on Rwanda; SC Res 1101 (1997) on Albania; SC Res 1031 (1995) and SC Res 1088 (1996) on BiH; SC Res 1291 (2000) and SC Res 1565 (2004) on DRC.

48 SC Res 678 (1990) which in para. 2 "authorized member States co-operating with the Government of Kuwait … to use all necessary means to uphold and implement resolution 660 (1990) and all subsequent relevant resolutions and to restore international peace and security in the area."

49 *The Responsibility to Protect, Report of the International Commission on Intervention and State Sovereignty* (2001); *A More Secure World*, paras. 199–203; *In Larger Freedom: towards development, security and human rights for all*, Report of the Secretary-General A/59/2005; 2005 World Summit Outcome GA Res A/60/L.I (20 September 2005); SC Res 1674 (2006).

50 *The Responsibility to Protect, Report of the International Commission on Intervention and State Sovereignty* (2001), viii and paras. 2.7–2.15; Catherine Lu, "Whose Principles? Whose Institutions? Legitimacy Challenges for 'Humanitarian Intervention'," in *Humanitarian Intervention*, ed. T. Nardin and M.S. Williams (New York: New York University Press, 2006), p. 188, at pp. 195–99.

51 *The Responsibility to Protect, Report*, paras. 2.28–2.33; *A More Secure World*, para. 201.

this is not possible, should it endorse such interventions.[52] Moreover, there are a number of criteria that can guide the SC in granting such authorizations. These criteria can be summarized as just cause, right authority, right intention, last resort, proportionality, and balancing of consequences.[53]

With the "R2P" doctrine, the UN projects itself as the forum that confers the "stamp of collective legitimacy"[54] on forcible humanitarian actions either through the SC or when the latter fails, through the General Assembly on the basis of the "Uniting for Peace" Resolution.[55] At the same time, the UN is enhancing its cosmopolitan legitimacy by vesting in itself the role of protecting human beings when their own state fails.[56] As noted above, cosmopolitan theories of all variants treat individual human beings as the ultimate unit of moral, legal, or political concern. Such concern usually stopped at state borders but, with the responsibility to protect, the UN projects itself as the legitimate guardian of human beings on a global scale, albeit in extreme circumstances of state failure.

Another area where the UN projects itself as dispenser of legitimacy is with regard to pre-emptive self-defence. The UN collective security system confines self-defence to cases of actual armed attack.[57] However, modern security threats emanate from diverse sources and manifest themselves in different forms and degrees. This situation has put immense pressure on the rules on the use of force that underpin the UN collective security system because states have often used the language of self-defence to justify their responses to various security threats even in the absence of an actual attack.[58] As a result, a "legitimacy gap" emerged between the UN Charter's stipulation of self-defence

[52] *A More Secure World*, p. 17, paras. 29–30 and paras. 199–207; *In Larger Freedom*, paras. 127–52; 2005 World Summit Outcome, GA Res A/60/L.I (20 September 2005), paras. 138–39.

[53] *The Responsibility to Protect, Report*, paras. 4.15–4.43.

[54] *The Responsibility to Protect, Report*, para. 6.8.

[55] *Responsibility to protect*, pp. 53–54.

[56] See Tan, "Enforcing Global Justice."

[57] Art. 51 of UN Charter.

[58] *Case Concerning Military and Paramilitary Activities in and against Nicaragua, (Nicaragua* v. *United States of America)*, I.C.J. Rep., (1986), p. 14, paras. 194–95, 210–11, 247–49; *Case Concerning Oil Platforms (Islamic Republic of Iran* v. *United States of America)*, I.C.J. Rep. (2003), p. 161, paras. 50–78; *Legal Consequences of the Construction of a Wall in the Occupied Palestinian Territory Advisory Opinion of 9 July 2004*, I.C.J. Rep. (2004), p. 200, paras. 138–39 and Dissenting Opinion of Judge Higgins, *ibid.*, para. 33. Yoram Dinstein, *War, Aggression and Self-Defence*, 4th edn. (Cambridge: Cambridge University Press, 2005), pp. 175–251.

and states' perceptions of legitimate self-defence. Such discrepancies became even more pronounced after "9/11" and the new US doctrine of pre-emptive self-defence.[59] The UN responded to such challenges by reviewing the whole question of legitimate self-defence. According to the UN report *A More Secure World*, pre-emptive self-defence is permissible when the threat of an attack is imminent[60] but with regards to "non-proximate" and "non-imminent" threats, the Report urges states to put their evidence to the SC which, if satisfied about the credibility of the threat, can authorize the use of force.[61] Once more, the UN responds to changes in the security environment but at the same time it retains for itself the role of universal dispenser of legitimacy with regards to preventative self-defence.

The UN also acts as legitimator or delegitimator of the consequences of illegal uses of force. The international society's sanction against unlawful uses of force is the non-recognition of the situation created by such unlawful acts and the obligation not to provide any aid or assistance that could help to maintain the unlawful situation.[62] This is however a decentralized sanction of dubious effectiveness because each state makes its own assessment as to whether there has been an unlawful use of force in the first place as well as whether it wants to apply this sanction. Hence, the UN's role as dispenser of legitimacy is critical in this regard due to its *erga omnes* validity. For example, when Iraq annexed Kuwait, the SC mandated all states not to recognize such annexation, and that decision had *erga omnes* validity.[63] In other cases, the SC removed the sanction of non-recognition or the sanction of not rendering aid or assistance by authorizing follow-up actions. This

[59] *The National Security Strategy of the United States of America*, (September 2002), p. 15, available at: www.whitehouse.gov/nsc/nss/2006/nss2006.pdf.

[60] *A More Secure World*, para. 188; *Caroline Case*, British and Foreign States Papers 1841–1842, vol. 30, 1858, p. 193; Nicholas Tsagourias, "The Shifting Laws on the Use of Force and the Trivialization of the UN Collective Security System: the Need to Reconstitute It" (2003) 55 *Netherlands Yearbook of International Law*, 55 at 70–75.

[61] *A More Secure World*, para. 190.

[62] Art. 41(2) in conjunction with art. 40 of Draft Articles on Responsibility of States for Internationally Wrongful Acts adopted by the International Law Commission at its fifty-third session (2001); James Crawford, *The International Law Commission's Articles on State Responsibility*, (Cambridge: Cambridge University Press, 2002), pp. 249–53; *Legal Consequences for States of the Continued Presence of South Africa in Namibia (South West Africa) Notwithstanding Security Council Resolution 276 (1970)*, I.C.J. Rep. (1971), p. 2, para. 122; *Legal Consequences of the Construction of a Wall in the Occupied Palestinian Territory Advisory Opinion of 9 July 2004*, I.C.J. Rep (2004), p. 200, para. 159.

[63] SC Res 662 (1990) paras. 1 and 2.

is what happened in Iraq (2003) and in Kosovo. In both cases, the SC authorized the post-conflict actions[64] and laid down the legal and political framework that regulated them. By doing so, it brought the situations that emerged after the initial action within the collective security system and dispensed legitimacy to follow-up actions.

Current challenges, proposals for reform and legitimacy

What transpires from the foregoing discussion is that the UN responds to exogenous or endogenous, normative or factual challenges by constantly adjusting itself in order to restore and maintain its legitimacy. The challenges are however persistent and in this section some of the more serious challenges currently facing the UN will be registered, proposals for reform will be reviewed, and their impact on UN legitimacy will be assessed.

A recurrent theme in any debate about UN legitimacy is the unrepresentative character of the SC and the veto power of its permanent members.[65] The former is held responsible for the SC's disconnection from the rest of the UN membership, and the latter for its operational ineffectiveness. Current proposals for SC reform envisage wider SC membership but there is no agreement on the number or the names of the new permanent or non-permanent members. As far as the veto power is concerned, current reform proposals either try to abolish the veto power or expand the number of veto-holders or indicate areas where the veto cannot be cast as, for example, in cases of genocide or of large-scale human rights abuses.[66]

The idea behind such proposals is that a more representative membership will enhance the legitimacy of the SC and of its decisions, because the SC will be in tune with the demands, needs, and understandings of wider sections of UN membership and thus create a sense of ownership of its processes and of its decisions.[67] Also, introducing benchmarks according to which authorizations to use force can be granted tries to instill a sense of common purpose and responsibility and, in general, make the SC more cohesive and effective. All of the above can also enhance the UN's role as dispenser of legitimacy because the SC

[64] SC Res 1244 (1999) on Kosovo ; SC Res 1483 (2003) and SC Res 1511 (2003) on Iraq.

[65] *A More Secure World*, paras. 244–60; *In Larger Freedom*, para. 170.

[66] *More Secure World*, para. 256. For a similar attempt with regard to double veto see Doc 852, III/1/37 (1), *UNCIO* vol. 11, pp. 711–14.

[67] Tsagourias, "The Shifting," p. 82.

will be able to combine "impartial" with "cross-sectional" jurying, since its membership will represent wider sections of the international society.[68]

It should be said at this juncture that the SC has recognized the need for "reaching out" and occasionally invites non-members to its sessions or convenes open sessions. Such initiatives have received positive remarks. For example, the Irish representative, commenting on behalf of the EU, said that the open debate on the Counter-Terrorism Committee strengthens the SC's "perceived legitimacy with all members of the United Nations family."[69] That said, participation in such debates is not formalized and, above all, participation does not extend to participation in decision-making. Moreover, what all these proposals or initiatives overlook is that broader membership does not necessarily imply convergence because "political convergence precedes institutional change, not the other way around."[70] In fact, there is little evidence of a common political and security ethos among current or future SC members or of overlapping consensus on the UN principles and values. This is best illustrated in the same debates about SC reform which have been hijacked by states' real or imagined projections of power and prestige.[71] Thus, to the extent that no common mindset exists, such proposals cannot attain their underlying objective but may cause even more hardship by making SC decision-making more cumbersome.

Another challenge facing the UN is that of defining, aligning, and operationalizing its values and principles. It is one thing to declare principles or reaffirm values which in their generality can attract widespread

[68] Franck, "Legality and Legitimacy in Humanitarian Intervention," in *Humanitarian Intervention*, ed. Terry Nardin and Melissa S. Williams, (New York: New York University Press, 2006), p. 153. Also see Lu "Whose Principles? Whose Institutions," *ibid.*, pp. 199–206; Brian D. Lepard, "Jurying Humanitarian Intervention and the Ethical Principle of Open-Minded Consultation," *ibid.*, pp. 223–36; Melissa S. Williams, "The Jury, the Law, and the Primacy of Politics," *ibid.*, p. 244.

[69] S/PV.4921, at 19.

[70] Edward C. Luck, "How Not to Reform the United Nations," (2005) 11 *Global Governance* 407 at 410–411.

[71] See "Question of Equitable representation on and Increase in the Membership of the Security Council and Related Matters," UN Doc A/59/L.64, L.67 and L.68. Edward C. Luck, "Reforming the United Nations: Lessons from a History in Progress" in Jean E. Krasno (ed.), *The United Nations: Confronting the Challenges of a Global Society*, (Boulder: Lynne Rienner, 2004), p. 364: "… much of the reform debate, at its basest level, is a struggle over political turf, over who is perceived to gain or lose influence within the organisation if the proposed changes are enacted or implemented."

consent and another to agree on their meaning, their relationship, or their implementation. For example, the *Report on a More Secure World* mentions six clusters of threats[72] – economic and social threats including poverty, infectious diseases, and environmental degradation; interstate conflicts; internal conflicts including civil war, genocide, and other large scale atrocities; threats from nuclear, radiological, chemical, and biological weapons; terrorism; and transnational organized crime – over which there seems to be widespread consensus, but such consensus breaks down at the point of interpretation or of policy implementation. Such disagreements inevitably affect the decision-making process with the UN swinging between inaction, as the SC prevarication over Rwanda[73] or Darfur demonstrates; inconsistent action, as the UN peacekeeping operations in Bosnia show, or non-action.

Regarding the alignment between UN values and principles, some of them appear in opposing pairs. For example, justice in the form of human rights may conflict with the principle of state sovereignty and non-intervention. Whereas the "responsibility to protect" doctrine tries to reconcile the principle of sovereignty with that of human rights by protecting the former only if it is translated as responsibility towards peoples,[74] a large number of states have opposed this principle by prioritizing the principle of sovereignty. For example, the Non-Aligned Movement rejected the:

> ... so-called "right" of humanitarian intervention, which has no basis in the United Nations Charter or in international law ... they also observed similarities between the new expression "responsibility to protect" and "humanitarian intervention" and requested the Co-ordinating Bureau to carefully study and consider the expression "responsibility to protect" and its implications on the basis of the principles of non-interference and non-intervention as well as the respect of territorial integrity and national sovereignty of States.[75]

In contrast, the United States "were pleased that the Outcome Document underscored the readiness of the Council to act in the face of

[72] *A More Secure World*, at p. 23.

[73] *Report of the Independent Inquiry into the Actions of the United Nations during the 1994 Genocide in Rwanda*, December 16, 1999.

[74] *The Responsibility to Protect, Report*, paras. 2.7–2.15; Lu, "Whose Principles? Whose Institutions?" in *Humanitarian Intervention*, ed. Terry Nardin and Melissa S. Williams, pp. 195–99.

[75] XIV Ministerial Conference of the Non-Aligned Movement, Durban, South Africa, 17–19 August 2004, para. 8, available at: www.nam.go.za/media/040820.pdf.

such atrocities, and rejected categorically the argument that any principle of non-intervention precludes the Council from taking such action."[76] Some other states did not oppose the doctrine, but were rather skeptical as to whether the proposed criteria would constrain their power to decide when and how to use force, whereas some other states tried to water down the reach of the doctrine.[77] It is thus apparent that states have their own understandings of what this doctrine means or requires. Neither should any illusion exist about the readiness of the SC to discharge its responsibility to protect. For example, nothing compelled the SC to mend its moral or political differences and act decisively when faced with a humanitarian catastrophe of Darfur proportions. Instead, the SC reaffirmed the sovereignty and territorial integrity of Sudan and tried to cooperate with the Sudanese government[78] even if it was that same government that had failed to provide protection to the peoples of Darfur.

Another challenge facing the UN is that of identifying its constituency. This has immense implications for its legitimacy because legitimacy judgements are collective judgments of those over whom power is exercised. The primary constituency of the UN is the aggregation of states because the UN is composed of states, is organized around states, and operates for the benefit of states. However, the problem is that the constituency of states is not homogenous but is normatively, politically, socially, and economically fragmented. As a result, it cannot pass univocal judgments on the legitimacy of the UN. On the other hand, UN activities impact on people's lives in many different ways, as the administration of territories and targeted sanctions show. The question then is whether peoples are also one of the UN's constituencies. It should be recalled at this juncture that the Preamble to the UN Charter opens with the words "We the People" and, as was said in previous sections, the UN is aware of the interests of human beings. That said, there is no *demos* within the UN, or indeed a global *demos*; neither do formal platforms exist where people can deliberate, form opinions, or express approval or disapproval of the UN. Even in those instances where the UN exercises direct power over people as in the case of territorial administrations or of targeted sanctions, the UN was less interested in generating legitimacy from local populations, but instead relied on the legitimacy that it enjoyed from and towards states. In other words, the UN's interest

[76] (2006) 100 *American Journal of International Law*, pp. 463–64.

[77] Alex J. Bellamy, "Wither the Responsibility to Protect? Humanitarian Intervention and the 2005 World Summit" (2006) 19 *Ethics and International Affairs* 151.

[78] SC Res 1755 (2007); SC Res 1769 (2007).

in human beings is indirect due to inherent structural and conceptual limitations.

The immediate question is whether the chain of legitimacy from the people to the UN can be mediated by states. This brings into consideration the nature of statehood and in particular the democratic credentials of UN members. A democratically-constituted UN could enhance the legitimacy of the Organization for a number of reasons. In the first place, there would be closer identification between the UN and its member states, and also between the UN and domestic audiences who are currently denied any input. Secondly, ideological affinity would enhance the substantive and procedural legitimacy of the UN. Thirdly, it would facilitate common action and thus enhance the legitimacy of the UN because it would be able to perform the tasks for which it was created. Fourthly, a democratically-constituted UN would diminish the risk of conflict to the extent that conflicts are often caused by political and normative differences.[79] As President Wilson observed "[a] steadfast concert of peace can never be maintained except by a partnership of democratic nations. No autocratic government could be trusted to keep faith within it or observe its covenants. It must be a league of honor, a partnership of opinion."[80] In the same vein, Fukuyama maintains that the UN should be reconstituted as a league of truly free states brought together by their common commitment to liberal principles.[81]

The UN is not oblivious to such arguments and has engaged in democratization policies.[82] For example, it has established peacekeeping operations with electoral or democratic transition mandates and, above all, has exercised territorial administration with a view to creating stable democratic states.[83] Also, the UN's human rights policies deal indirectly with democracy. That said, the UN's democratization policies

[79] John C. Pevehouse, Bruce Russett, "Democratic Intergovernmental Organizations Promote Peace" (2006) 60 *International Organization* 969; Robert O. Keohane, Andrew Moravscik, Anne-Marie Slaughter "Legalised Dispute Resolution: Interstate and Transnational" (2000) 54 *International Organization* 457.

[80] Woodrow Wilson, *War Messages*, 65th Cong, 1st Sess. Senate Doc. No. 5, Serial No. 7264, 1917, 3, p. 8.

[81] Francis Fukuyama, *The End of History and the Last Man*, (New York: The Free Press, 1992), p. 283

[82] *An Agenda for Peace*, para. 59: "There is an obvious connection between democratic practices ... and the achievement of true peace and security in a new and stable political order." *An Agenda for Democratisation*, A/51/761 (1996); *Prevention of Armed Conflict*, A/55/985-S/2001/574 (7 June 2001), para. 79.

[83] SC Res 1244(1999) on Kosovo; *Report of the Secretary-General of the United Nations Interim Administration on Kosovo* S/1999/779 (12 July 1999); SC Res 1272 (1999) on East

suffer from a number of weaknesses. Democratization is not a mainstream policy but is often part of the UN's peace and security mandate. This makes it an extraordinary policy. Furthermore, as part of its human rights policy, it lacks bite because the UN's competence is limited to promoting and encouraging respect for human rights.[84] Again, it is only in cases where violations of human rights are so severe that they threaten international peace that the UN can take direct action.[85] More than that, the UN's democratization policies and initiatives are usually ambiguous because the UN is not a conglomeration of democratic states and considerable differences of opinion exist as to the desirability or the meaning of democracy. This is evident in the membership criteria of the newly established Human Rights Council[86] as well as in SC Res 1483 (2003) on Iraq which is replete with contradictions; supporting at the same time democratic change and the status quo.[87]

Regarding the UN's role as dispenser of legitimacy, the UN has tried to enhance its role by responding to new challenges and this is what the "responsibility to protect" or authorizations of preventive self-defence try to do. However, in order for the UN to be able to act as dispenser of legitimacy, there must be agreement on the importance of the norms and values at stake as well as on the action to be taken. In the absence of such agreement, the UN will not be able to authorize actions and play its role as dispenser of legitimacy. To give an example, the UN was able to authorize the Allied action against Iraq in 1991 because there is overwhelming agreement that territorial conquest is impermissible, but authorizations of humanitarian operations, on the other hand, are more difficult to obtain because the necessary normative consensus is lacking. If the SC fails to authorize an operation, states may invoke a number of normative configurations drawn from the UN system in order to justify their actions, or they may appeal to other institutions for legitimacy.[88] In the first instance, states may claim implicit SC

Timor; *Report of the Secretary-General on the Situation in East Timor* S/1999/1024 (4 October 1999).

84 Articles 1(3) and 55, 56 of the UN Charter.

85 Louis Henkin, "International Law: Politics, Values and Functions," 216 *Recueil des Cours* (1989 IV), pp. 214–16.

86 *In Larger Freedom*, paras. 181–83; GA Res. 60/251 (2006) establishing the Human Rights Council.

87 Russell Buchan, "International Community and the Occupation of Iraq" (2007) 12 *Journal of Conflict and Security Law* 37.

88 *Responsibility to Protect, Report*, xiii: "If the Security Council fails to discharge its responsibility to protect in conscience-shocking situations crying out for action, concerned

authorization. In such cases, there is an initial SC determination that there is a threat to the peace from which authorization is implied. For example, with regard to NATO's operation in Kosovo, the US argued before the ICJ that the Kosovo action was implicitly authorized by "[t]he resolutions of the Security Council, which have determined that the actions of the Federal Republic of Yugoslavia constitute a threat to peace and security in the region and, pursuant to Chapter VII of the Charter, demanded a halt to such actions."[89] Similar arguments were used in relation to the US/UK operation against Iraq in 2003. It was claimed that the operation was based on previous SC resolutions such as SC Res 1441 (2002) and SC Res 687 (1991) that implicitly authorized the 2003 operation.[90] Alternatively, states may invoke UN principles in order to justify their actions. For example, President Clinton stated with regard to Kosovo that "[t]he actions of NATO in Kosovo helped to vindicate the principles and purposes of the Organization's Charter ...,"[91] and NATO claimed that the principle of sovereignty frustrates UN action and that human rights should be prioritized, and trump state sovereignty.[92] In the scenarios mentioned above there is no total repudiation of the UN system because the actions are presented as being in sync with UN collective security, although the power of the SC to actually authorize an operation is undermined. More serious are those cases where other organizations claim for themselves the power to use force. For example the African Union (AU) can intervene even without SC authorization "in respect of grave circumstances, namely: war crimes, genocide and crimes against humanity."[93] In this case, an organization

sates may not rule out other means to meet the gravity and urgency of that situation-and that the stature and credibility of the United Nations may suffer thereby."

89 *Legality of Use of Force (Yugoslavia v. United States of America)* Verbatim Record, 11 May 1999, CR 99/24; *Legality of Use of Force (Yugoslavia* v. *Belgium)* Verbatim Record, 10 May 1999 CR 99/15.

90 *Iraq: Legal Basis for the Use of Force* (17 March 2003) www.fco.gov.uk.

91 Press Release GA/9599 (21 September 1999).

92 Statement by the North Atlantic Council on Kosovo (30 January 1999) available at: www.nato.int/docu/pr/1999/p99-012e.htm. Also see *Independent International Commission on Kosovo: The Kosovo Report*, p. 2: "The Commission concludes that the NATO military intervention was illegal but legitimate. It was illegal because it did not receive prior approval from the United Nations Security Council. However, the Commission considers that the intervention was justified because all diplomatic avenues had been exhausted and because the intervention had the effect of liberating the majority population of Kosovo from a long period of oppression under Serbian rule."

93 Art. 4(h) *Constitutive Act of the African Union* (2002). Also see arts. 22(c) and 53(3) of the *ECOWAS Protocol Relating to the Mechanism for Conflict Prevention, Management, Resolution, Peace-keeping and Security*, available at: www.sec.ecowas.int.

other than the UN dispenses legitimacy to forcible actions. The challenge is even more serious when institutions project themselves as dispensers of legitimacy by discrediting the UN at the same time. For example, NATO mounted a direct attack on the UN in order to justify its operation in Kosovo. More specifically, it questioned the democratic credentials of SC members and admonished the UN for being biased in favour of sovereignty. In contrast, NATO was presented as an organization of democratic states enjoying procedural as well as substantive legitimacy to act as dispenser of legitimacy. The UN responded to such a challenge through institutional or doctrinal changes; as, for example, by adopting the "responsibility to protect" doctrine. That said, states will continue to look for alternative forms and arenas to legitimize their actions as long as UN membership is diverse, UN principles and values are subject to diverse interpretations, and membership of and allegiance to the UN is not the only *raison d'être* of states. For these reasons, the emergence of alternative poles of legitimacy cannot be prevented, neither can their availability be suppressed. Indeed, not only their existence, but also their role has been acknowledged by the former UN Secretary-General Kofi Annan who, in the wake of NATO's action in Kosovo, said that 'there are times when the use of force may be legitimate in the pursuit of peace'[94] and went on to say:

> Imagine for one moment that, in those dark days and hours leading up to the genocide [in Rwanda], there had been a coalition of states ready and willing to act in defence of the Tutsi population, but the Council had refused or delayed giving the green light. Should such a coalition then have stood idly by while horror unfolded?[95]

Legitimacy, cosmopolitanism, and constitutionalism

In this section I will examine the constitutional character of the UN as the material manifestation of its cosmopolitanism. In the first place it should be said that there is an intricate relationship between legitimacy, constitutionalism, and cosmopolitanism. Legitimacy and constitutionalism are linked in that they are both concerned with the relationship between the ruler and the ruled.[96] If legitimacy is about the substantive and procedural justification of power, constitutions,

[94] Kofi Annan, "Two Concepts of Sovereignty," *Economist*, (18 September 1999), 49
[95] *Ibid.*
[96] Hilaire Barnett, *Constitutional and Administrative Law*, (London, Cavendish, 1999), p. 5.

irrespective of their form, are about the structural and normative premises that underpin political orders and justify their authority.[97] Constitutionalism and cosmopolitanism are also related. As was said above, cosmopolitanism is about the principles and values that govern all members of a single, albeit global, unit. It follows that some framework is needed according to which cosmopolitan ideals will be practiced. Thus, moral cosmopolitanism leads to political cosmopolitanism. Political cosmopolitanism can lead to institutionalization manifested, for example, in the creation of institutions such as the UN. However, it is not just the institution that is important but equally important are the rules, principles, structures, and organs of the cosmopolitan project that the referent institution represents. This, in its turn, alludes to constitutionalism. Although the need for a constitution to fulfill the cosmopolitan project is not accepted by everyone,[98] it can be said that, unless cosmopolitanism is to remain an abstract promise, it needs some form of constitution. Thus, the cosmopolitan project represented by the UN can in principle support the constitutionalization of the UN. I will thus examine in this section the constitutional character of the UN and, contrary to a number of commentators who maintain that the UN exhibits constitutional characteristics,[99] I will express several of reservations.

To begin with, constitutions require some degree of normative, political, or social integration and a shared image as to what the constituted entity should be. The UN however lacks the compensating power of such normative integration. Instead, it is a conglomeration of politically, normatively, and socially diverse states with weak affinities and little, if at all, affection. Furthermore, there is little or no convergence of interests as to what the UN is or should be. The impact of such alienation on the constitutional reading of the Charter has been noted by Dupuy, who contrasted the "normative and organic integration attached to the ideal of constitution" with the dissemination of sovereign power

[97] Nicholas Tsagourias, "Introduction: Constitutionalism: A Theoretical Roadmap," in Nicholas Tsagourias (ed.), *Transnational Constitutionalism: International and European Models*, (Cambridge: Cambridge University Press, 2007), pp. 1–2.

[98] Hans Reiss (ed.), *Kant's Political Writings*, (Cambridge: Cambridge University Press, 1986), p. 16; Charles Beitz, "International Relations, Philosophy of," Edward Craig (ed.), *Routledge Encyclopedia of Philosophy*, (London, Routledge, 1998) vol. IV, p. 831.

[99] Bardo Fassbender, "The Meaning of International Constitutional Law," in Tsagourias (ed.), *Transnational Constitutionalism*, p. 307; Wouter Werner, "The Never-ending Closure: Constitutionalism and International Law," in Tsagourias (ed.), *Transnational Constitutionalism*, p. 329; Simma, "From Bilateralism," pp. 256–84.

between competing states which characterizes the international.[100] If the forgoing observations are applied to collective security, it means that it is not only structures, rules, and tools that are needed but what is needed, above all, is a common mindset. Members of a collective security system need to share some common understandings about security and about methods or aims in order to transcend individual and parochial interests. If no "*esprit de corps*" exists, any security system is doomed to fail.[101] One may then question the degree of integration, collegiality, and solidarity among members of the UN collective security system when these members are either traditional foes or incidental enemies. The League of Nations, as the UN predecessor, suffered from the same problem, which led Lauterpacht to admit that collective security can only be "resuscitated" by a group of states of "sufficient community of outlook and interest." As he further noted "a community both of outlook and of interest must … be the indispensable basis of that close association of collective security."[102] In similar vein Brierly noted that "organic type" institutions require far more integrated societies, and went on by saying that "we need a society where members have the same sort of confidence in one another's intentions and policies and the same absence of fundamental diversity of interests that the states of a federation must have if their union is to endure."[103]

This hints at another problem. Relations among member states and between member states and the UN are primarily horizontal and often conflictual. Member states do not view their existence, relations, or activities as being subordinated to the UN Charter neither do they always view their relations with fellow members or with the UN as being part

[100] Pierre-Marie Dupuy, "The Constitutional Dimension of the Charter of the United Nations Revisited" in (1997) 1 *Max Planck Yearbook of United Nations Law* 1 at 2 and 30.

[101] As Viscount Cecil said with regard to the League of Nations, there "has been a lack of solidarity, of *esprit de corps*, in the League powers which should have induced them jointly and almost automatically to resist an armed attack on any of their number. That is partly due to want of imagination caused by geographical remoteness or other considerations, partly to the unfamiliarity of the truth that peace is in itself the greatest of national interests, and partly to the want to vigour and precision in the League organization." Robert Cecil, *A Great Experiment: An Autobiography* (London: J. Cape, 1941), p. 348; *In Larger Freedom*, para. 126.

[102] Elihu Lauterpacht (ed.), *International Law; Being the Collected Papers of Hersch Lauterpacht*, (Cambridge: Cambridge University Press, 1977) vol. 3, ch. 5 "The League of Nations" 575, at 586. Also Matti Koskenniemi, *The Gentle Civiliser of Nations; The Rise and Fall of International Law 1870–1960*, (Cambridge: Cambridge University Press, 2001), pp. 376–82.

[103] James L. Brierly, "The Covenant and the Charter" (1946) 23 *British Yearbook of International Law* 83 at 92–93.

of a common project. Instead, they pursue their interests and reaffirm their power inside or outside the UN or compete with each other and with the UN for the same issues or goods. Furthermore, states have created a plethora of institutions which exercise parallel functions with the UN. These institutions whose membership is more circumscribed and are often more integrated than the UN have appropriated state affections and interests. What is more, as NATO's attack on Yugoslavia shows, such institutions often target UN members in order to promote their own agendas, whereas the UN remains silent. In sum, states have not transferred all their loyalties to the UN or their affections to their fellow members nor do they view the UN as the exclusive locus of their existence or as the main orientation pole of their activities.

Furthermore, there is no formal forum inside or outside the UN where constitutional ideas or proposals about the UN can be debated by those for whom the UN has some pertinence. These can be states, but also individuals, as well as other IOs, NGOs, etc. Although issues of legitimacy can be discussed in different global spaces and by different participants, such discussions lack formal recognition by the UN which remains a state-oriented organization. That is why reform proposals are produced by states, and their negotiation takes place at state forums and is subject to the procrustean measurements of national governments.[104]

The UN also does not have inbuilt mechanisms such as courts or institutions that could engineer or support any process of constitutionalization. Relations among and between its organs and members are disjointed. This can be contrasted with the constitutionalization of the EU where its constitutional transformation has often been engineered by its own institutions such as the European Parliament or the European Court of Justice.

Last but not least, one should not underestimate the acute political character of constitutionalism and the different reactions to which it may give rise. It would be interesting to mention here the disagreements that surrounded the proposed EU constitutional treaty. Whereas European integration was successful as long as it concerned defined and technical objectives, when integration became political and was dressed in constitutional language, it revealed the differences of opinion and the divisions between the member states. If this can happen in a community of twenty-seven states with extensive political, social,

[104] As the former Secretary-General Boutros Boutros-Ghali said: "The United Nations is a gathering of sovereign States and what it can do depends on the common ground that they create between them." *An Agenda for Peace*, para. 2.

economic, and legal interrelationships and commonalities, what will happen among nearly two hundred sometimes radically different states is not difficult to predict.

Conclusion

In the previous sections I presented the promise and the reality of UN cosmopolitanism, constitutionalism, and reforms in rather stark terms. Against this background, the question of what sustains the UN and, more specifically, what sustains its legitimacy remains. I believe that ambivalence is the answer and such ambivalence derives from the contradictions that riddle the UN. To begin with, the UN and its collective security system are "neither contractual nor constitutional"[105] and whereas structures, rules, principles, and practices may resemble one or the other – either a contract or a constitution – they are different from either. In the same vein, whereas the UN projects a cosmopolitan air, in reality it has not abandoned statism or power politics. As far as its legitimacy is concerned, the UN has various clusters of legitimacy that appeal to different sections of its constituency. Its overall legitimacy is the sum of these micro-legitimacies which co-exist but remain uncoordinated. UN actions are also ambivalent because they try to balance multiple perceptions of legitimacy. As a result, the stakeholders of UN legitimacy confer or withdraw their support for different issues and at different times, but at no time is there total repudiation by the totality of its stakeholders.

Thus, it is my feeling that the UN will carry on regardless, because no actor has completely withdrawn their support; changes in the general assumptions that underpin the UN are not orderly or uniform; the incentives for reform are fragmented; and, above all, everyone frets about opening the Pandora's box of radical reforms, or of negotiating a new World Order. What can be expected therefore are some incremental and modest developments, and some patchy reforms. The latter will continue to form part of UN rituals because they are necessary in managing the legitimacy of the Organization. My prediction then is that no radical mutation of the Organization is to be expected in the foreseeable future, nor any fatal assault on its legitimacy.

[105] Alfred Zimmern, *The League of Nations and the Rule of Law 1918–1935*, (London: Macmillan, 1945), pp. 290–91.

7

Enforcing cosmopolitan justice: the problem of intervention

KOK-CHOR TAN

Introduction

The worry may be raised that the more demanding a conception of global justice is with respect to how states may treat their own citizens, the more readily a rationale is provided for states to intervene against each other in the name of upholding justice. Accordingly, it may be thought that to the extent that liberal cosmopolitanism, as we may call it, understands the limits of global toleration to be determined not just by how states respect and honor the basic rights of their citizens (such as the right to life, bodily integrity, basic protection of the law, basic subsistence) but also by how they promote and protect their liberal democratic political rights (such as the right of free speech and expression, democratic political participation and so on), it is a conception of global justice with strong interventionist tendencies.[1] In contrast to liberal cosmopolitanism (henceforth also "cosmopolitanism" for short), some commentators propose a more cautionary and modest conception of liberal global justice, one which is committed to a shorter list of universal human rights, limited to basic human needs and security. Rawls's "Law of Peoples" is one key example of this more modest liberal internationalism.[2] Rawls's liberal internationalism does not require all societies to

Thanks to Roland Pierik and Wouter Werner for their very helpful criticisms, suggestions, and comments on earlier drafts.

[1] For some examples of liberal cosmopolitanism, see Darrel Moellendorf, *Cosmopolitan Justice* (Boulder, CO: Westview Press, 2002); Thomas Pogge, *World Poverty and Human Rights* (Cambridge: Polity Press, 2001); Simon Caney, *Justice Beyond Borders* (Oxford: Oxford University Press, 2005); Allen Buchanan, *Justice, Legitimacy and Self-Determination* (Oxford: Oxford University Press, 2004), Charles Beitz "Rawls's Law of Peoples," *Ethics* 110 (2000): 669–96, and my *Toleration, Diversity and Global Justice* (University Park, PA: Penn State Press, 2000) and *Justice Without Borders* (Cambridge: Cambridge University Press, 2004). See editors' introduction in this volume for helpful taxonomy of the concept of "cosmopolitanism."

[2] John Rawls, *The Law of Peoples* (Cambridge, Mass.: Harvard University Press, 1999).

be liberal as a matter of justice. It recognizes that certain nonliberal but decent societies can qualify as equal members in good standing in a just Society of Peoples. Roughly, societies are judged under Rawls's theory to be decent so long as they honor basic human rights and are peaceable towards other societies; but they do not need to honor liberal principles of justice within their jurisdiction. One way the fundamental difference between Rawls and the cosmopolitans can be put is that Rawls is more concerned literally with inter*national* justice, that is justice between states, whereas the cosmopolitans are more truly concerned with global justice, that is justice *among persons* beyond borders.[3] Compared with Rawls's more accommodating idea of international justice, liberal cosmopolitanism appears dangerously interventionist to its critics.

This concern over the interventionist tendency of cosmopolitanism is understandable. Any defensible conception of global justice cannot treat intervention frivolously, and lower the bar for permissible intervention instead of keeping a tight reign on this practice. But I think the worry that liberal cosmopolitanism dangerously greases the path of intervention is unfounded. The worry conflates the making of a critical judgment with a specific method of enforcing that judgment. Liberal cosmopolitanism identifies principles of justice that, among other things, define the conditions of state moral standing and legitimacy and membership in a moral international order. That is, liberal cosmopolitan principles provide one benchmark for evaluating the legitimacy, or its lack thereof, of states. On both the liberal cosmopolitan and Rawlsian liberal internationalist views, as distinct from the tradition of international realism, the way a state treats its own citizens is one necessary condition of its legitimacy. But principles of legitimacy in themselves do not entail, or necessarily permit, a particular method of enforcement when these principles are not honored. How cosmopolitan principles are to be enforced is a further question, and is distinct from what these principles are. On the contrary, basic liberal morality will set constraints on how principles of justice may be properly enforced. Principles of justice shape our critical evaluation and judgment of a state of affairs, and so, on the cosmopolitan ideal, a society that fails to respect the basic liberal rights of its members will elicit critical disapproval. But how that disapproval is to be expressed and, more importantly, how compliance is to be enforced, is a further question the answer to which will depend on a host of other considerations, including competing moral principles. In short a distinction must

[3] See my *Justice Without Borders*, p. 35.

be noted between making a critical judgment (by reference to certain principles of justice) and the enforcement of that judgment.[4]

Humanitarian intervention – and by this term, and the term "intervention," I mean specifically intervention by military means to defend human rights – is a special means of enforcing the demands of global justice. But whether an intervention is going to be a good strategy of protecting human rights or, more relevantly to our discussion, a morally permissible method of protection will depend on various factors and conditions, as well as the availability and feasibility of alternative non-military means of enforcement. This distinction between taking an evaluative stance on the one hand, and acting on that stance on the other is obvious enough. But it is worth explicating in the context of humanitarian intervention given the common worry that the universalistic aspirations of liberal cosmopolitanism render it intervention-prone.

The aim of this chapter, then, is to clarify that cosmopolitan liberalism is not in principle more interventionist than other forms of liberal internationalism such as Rawls's. To this end, I recount the well-known conditions under which intervention is generally agreed by most moral theorists to be morally permissible for the purpose of highlighting the very special and stringent conditions of permissibility. I explicate these well-rehearsed points for the purpose of clarifying that liberal cosmopolitanism can accept these common conditions of permissibility. My central claim is that liberal cosmopolitanism does not depart from commonly accepted accounts of just intervention.

The morality and legality of intervention

As I will argue, cosmopolitanism accepts many of the fundamental tenets of common morality concerning just war and the limits of intervention.[5] Yet, common morality notwithstanding, the appropriateness of humanitarian intervention is not without controversy especially in light of recent and historical occurrences of intervention. I begin then with some brief reflections on some of this concern. Specifically, I will look at those worries that stress the potential pitfalls of permitting intervention for international relations in practice and international law.[6]

[4] I discuss this also in *Toleration, Diversity and Global Justice*, pp. 32–33; 59–64.

[5] See Terry Nardin, "The Moral Basis of Humanitarian Intervention," *Ethics and International Affairs*, 16, no. 1 (2002), pp. 57–71.

[6] As is the theme of this volume, I am especially interested in the gap between the morality and the legality of intervention, between intervention as a practice and the institutionalizing of intervention.

First, one might point to historical examples of interventions that are quite clearly unjust to remind proponents of the dangers of the practice.[7] The 2003 US invasion of Iraq provides a vivid example of an intervention widely seen as unjust, that has also, as it turns out, failed even in its political objectives. A reason why this intervention is considered unjust is that while the Saddam regime was indeed tyrannical, it is also clear that the other standard conditions for a just intervention – last resort, proportionality, urgency – had not been met.[8] Yet, it is important that a recent vivid experience does not cloud our general moral assessment of the practice of intervention. It is natural that the ongoing situation in Iraq, one that looms so large in the international public consciousness, tends to dominate our thinking and discussion of intervention and render the practice of intervention highly suspect. But it is important that a recent bad example does not distort our analysis of the permissibility of intervention.[9] The case of Iraq only shows that immoral (and in this case also illegal) interventions can occur; it does not show that all interventions are as a rule morally unacceptable.

While it is of course true that there have been abuses of cosmopolitan principles historically to rationalize military interventions, the question is whether absent these principles these immoral and illegal interventions would not have occurred. A blanket prohibition against *humanitarian* intervention would eliminate one (albeit convenient) rationalization for intervention; but it doesn't follow that other pretexts couldn't be cooked-up if the government of a country has already set its mind on invading another. The US would have invaded Iraq even if the

[7] Martti Koskenniemi, *The Gentle Civilizer of Nations* (Cambridge: Cambridge University Press, 2001). Koskenniemi for example calls rightly to great effect the 1965 US intervention in the Dominican Republic in the name of universal humanitarian principles as a case of such an abuse, see p. 480.

[8] I will return to this point in more detail below. My aim here is not to establish the injustice of the Iraq intervention but to note, as in the text, that the widely perceived injustice of that intervention has prompted increased skepticism towards interventions more generally in recent thinking.

[9] Recall the opposite public reaction following the NATO intervention in Kosovo. Here the mood was more optimistic, and that intervention was celebrated by some commentators as the closest real world example of an altruistic intervention or pure humanitarian intervention. Academic debates following that intervention were dominated not by questions concerning the morality of intervention but over the tension of a morally permissible but illegal intervention. See, for example, several of the papers in *Humanitarian Intervention: ethical, legal and political dilemmas*, ed. J.L. Holzgrefe and Robert Keohan (Cambridge: Cambridge University Press, 2003).

humanitarian argument weren't available; in fact the arguments from security and fight against terrorism dominated the war discourse.[10]

Now one might say that in general intervention has caused historically more harm than good, and so an absolute prohibition against it is desirable. But it is far from obvious how such a claim, based as it is on counterfactuals, can be properly evaluated. For one can as well construct counterfactuals to show that a world in which states simply minded their own business and not intervene would be far worse. If anything, history shows that the last presents a worse scenario. The formation of the UN, the introduction of the Universal Declaration of Human Rights, the adoption of the Genocide Convention and so on, were precisely to leave behind such a world, a world in which states could and ought to mind their own business, which the experience of WWII has proved to be morally untenable.[11] More specifically, there are several historical examples of moral but illegal interventions that successfully put an end to gross human rights violation: Tanzania's intervention in Uganda that toppled Idi Amin's brutal dictatorship; India's intervention in East Pakistan (which then gained independent statehood as Bangladesh), and Vietnam's invasion that ended the killing fields of Cambodia. These interventions, quite uncontroversially, succeeded in putting an end to unspeakable atrocities. These are classic textbook examples of morally permissible interventions, so there is no need to belabor their case here, suffice to note that, compared with the Iraq intervention, there were occurring wide-spread atrocities whose

[10] My point here is not to be pessimistic about international relations; on the contrary I hold that principles and concerns for justice can move citizens to evaluate the policies and actions of their own states. I meant only to stress that a general moral prohibition on intervention is not going to make the world any safer for aggressive states aren't moved by moral arguments.

[11] David Kennedy draws attention to the dangers, what he calls "the dark sides," of enforcing abstract humanitarian principles in *The Dark Sides of Virtue* (Princeton: Princeton University Press, 2005). But Kennedy's warning that agents take heed of the implications of intervention ("the pragmatism of consequences" as he calls it) and maintain "a clear-eyed focus on the purpose of our work" ("the pragmatism of intent") against a blind and impulsive enforcement of humanitarian principles is a point cosmopolitans can surely agree with (p. xx). As I suggest above, there are moral reasons why cosmopolitans will refrain from intervention just because a state is deemed intolerably unjust. That a given intervention will make matters worse is, of course, one important moral consideration against it. Kennedy's warning of the dark sides of humanitarian enforcement is not a blanket dismissal of universal humanitarian principles, but an exhortation that salient competing moral considerations not be overlooked by humanitarian agents. See Kennedy, *The Dark Sides of Virtue*, ch. 9.

seriousness required immediate action rather than more attempts at diplomatic solutions which had hitherto failed to put an end to the human misery.

Another objection is that non-military alternatives for protecting human rights are preferable.[12] This point is worth stressing, even if it is quite obvious. Clearly no one should prefer war when humanitarian assistance (or for that matter politics) by other means is available. This is precisely why there is a last resort condition for a permissible intervention, and why any plausible theory of just war observes this point. But it does not follow from this that we affirm the general rule that only non-military responses to humanitarian crises are morally acceptable. Imagine that there is genocide going on in country X and till now no diplomatic attempts have succeeded in putting an end to it and imagine that an intervention would correct the situation. How long more do we sit back and wait for a non-military option to present itself? Wasn't this the lesson of Rwanda, and of Darfur at the moment? To be sure, in many historical and ongoing cases, no serious attempts were made to consider non-military methods of protection, so the exhortation that the non-military option be taken seriously is certainly well-taken and serves as an important reminder to any party contemplating humanitarian rescue. But it is another thing to conclude that intervention is never permitted and that we are morally required always to consider non-military options regardless of the situation at hand. The last, taken as a general rule will have the effect of excusing inaction.

Some may say that it is more important to preempt humanitarian crises from arising, and so our attention should be on preemption of intervention not intervention.[13] For example, in the case of the genocide in Rwanda, one might say that among other things, it was European colonialism that laid the kindling for the events that enflamed some decades later. Indeed, a commentator might say that the past intervention by Europeans left behind the precarious political-ethnic situation in Rwanda that tipped over so easily into genocide at the slightest provocation. Leaving aside the merits of these particular causal claims (there is probably some truth to all of them), I accept that engaging in serious analysis of, and being sensitive and responsive to, historical events is

[12] See Anne Orford *Reading Humanitarian Intervention: Human Rights and the Use of Force in International Law* (Cambridge: Cambridge University Press, 2003).

[13] *Ibid.*; see also Thomas Pogge; "Preempting Humanitarian Intervention," *Humanitarian Intervention: moral and philosophical issues*, ed. Aleksandar Jokic (Peterborough, ON: Broadview Press, 2003).

important for various obvious reasons, one of which being that we can try to learn (if we care to) how to avoid such future fatal potentialities. And it is of course morally imperative that we try to prevent bad things from happening. Still it seems equally obvious that when a situation in front of us is pressingly urgent, some immediate action may be called for regardless of how we thought the situation had come to be. Imagine offering the following response to a people in urgent need of humanitarian rescue: "We see you are in need of rescue (and we are certainly in a position to help you). But as we can all also see, it was because of certain past injustices, indeed regretfully injustices on our part, that you are now in such dire straits. The lesson to be learned is that we should not act unjustly in this way again, and will also do what we can to prevent such injustices from occurring elsewhere. There is nothing we can do for you now because our intervening will not address the root cause. That's all in the past." Surely this is an absurdity, and more so if the respondent was also the party responsible for the current dire state of affairs.

Again, to stress, I don't claim that any talk of the past is irrelevant and of no use whatsoever. Of course understanding the past is useful and important for a variety of reasons too obvious to state. But the fact that it is important to understand historical causes of a bad situation and better to prevent this from arising does not eliminate the fact that some atrocities are now occurring that call out for a response. To be sure, humanitarian defenders must realize that intervention is only a band-aid solution, but band-aids are sometimes useful and needed.

Perhaps the most challenging worry concerns the possible implications of intervention for international law.[14] That is, what makes

[14] Currently, there is no explicit provision under international law for "pure humanitarian intervention." Article 42 (7) of the UN Charter that is invoked to justify military action notes that the international community "may take action by air, sea, or land forces as may be necessary to *maintain or restore international peace and security.*" The italicized portion (mine) is significant. Thus an intervention intended strictly to put a end to some violation of human rights would not be justifiable under current UN charter. This, of course, does not mean that humanitarian intervention cannot be sanctioned and in effect enacted under the present international legal regime. The built-in loop hole here is obvious: since it is not difficult to claim that a grave human rights situation in one country will have destablizing regional and global effects, Article 42(7) can be and has been invoked by the UN to justify various humanitarian interventions. For some discussion on how the concept of "the threat to peace" has been given a broad reading, see Nicholas Tsagourias, "Cosmopolitan Legitimacy and UN Collective Security," this collection. But technically no intervention for the sole purpose of defending the human rights of the inhabitants of a country, i.e. "pure humanitarian intervention," can be justified under

intervention morally objectionable is not so much the act of an intervention itself, which taken in isolation may be granted as morally permissible. What is problematic is the impact of such actions on international law and practice. Here are two possible impacts. One is that we keep international law as it is, that is, in general, outlaw purely humanitarian intervention, but allow for its legal exemption on a case-by-case basis. On this approach, when we have a case for a morally permissible intervention, we say that the law has run out and a situation like a supreme emergency is in effect, and the law can be suspended. Or, two, we can urge that international law be reformed to grant legality to intervention, and this involves some codification of terms and conditions of a legally just intervention. On this approach, we bring closer together law and morality.

The first option may appear to some as a rather unattractive position because it displays a certain disregard and contempt for the rule of law. Moreover, it seems also to allow states to unilaterally invoke moral reasoning that purportedly transcends the law, thereby dangerously opening the way for states to disregard the sovereignty of other states.[15] This would suggest that we reject this possibility and accept the second option, that of reforming international law to make space for intervention. Still some assuaging remarks in defense of the first option can be made: first, it is not clear that defying the law is by definition a mark of disrespect for the rule of law. The philosophical literature on civil disobedience is instructive here.[16] Furthermore on the matter of intervention, Thomas Franck has proposed an international jurying process by which to determine when a legal exemption is acceptable to allow for a morally permissible intervention.[17] If Franck's proposal can be implemented, then the worry that making space for morally permissible

this clause. Legalizing pure humanitarian intervention would require providing legal provisions for the use of force solely for the purpose of defending human rights without the pretext that is necessary for protecting world peace.

[15] See Pratap Mehta, "From State Sovereignty to Human Security (via institutions?)," in *Humanitarian Intervention*, ed. Terry Nardin and Melissa Williams (New York: New York University Press, 2005).

[16] See Rawls's discussion on civil disobedience. The philosophically interesting feature of civil disobedience is that it involves the rejection of a law while maintaining a general respect for the rule of law. *Theory of Justice* (Cambridge: Harvard University Press 1971), pp. 36–91.

[17] Franck, "Legality and Legitimacy in Humanitarian Intervention," in *Humanitarian Intervention*, ed. Terry Nardin and Melissa Williams (New York: New York University Press, 2005).

interventions *through legal exemptions* will lead to problematic unilateralism in intervention is unfounded. Instead of allowing a single state to determine when it may transcend the law on moral grounds, there will be an international legal procedure in place to determine when the law ceases to apply or when an exception is to be permitted.

At any rate, even if the worry about illegality in intervention persists, there is the second option, that of attempting to make the law as it is written more consistent with moral views about the permissibility of intervention. That is, change the law to make space for pure humanitarian interventions, which I believe also to be the more attractive route.[18] A possible worry with this idea is that codifying humanitarian intervention will pave the ground further for its abuse. A critic might be prepared to grant that there are morally permissible interventions under the right conditions, but still worry that institutionalizing such a practice will have morally objectionable consequences. That is, one might think that even though interventions could be morally permissible per se, to make room for them within the law would be morally objectionable. The objections here are what we might call institutional rather than moral. This line of argument parallels an argument often made against institutionalizing and legalizing physician assisted suicide. Even if physician assisted suicide can be shown to be morally permissible, it would be a grave mistake to allow society to legalize and institutionalize such a practice. Some reasons for this conclusion are that legalizing such a practice would lead to abuses and misapplication; that it would put pressure on both patients and doctors to make rash decisions, and so on. But this institutional objection against active euthanasia works only if it can be shown that there are no feasible countervailing institutional mechanisms to block abuses and slippery slopes.[19] Likewise, the claim that codifying intervention has unacceptable social and legal implications holds only if there are indeed no feasible and practicable

[18] Such a reform will include revising Article 42 (7) of the UN Charter to say something like the international community "may take action by air, sea, or land forces as may be necessary to maintain or restore international peace and security *or to defend basic human rights.*" In this volume, Tsagourias has incisively noted the legitimation crisis within the UN and argues that reforms within the UN will be difficult. I don't disagree with Tsagourias that there are difficulties; my point here is only to illustrate the difference should there be a UN Charter endorsement of pure humanitarian intervention.

[19] Dan W. Brock, "Voluntary Active Euthanasia" Hastings Center Report 22, no. 2 (1992), pp. 10–22; Johannes J.M. Van Delden, "Slippery Slopes in Flat Countries – a response," *Journal of Medical Ethics* 25, no. 1 (1999), pp. 22–24.

institutional safeguards that can be put in place to prevent misuses and the slide down the path to excessive intervention. This is still an open matter and calls for more discussion and examination, instead of being ruled out of court.

Moreover, it is far from clear that the world is any safer from immoral interventions in the absence of legal codification. As mentioned earlier, when countries invade one another immorally it is not the case that absent legal and moral principles no such interventions would have occurred. Abuses can take place with or without the law. Indeed, it is the gap between international law and morality that creates the widest avenue for abuses. Parties feel entitled to act on morality alone since the law seems inappropriate (or is silent) and hence feel entitled to act unilaterally as per their moral view. Codifying a law of intervention would remove this moral licensing of intervention. It will not be enough then to simply consult morality and ignore the law on the grounds that it has failed morally; a law of intervention that reflects moral sensibilities on this matter can thus better reign in and regulate its practice. Indeed, as it might be argued that legalizing certain acts such as euthanasia or abortion is morally preferable because it allows for the control and regulation of activities that would occur anyway, so one might say that establishing the legal terms of intervention rather than setting us on the slippery slope towards an interventionist world would allow for better means of controlling a dangerous but sometimes necessary practice.

In sum, it seems hard to make the case for a blanket prohibition against intervention. Not only is such a blanket claim conceptually impossible to make, for examples can easily be concocted that will strain the claim, but there have been in fact historical examples where it would be a stretch to deny that an intervention was or would have been permissible if not even required (for example, an intervention to end the Nazi Holocaust). One rather suspects that objections against intervention are really objections against this or that particular intervention, and indeed defenders of humanitarian intervention will readily agree that historically there have been too many immoral interventions. But to conclude from this fact that there should be a general absolute prohibition against intervention is not only to argue fallaciously but to support a position that is morally counter-intuitive, holding that even when force is reasonably the last resort, it still may not be used to end some wide-spread systemic violations of human rights.

Cosmopolitanism and intervention

In *The Law of Peoples*, Rawls asks, rhetorically: under what conditions might a military intervention to protect persons against their own state (or the state's failure to protect them against elements within the state) be permitted? He continues: "Is there ever a time when forceful intervention might be called for? If the offenses against human rights are egregious and the society does not respond to the imposition of sanctions, such intervention in the defense of human rights would be acceptable and would be called for."[20] In such a case, a "people's right to independence and self-determination is no shield from that condemnation, nor even from coercive intervention by other people in grave cases" (*ibid.*, p. 38). Notice that it is not just human rights violations that will trigger the call for intervention, but "egregious" or "grave" violations *and* that the violators are not responsive to non-military attempts to end the violence.

So even on Rawls's internationalism, where basic human rights set the limits of state legitimacy, violation of or disrespect for basic rights per se do not warrant forceful sanctions or military action. The society that fails to honor human rights forfeits its status as a member in good standing in the Society of Peoples, but what the appropriate response is on the part of members of the Society of Peoples is a separate question. As Rawls puts it: "What to do on these questions is, however, essentially a matter of political judgment and depends upon a political assessment of the likely consequences of various policies" (*ibid.*, p. 93). The fact that principles of international justice have been violated is not sufficient cause for taking a particular kind of enforcement action against the violator. We have to evaluate the seriousness of the violation, the urgency of the situation, the available range of responses, and their respective potential consequences to determine the right and effective course of action, and here the exercise of good judgment is indispensable.

Intervention is limited to only extreme or egregious instances of basic rights violation that are not responsive to non-military attempts to halt them. On the last point, sound political judgment is most crucial: are there still possible alternative means of ending the violation short of military action relative to the urgent need to put an end to the violation?

[20] Rawls, *The Law of Peoples*, p. 94, fn. 6; see also the following remarks: "An outlaw state that violates these rights is to be condemned and in grave cases may be subjected to forceful sanctions and even to intervention," *ibid.*, p. 81.

If not, is an intervention going to be less costly, morally speaking, than the harm it is meant to halt? To paraphrase the common slogan, we don't want to bomb an entire village and its inhabitants in the name of protecting their human rights.

For Rawls, the permissibility of intervention under extreme cases is seen as an exception to the general rule *prohibiting* intervention. Recall that one of the eight stated principles of Rawls's internationalism holds that "Peoples are to observe a duty of non-intervention" (*ibid.*, p. 37). Rawls's discussion of intervention does not rescind the general principle of non-intervention but identifies conditions under which a departure from this general principle is acceptable. What is relevant for our purpose is that the exception is not granted simply when basic human rights are violated but only when they are violated in a particularly egregious way *and* that military offensive to stop the violation is the last resort and a proportionate response.

It is useful here to note that Rawls's view on intervention is sensibly cautious, and substantively rather similar to that of Michael Walzer's, which has been criticized by some commentators as being too protective of state sovereignty.[21] For Walzer, the general norm is that only wars of self-defense are justifiable.[22] The key reason for this general prohibition stems from the importance of respecting the self-determination and communal integrity of political societies. Hence the principle of non-intervention is a default principle. Yet, "when the violation of human rights within a set of boundaries is so terrible that it makes talk of community or self-determination or 'arduous struggle' seem cynical and irrelevant, that is, in cases of enslavement or massacre" an exemption can be made to the general rule of non-intervention (p. 90). Thus in Walzer's view, as in Rawls's, human rights violation is not a sufficient cause for intervention. What is necessary is that the rights violation be recognized as egregious or grave, or such as to shock the conscience of humanity, or such as to render cynical the idea of self-determination of a community. But even gross violations don't provide a sufficient condition for intervention. What is required are also the common conditions of just war, for examples the so-called "last resort" condition (Walzer, p. 84) and the conditionality of proportionality and so on.[23]

[21] See for one example, David Luban, "The Romance of the Nation-State," *Philosophy and Public Affairs* 9 (1980): 392–97.

[22] Walzer, *Just and Unjust Wars* (New York: Basic Books, 1977), pp. 61–63.

[23] As Walzer notes in *Just and Unjust Wars* (pp. 212–13) there is no literal last resort. What the condition demands is that reasonable non-military options have been put to test and

Some might add to the egregiousness and last resort conditions a right authorization condition. For instance, adapting from the Thomist just war tradition, one might say that a morally permissible intervention must also have the proper authorization from some global body such as the United Nations. Yet, so it seems to me, the purpose of right authorization with respect to intervention is to help ensure that interventions are not undertaken for nationalist geopolitical reasons.[24] The requirement of right authorization serves as a useful institutional check against this problem. But perhaps this should not be treated as a moral condition in itself. For example, right institutional authorization becomes less significant and is indeed dispensable when, in spite of overwhelming moral considerations in favor of intervention, proper authorization is not forthcoming because of the ulterior interests of members of the authorizing entity. To insist on proper authorization when it is obvious that such an authorization is not going to be granted because of specific geopolitical factors is a procedural fetishism of sorts, for it confuses the means (a means of safeguarding abuses against a moral condition) for the end (that is, the moral condition itself).[25] These remarks are consistent with Allen Buchanan's rejection of "legal absolutism," the view that "it is virtually never justifiable to violate international law, or at least not the most basic norms of international law, even for the sake of protecting human rights."[26] For Buchanan, there can be moral reasons, the necessity of protecting human rights for one, for by-passing what the law regards as necessary proper authorization, and indeed morally grounded cases of overriding prevailing laws or legal norms can provide impetus for international legal reform.

The moral relevance of right authorization is of course a complex issue and in need of more discussion. I meant only to flag some problems with insisting on it as a necessary condition of permissibility. Perhaps at best, the requirement of right institutional authorization should be seen as an "operational" requirement, meaning by this that it is a requirement not of morality per se but of the limits of putting morality into practice. Moral

have failed to produce results, and the urgency of the situation does not allow further attempts.

[24] Recall here Franck's jurying procedure as one safeguard in his "Legality and Legitimacy in Humanitarian Intervention."

[25] See my "The Unavoidability of Morality," in *Humanitarian Intervention*, ed. Terry Nardin and Melissa Williams (New York: New York University Press, 2005). There is also helpful discussion of this in Nicholas Tsagourias, "Cosmopolitan Legitimacy and UN Collective Security," this collection.

[26] Buchanan, *Justice, Legitimacy and Self-Determination*, p. 441.

reasoning does not depend on institutional authorization for its soundness; morality stands above what institutions require or don't require. However, given the epistemic limitations of agents as well as the distorting influence of agents' diverse experiences and interests, and given the very high risks and costs of war, proper institutional authorization, appropriately defined, can be seen as a *real world* safeguard against misapplication of moral reasoning towards the end of war. Still, in this view, it remains important not to lose sight of the moral ideal and forget why institutional authorization is important in the first place. Institutional authorization is needed to help ensure that moral reasoning is adhered to in real world practice, but it does not replace moral reasoning itself. Moreover, what counts as right authority will depend on how we understand the moral basis for such an authority in the first place. It is by reference to moral reasoning that we can say of a particular practice of authorization that it is inadequate and needs to be reformed.[27]

At any rate, my general point is unaffected, namely, the standards by which moral legitimacy of a state is determined (basic human rights for Rawls) do not themselves furbish an answer to the question of whether it would also be legitimate to intervene against that state. Those who take the respect for basic human rights to be the benchmark of state moral legitimacy do not take the criterion of legitimacy alone to define the legitimacy of an intervention. At the very least the condition of "last resort" which is in turn tied to some judgment of the "urgency" of the situation and the idea of proportionality will have to be satisfied.[28]

The conditions noted above, under which the general prohibition against intervention is overruled, do not derive specifically from liberal morality but from more widely shared views about the morality

[27] None of this is to deny the importance of institutions as constraints on action or indeed the basic point that institutions be the subject of justice. The point merely is that there ae sometimes institutional requirements on actions that are primarily for the purpose of providing safeguards and it is important to recognize these for what they are, rather than as the moral objective in themselves. See Buchanan's remarks that institutions not be neglected (Buchanan 2004: 30). Moreover, institutionalization is significant in other regards. I have argued that to properly realize the responsibility to protect (i.e. the duty to intervene to protect human rights), the international community should put in place (i.e. institutionalize) a standing humanitarian defense force. See my "The Duty to Protect."

[28] Contra Thomas Mertens, these limiting conditions are not simply practical or pragmatic. The conditions of permissible intervention are moral conditions, and it establishes the moral (and not pragmatic political) limitations against intervention. Mertens, "Defending the Rawlsian League of Nations," *Leiden Journal of International Law* 18 (2005), pp. 711–15.

of war.[29] As long as one accepts some notion of basic individual rights (on whatever philosophical grounding) to life, security of persons, bodily integrity, and the like, and that there are situations where most can agree that violations against these rights are occurring, the just cause condition is satisfied. The rightness of using armed means to defend basic human rights from systemic violation when this is urgent and the last resort is not uniquely a liberal moral idea. A liberal internationalist is not any more interventionist than other conceptions of global morality that affirms (and which plausible conception does not?) some idea of the inviolability of persons. Liberal internationalism, as least in the version offered by Rawls, does not open the floodgates to intervention but is in fact in line with common morality on this matter.[30]

Some may note that this modesty of Rawlsian Liberal Internationalism is precisely its appeal over a more *cosmopolitan* liberal position. Liberal cosmopolitanism, as I am defining it, advances an account of global justice that effectively takes liberal principles to have global validity and application for all societies. Unlike Rawls, cosmopolitans set the limits of global toleration higher. For liberal cosmopolitans, such as Buchanan, Caney, Mollendorf, it is not the case, contra Rawls, that societies that do not affirm liberal principles (including the respect for the political liberties and freedoms and basic democratic rights that citizens of liberal

[29] For some discussion, see Joseph Boyle, "Traditional Just War Theory and Humanitarian Intervention" in *Humanitarian Intervention*, ed. Terry Nardin and Melissa Williams (New York: New York University Press, 2005); Nardin, "The Moral Basis of Humanitarian Intervention."

[30] Ronald Janse has argued that it is not clear why liberal peoples should not, contra Rawls, want other non-liberal peoples to adopt liberal values. "The Legitimacy of Humanitarian Interventions," *Leiden Journal of International Law* 19 (2006), pp. 669–92. As a comment on what it is that liberal peoples should aspire toward vis-à-vis non-liberal peoples, I agree with Janse. But as an implicating comment about intervention, that is, that liberal peoples would want to *forcefully* impose their values on non-liberal peoples, I disagree (as argued for in the text above). There is no logical necessity that just because an agent is committed deeply to certain values that she has to go about forcefully imposing these values on others. (And as said, Rawls is clear too that it does not follow that liberal and decent peoples have a default right to intervene against tyrannical societies even thought tyrannical societies are deemed to be outlaws.) Janse seems to think that by default a commitment to some values entails that you enforce these values by military means if necessary, and hence he worries that unless there are strong counteracting reasons acceptable to liberals, liberals would be liable to intervene. But if we keep clear that value-commitment has no immediate logical connection to value-enforcement, Janse's worry is muted. That is, rather than say that absent good counteracting reasons liberals should go about enforcing liberal values abroad (Janse's worry) we say, instead, that absent good reasons, liberals should not go about enforcing liberal values abroad.

states enjoy) fall within the limits of liberal global toleration and be counted among the societies in good and equal standing in the society of peoples.[31] The question here, however, is whether this means that cosmopolitanism has also lowered the threshold of permissible intervention.

To begin with, it is first worth noting that cosmopolitanism does not take intervention to be a general rule, but also treats it as a general prohibition to which exceptions can be made. Cosmopolitans can as well take seriously the importance of self-determination, communal integrity, and so on. More to the point, given that war is an act of violence and highly destructive of people's lives, it is not a course of action to be taken lightly but can be justified only under extreme circumstances. The fact that liberal cosmopolitanism sets a higher standard for state moral legitimacy does not mean that it puts the burden of proof on states to justify why they should not be intervened against. The burden of proof is still on intervening states, even though the condition of legitimacy is stricter. The key issue then is whether the burden of proof for intervening is easier met under cosmopolitanism given its stricter account of what is tolerable in international affairs.

In response, it can be pointed out that the stricter conditions of state legitimacy under cosmopolitanism do not mean that justification for intervention is easier to come by. Even if the failure to attain legitimacy satisfies the just cause condition, it does not follow immediately that the other conditions of permissibility are also satisfied. Recall the other conditions noted above, that of "last resort" and "proportionality." Even if a society's failure to respect the liberal democratic rights of its citizens constitutes a just cause for intervention, it has to be shown that intervention is the last option in the sense that feasible non-military and political and economic means have been attempted unsuccessfully, and that the urgency of the situation does not permit further waiting. Furthermore, it must also be reasonably predictable that the intervention is not going to do more harm than good and be in fact successful as a humanitarian response. As Moellendorf writes, "just cause is not a sufficient condition for intervention … because it does not require that there be good reason to believe that action will remedy the injustice, that such action is necessary to remedy the injustice, and that the greater harms will not also be done in the course of attempting to remedy the injustice" (p. 118–19).

[31] Buchanan, *Justice, Legitimacy and Self-Determination*; Caney, *Justice Beyond Borders*; Moellendorf, *Cosmopolitan Justice*; also my, *Toleration, Diversity and Global Justice*.

Indeed, the point about last resort can be more strongly made. Given the nature of the failure of legitimacy (on the cosmopolitan view) in the case of a society that respects the basic human rights of its citizens but fails to provide them with the full range of standard liberal rights (what Rawls would call a decent non-liberal society), it is hard to see how military action can be defended as a last resort. After all, what counts as a last resort is directly dependent on the urgency and nature of a situation; there is no literal last resort as more diplomacy and non-violent measures can always be further attempted. What the last resort criterion highlights is that relative to the urgency of the situation and given that different methods of resolution have been sincerely tried and tested, further deliberation is no longer acceptable and some forceful action is now imperative. In the case of systemic and widespread violations of human rights, such as genocide, mass murder of civilians, etc., it is easy to see how the wait for the right diplomatic response cannot be too long, if any waiting at all is appropriate. But in the case of a Rawlsian decent society where basic human rights are protected (but where liberal rights are not honored), it is hard to see how non-military means can be said to have run its course and a violent response to the failure of justice is now called for. Moreover and relatedly, it is also unclear how the proportionality condition can be satisfied for the purpose of intervening against a decent society. Intervention comes at great costs, as any military action does, not just for the intervening state but for members of the intervened state, including those whom the intervention is meant to rescue. Even surgical strikes will normally have collateral effects impacting negatively the very individuals that the intervention is meant to rescue. Intervention to prevent further acts of genocide presumably can meet the test of proportionality in the right context; but it is quite obvious that an intervention for the purpose of defending greater press freedom, freedom of speech, or democratic rights is going to be out of proportion. None of this means that liberal cosmopolitans either intervene or stand helplessly by. There are a slew of non-military options that can assist in liberal reforms between the poles of inaction and military action.

The above discussion proceeded as if failure to meet cosmopolitan justice constitutes a just cause for intervention; and that what is preventing intervention is the fact that other necessary conditions are rarely met in cases where states merely fail to honor liberal justice. But even this presumption might be too strong. To qualify further, a cosmopolitan can hold that a state that fails to meet liberal standards fails the legitimacy test, but failure of legitimacy in itself need not even meet the just cause condition. It is the *kind of failure* of legitimacy that is relevant, how a state is illegitimate and not just that it is illegitimate. Illegitimate states are of course all open to outside criticism and some appropriate response. But whether a state's illegitimate status provides a just cause for a particular form of response depends on the nature of the failure of legitimacy. Cosmopolitans can accept that it is only in cases of egregious rights violations that the just cause condition for intervention as the appropriate response is met (and then it remains to be seen, as discussed above, whether the other necessary conditions are met). There are a number of ways a state can be illegitimate, and under liberal cosmopolitanism, Rawls's decent societies will be deemed illegitimate. But it is only illegitimacy of certain kinds, that involving grave violations of human rights, that the just cause criterion for military intervention is met. As in Rawls's liberal internationalism, cosmopolitanism need not depart from common morality on the question of intervention. As a conception of justice, cosmopolitanism establishes the principles of a just global order. But it need not contradict common moral views on how principles of justice may be militarily enforced.[32]

To be more precise then, one could say that a forfeiture of legitimacy does not by itself give just cause for any third state to intervene. There is no just cause because the failure of compliance, in the case of a decent society, is not egregious or so extreme as to shock the conscience of humankind. Intervention is a special kind of response for specific types of non-compliance. It involves the use of selective violence strictly for the purpose of countering ongoing violence of certain kinds. Other kinds of non-compliance with justice do not merit this violent response. That is to say, it is open to the cosmopolitan view to hold there is just cause only when the failure of legitimacy is of an extreme kind.

To illustrate some of the points above, consider the US invasion of Iraq, and for the purpose of discussion, let's focus on the rhetoric that the invasion was a humanitarian intervention whose purpose was to "liberate the Iraqi people." Is cosmopolitanism committed to this intervention?[33] Do its principles support it? It is far from obvious that

[32] For more discussion on common morality and intervention, see Nardin, "The Moral Basis of Humanitarian Intervention."

[33] That war was also rationalized as a just war of self-defense and a global war against terrorism. But I focus here on its presentation as a humanitarian war. Just for some legal background, it is worth noting that UN Security Council Resolution 1441 (November 2002) did not unequivocally authorize the right to wage war against Iraq for its failure

they do. Saddam's regime was clearly tyrannical and illegitimate, and the cosmopolitan and liberal internationalist positions allow us to make this evaluative claim. But does it follow from this claim of illegitimacy and tyranny that military intervention is warranted? What were the gross human rights violations that the intervention is meant to solve and what is the urgency of coming up with an immediate resolution? Is the intervention likely to do more harm, harm to the individuals the intervention is meant to rescue, than good? And most significantly, what alternatives were available for criticizing and challenging Saddam's tyrannical regime and even supporting efforts at regime change from within besides sending in foreign troops? Considerations of these questions do not immediately suggest the right to intervene. On the contrary, they suggest the impermissibility and counter-productiveness of the intervention.

Cosmopolitanism thus shares the Rawlsian Internationalist view (as I have interpreted that view) that the invasion of Iraq was unjustified. On the Rawlsian account, Saddam's regime counts as an outlaw regime. But in Rawls's theory of just war, the invasion can't be justified, as we can see from the earlier discussion. Again, the legitimacy of a state is one thing, the right to legitimately intervene militarily against it is another, and Rawls certainly does not hold that all tyrannical societies may be intervened against. Similarly with Walzer: while Walzer agrees that Saddam's regime is tyrannical (indeed it is hard to dispute this), he also holds that the intervention was morally unjustifiable. His main reason is that although Saddam was clearly a brutal dictator, there wasn't any wide-spread humanitarian atrocity at the time of the invasion.[34]

This decoupling of legitimacy from military intervention is important. It allows for a stronger and more demanding ideal of state legitimacy without the attendant worry that this also relaxes the condition of just intervention, hence paving the way for liberal interventionism. It also frees us to operate with a more extensive ideal of universal individual rights and freedoms without the corresponding worry that this more demanding ideal also gives states the license to intervene

to comply with UNSC Resolution 687 (April 1991) that sets the terms for a ceasefire to the Gulf War of 1991. Rather the Resolution resolves that the Security Council will discuss any further breach by Iraq. As the US Representative John Negroponte himself puts it in his remarks to the Security Council: "If there is a further Iraqi breach, reported to the Council by UNMOVIC, the IAEA or a Member State, the matter will return to the Council for discussions as required in paragraph 12."

[34] Michael Walzer, *Arguing About War* (New Haven: Yale University Press, 2006).

militarily against other states under the guise of protecting these rights. Cosmopolitans can affirm the universality of liberal democratic principles while side-stepping the charge that this gives liberal democratic states permission to forcefully interfere with the affairs of other (non-liberal) states. All cosmopolitanism licenses liberal states to do is to take a critical judgmental stance towards non-liberal societies; how this criticism is to be expressed through foreign policy is to be further determined by the nature of the injustice, the means for redress available, and so on. In most cases of failures of justice, non-military responses, including the offering of trade incentives, foreign aid provisions, negotiation and diplomatic pressures, short-term and selective sanctions are both more effective and morally appropriate as responses. This last point is important to keep in mind, for a non-interventionist cosmopolitanism is not irresponsive to its own commitments. It does not say that we either intervene militarily or do nothing at all.

It is worth noting the real difference between cosmopolitanism and Rawls's liberal internationalism. For cosmopolitans, the real failure of Rawls's theory, and of a theory like Walzer's, is not that it isn't interventionist enough. As I have tried to suggest, liberal cosmopolitans can accept the limitations on intervention found in both Rawls's and Walzer's accounts. The disagreement is over what the relevant principles are, not how these principles may be enforced. Against Rawls, cosmopolitans want a more exacting standard of legitimacy, even as they agree with Rawls that military enforcement of principles is limited to very extreme cases.[35]

The key point, that there is a distinction between principles by which to pass judgments on the one hand and methods or means of enforcing a judgment on the other, is rather obvious. But it is worth stressing especially in the context of global justice and intervention because of the common misplaced worry that cosmopolitanism is an interventionist doctrine compared to, say, the more modest internationalism of Rawls. It is also worth noting that the fear of excessive intervention is not really Rawls's reason for his more moderate internationalism. His reasons have to do with the kinds of judgments that liberal peoples may make, and

[35] To be sure some cosmopolitans reject Walzer's conditions of permissible intervention. See for example Luban. But these objections either seem to problematically lower the bar for intervention or are better seen as objections to Walzer's account of legitimacy rather than to the limits of intervention as such. In part this is because, as mentioned above, Walzer seems to run together a state's moral standing and the right to intervene against it, at least in the discussion in "The Moral Standing of States."

the principles to which they may appeal when making these judgments, with respect to non-liberal peoples. The dividing philosophical issue is essentially that of philosophical reasonableness, not of enforcement. At any rate, my claim is that liberal cosmopolitans can agree entirely with Rawls's remarks on intervention in Part III of *The Law of Peoples*, and accept that intervention, given its great costs, be permitted only under extreme and special circumstances. The real debate concerns that of right and not might. Indeed the conditions specified there, and in other theories (like Walzer's) are consistent with and required by the more general features of common morality concerning the appropriate use of coercive force against persons. Intervention is an emergency measure to be reluctantly and cautiously carried out, and only when warranted by the urgency and seriousness of a situation. Cosmopolitan justice does not deny this. It has a distinctive account of what global justice is, and a more demanding one that is true, but it does not hold a dangerously cavalier view of how to enforce global justice.

PART IV

International Criminal Court

8

Rawls's Law of Peoples and the International Criminal Court

STEVEN C. ROACH

Introduction

John Rawls's *Law of Peoples* has been widely criticized for not properly extending the liberal egalitarian principles of his domestic theory of justice to the international level.[1] Cosmopolitan critics refer to his conception of international politics as "utopian realism."[2] They argue that Rawls's minimalist conception of human rights, and his attendant adoption of bounded state sovereignty, are too statist (Westphalian state sovereignty) to do justice to the needs of individuals. Moral cosmopolitans, for instance, focus on the ideals of equal respect and the inclusiveness of all individuals. Their emphasis on these ideals places them at odds with Rawls's insistence that international society is made of peoples, not individuals. Yet those sympathetic with Rawls's statist conception in the Law of Peoples contend that this conception downplays "the fact that individual human persons share globally no self-understanding or idea of persons as free equals morally and politically speaking."[3] This is not to say that we should ignore our responsibilities of encouraging non-democratic states to adopt the same political and economic liberties. Rather, it underscores the objective that peoples of such states must develop their own ethical self-understanding of equality and freedom.

[1] John Rawls, *The Law of Peoples* (Cambridge: Harvard University Press, 1999).

[2] See, *inter alinia* Allen, Buchanan, "Rawls's Law of Peoples: Rules for a Vanished Westphalian World," *Ethics*, 110 (2000), pp. 697–721; David Held, "Law of States, Law of Peoples: Three Models of Sovereignty," *Legal Theory*, 8 (2002), pp. 1–44; Onora O'Neill, *Towards Justice as Virtue* (Cambridge: Cambridge University Press, 1996); Andrew Kuper, "Rawlsian global justice: beyond the Law of Peoples to a Cosmopolitan law of persons," *Political Theory*, 28 (2000), pp. 640–74.

[3] David A. Reidy, "Rawls on International Justice: A Defense," *Political Theory* 32, (2004), p. 310.

In this chapter, I provide a limited (or qualified) defense of Rawls's Law of Peoples by stressing how social cooperation and the second-level formulation of the original principle can and should be considered as part of an emerging ethical world order. I argue that Rawls's Law of Peoples needs to be rooted in an evolutionary perspective on international law and justice: where the reflexive logic of international legal principles and procedures reveals the prospects and implications of social cooperation and the evolving functional modes of international criminal justice. Drawing on the legal framework and process of the International Criminal Court (ICC), I shall assess how the statist elements of the principles of complementarity and accountability support and promote the cosmopolitan dimensions of international criminal law (albeit in an uneven manner). In this way, I shall address the central challenge mentioned at the outset of this volume: how the institutional power of the ICC exposes the tensions between state politics and the ideals of equal moral concern and inclusiveness. Unlike Victor Peskin's claim in this volume, I contend that the evolution of the ICC offers an important, potentially transformative framework for the constitutivity of state politics. One of the central questions I address is whether we can expect the consistent application of the ICC's global juridical authority (coupled with state cooperation) to transform the political structures of non-democratic societies. I propose that Rawls's minimalist threshold of international justice sheds light on the challenges posed by state cooperation, thereby providing an important starting point for evaluating (the transformative effects of) the evolving institutional dynamics of the ICC.

Accordingly, in the first part of the chapter, I provide an overview of the Law of Peoples and assess the role played by human rights in Rawls's formulation of this law. I then move on to discuss the parameters of the ICC, including the complementarity principle and accountability. Here, I assess how these principles reflect the tensions between Rawls's idealism and moral realism, and assess the different ways in which the Law of Peoples applies to the ICC's development. In the last section, I discuss in greater detail the larger implications of applying the Law of Peoples and conclude that the Law of Peoples sheds important light on political tensions between state cooperation and the universal morality of the ICC.

Human rights and the Law of Peoples

The principles underlying the Law of Peoples, namely, social cooperation and equal respect, grow out of Rawls's own tacit account of justice across borders. While Rawls's treatment of justice in the domestic and international contexts differ, these differences are largely attributable to differences in international and domestic society. Where individuals are the primary moral agents within the single society, public culture at the international level, at least for Rawls, is undeniably statist. It is in this international public culture that Rawls situates the Law of Peoples for states rather than individuals. As such, Rawls predicted that a second original position consisting of states would select familiar principles of international law as the principles of justice that would govern the international system.

International human rights offers a crucial starting point for understanding the extension of the original position to international criminal law. Rawls conceives human rights in the following terms: "Human rights … is a proper subset of the rights possessed by citizens in a liberal constitutional democratic regime, or of the rights of the members of a decent hierarchical society."[4] Within this context, Rawls sets forth three conditions for understanding the importance of basic human rights in a society of peoples: (1) Their fulfillment is a necessary condition of the decency of a society's political institutions and its legal order; (2) they are sufficient to exclude justified and forceful intervention by states; (3) and they presume the worth of pluralism, or differing political conceptions of freedom and relative equality.

Given these conditions, human rights in the Law of Peoples can be said to function in both a prescriptive and proscriptive sense. The former refers to *inter alia*, personal property, equal protection under the law, and various meaningful cultural freedoms, including the right to practice one's religion. The latter, by comparison, characterizes the restrictions placed on the state vis-à-vis its citizens, including freedom from slavery and serious physical harm. In this way, Rawls derives his formulation of the Law of Peoples from a basic or minimalist conception of human rights. Only the rights mentioned above can be said to play some minimalist role in formulating a conception of justice or the common good.

Adopting a minimalist threshold of human rights is important precisely because many non-democratic states observe and recognize these basic rights of their citizens in their constitutions.[5] States must

[4] Rawls, *The Law of Peoples*, p. 37.

[5] See Steven C. Roach, "Value Pluralism, Liberalism and the International Criminal Court," *Journal of Human Rights* 4, no. 4 (2005) *op. cit.*, "Humanitarian Emergencies and the International Criminal Court: Toward a Cooperative Arrangement between

at least honor basic human rights, if they are to be considered a member of a society of peoples. Within this conception of human rights, we encounter the causal link between prescriptive and proscriptive accounts of human rights. Here the former refers to the moral duty of states to uphold the citizens' basic rights; while the latter underscores the use of international pressure or force to punish any state that fails to refrain from unduly harming its citizens (genocide and crimes against humanity).

The causal link between these two modes encompasses, in turn, three applicative aspects of human rights protection: (a) "the peoples' observation of a duty of non-intervention; (b) peoples have the right of self-defense but no right to investigate war for reasons other than self-defense; (c) and peoples have a duty to assist other peoples living under unfavorable conditions that prevent their having a just or decent political social regime."[6] Here, the duty of assistance and the justification of the use of force to reverse the state's harmful actions expose the boundaries between tolerance and intolerance in the Law of Peoples. As noted earlier, the Law of Peoples can be characterized as a political conception of right and justice, which expresses the limits and problems in international justice; it is intended, in this sense, to tailor the original position to a more specific and reasonable conception of justice as fairness at the international level. More than anything, this limited conception of state sovereignty can be attributed to Rawls's reluctance to embrace a global state. Rawls advocated that the Law of Peoples should extend to all states (willing to cooperate with and participate in international institutions) through a reasonable conception of international justice. Accordingly, humanitarian intervention, whether in the form of economic sanctions or military coercion, should be applied as an option of last resort.

For Rawls, then, sovereignty remains the central organizing principle of international justice. This means that military coercion as an option of last resort cannot be divorced from the evolving institutional modes of justice (*jus ad bellum*). In fact, it constitutes what I call a strained, albeit first-level evolutionary trait of Rawls's Law of Peoples. The predicament we face with this first-level trait is that it conveys the tacit right of intervention of rogue states that lack a hierarchical

the ICC and the UN Security Council," *International Studies Perspectives* 6, no. 4 (2005), pp. 431–46.

[6] Rawls, *The Law of Peoples*, p. 37.

consultative body for building consensus around social policies.[7] Such a tacit right seems to suggest an uneasy link between Rawls's conception and the imperialism that (unduly) politicizes the application of law, by allowing the law to serve the coercive and/or civilizing ends of Western states.

For some international legal scholars, Rawls's tacit right echoes the logic of reformism of the Victorian period (of civilizing the world), which led, as Martti Koskenniemi notes, to the emergence of "depoliticized legal pragmatism and the imposition of imperial policy agendas" (on the legal profession).[8] As Koskenniemi argues, the unfortunate results of the passionate thinking of international law during the late eighteenth century shows how "the limits of our imagination are a product of a history that might have gone another way."[9] Koskenniemi's point is that we need to contest existing theories of the law in order to interpret law as a contingent and open-ended process. My minimalist and pragmatic defense of Rawls's Law of the Peoples addresses this point by linking the efficacy of applied norms in international criminal law with the evolution of international law. In other words, if Koskenniemi is correct, then it is important that we see the new global contexts of international law as evolving functional modes of international criminal law. I should stress that evolving global contexts constitute a set of new opportunities for transforming international law through the ethical dimensions of discretionary power and the novel, institutional capacities of the ICC, most notably, the equal rights of defendants and the right of all victims to participate in the prosecutorial proceedings.

A second-level evolutionary trait in Rawls's Law of Peoples refers to the increasing social cooperation that reinforces existing and new legal norms and rules. In this sense, the link between social cooperation and the enforcement of human rights can and should be seen as an important condition of the transformation of international law.[10] With this

[7] Note that a crime against humanity refers to acts committed as part of a widespread or systematic attack with an organizational policy against any civilians with knowledge of the attack (and who have been accused of committing crimes against humanity).

[8] Martti Koskenniemi, *The Gentle Civilizer of Nations: The Rise and Fall of International Law 1870–1960* (Cambridge: Cambridge University Press, 2001), p. 5.

[9] *Ibid.*

[10] Hence a society of peoples can be decent without being liberal. This, however, underscores two types of domestic societies that Rawls refers to: liberal peoples and decent peoples. Both of these types constitute well-ordered peoples. And Rawls refers to two other types of societies to justify the extension of the original position and overlapping principles to non-liberal societies: societies burdened by unfavorable conditions and benevolent absolutions.

second criteria/level of the original position, we need to recognize that human rights norms reflect an overlapping consensus in which "society's politically active citizens and the requirements of justice are not too much in conflict with citizens' essential interests as formed and encouraged by their social arrangements."[11]

In sum, the difference between the first and second original position is one of logical specificity, rather than substantive teleological orientation. As Rawls states: "This makes the use of the original position at the second level a model of representation in exactly the same way it is at the first. Any differences need to be tailored given the agents modeled and the subject at hand."[12] From this perspective, the evolution of human rights reflects the ethical self-realization of peoples of different countries. Yet, it does not presuppose the emergence of one standard of equality to validate this realization. As David Reidy points out:

> True, Rawls's basic human rights fall well short of the full list included in the Universal Declaration of Human Rights or the two Covenants or other human rights documents or treaties. Nevertheless, they are not insignificant. Their realization would go a long way to eliminating the worst of human suffering, requiring a world within which all peoples were constituted as something like Kant's constitutional republics or Hegel's ethical states. Further nothing in Rawls's account of basic human right precludes the realization through political undertaking and positive law of additional rights as universal human rights.[13]

As this passage suggests, the Law of Peoples establishes a framework for understanding the internal and evolutionary logic of human rights and legal procedures (where more human rights are subsumed under a larger list of basic rights). Still, we need to be careful with how we apply Rawls to understand the evolutionary logic of the ICC's legal procedures. For, as Reidy correctly states, "non-agreement is what validates the lack of self-understanding that can be loosely and intuitively connected with the problematic political limitations of global enforcement."[14] Such limitations call attention to the evolutionary qualities of two central

[11] John Rawls, *Political Liberalism* (New York: Columbia University Press, 1993). Human rights scholars have extended this principle to explain, among other things, the consensus surrounding the compatibility of the International Rights Human Covenants; see Jack Donnelly, *Universal Human Rights*, 2nd edn. (Ithaca, NY: Cornell University Press, 2003).

[12] Rawls, *The Law of Peoples*, p. 311.

[13] Reidy, "Rawls on International Justice: A Defense," p. 311.

[14] *Ibid.*, p. 303.

principles of the ICC, namely, accountability and complementarity (via Rawls's Law of Peoples). As we shall see in the following section, such principles seem to suggest that the first and second-level interpretation of the original position will evolve through the ongoing procedural application of these principles.

Legal principles and the International Criminal Court

In turning to the ICC, it is important to stress its recent entry into force on July 1, 2002 and its formative development as a global institution. Many legal scholars, for instance, argue that state noncompliance will arguably limit, or at the very least unduly challenge the development of the ICC.[15] Still others have asserted that the entrenchment of the ICC's proscriptive norms will narrow the gap between international and domestic criminal legal systems, thereby facilitating the efficacy of the ICC, or its capacity to hold accountable the perpetrators of gross human rights violations.[16] In this section, I will address the principles of accountability and complementarity, showing how the Law of Peoples helps to substantiate these principles and the evolutionary dynamics of the ICC.

Complementarity and accountability

There are two basic structural ordering principles of the ICC: complementarity and moral accountability. When the framers of the ICC met in 1995 to adopt the final draft of the ICC statute, they had to find a compromise between universal jurisdiction and state sovereignty. Such a compromise would become known as the complementarity regime of

[15] See Allison Marston Danner, "Enhancing the Legitimacy and Accountability of Prosecutorial Discretionary at the International Criminal Court," *American Journal of International Law* 97, no. 3 (2003), pp. 510–52; Roy Lee (ed.), *The International Criminal Court: The Making of the Rome Statute* (The Hague: Kluwer Law International, 1999); Antonio Cassese, "The Statute of the International Criminal Court," *European Journal of International Law* 10 (1999), pp. 141–71.

[16] See, *inter alia* Benjamin Schiff, *Building the International Criminal Court* (Cambridge: Cambridge University Press, 2008); Bruce Broomhall, *International Justice and the International Criminal Court: Between Sovereignty and the Rule of Law* (Oxford: Oxford University Press, 2003); Steven C. Roach, *Politicizing the International Criminal Court: The Convergence of Politics, Ethics, and Law* (Lanham, MD: Rowman & Littlefield, 2006); M. Cherif Bassiouni "The Universal Model: The International Criminal Court," in *Post-Conflict Justice*, ed. M. Cherif Bassiouni (Ardsley, NY: Transnational Publishers, 2003), pp. 813–28.

the ICC. The complementarity principle, as understood in the preamble of the ICC Statute, allows states *prima facie* to investigate and prosecute any violation of the core crimes of the ICC Statute, which have been committed within their territorial borders. The ICC Prosecutor, however, can initiate/launch its own investigation into situations that have occurred within territorial states (state parties), or where the national courts of state parties have proved unwilling or unable to investigate or prosecute.

Procedurally, the legal scope of the complementarity principle ranges from judicial assistance to the ICC's request of surrender. In particular, Article 17(2) contains the conditions or rules of procedure in regards to the Court's jurisdictional prerogatives. It stipulates, *inter alia*, that the ICC can intervene when national courts 1) shield the defendant from investigation and prosecution; 2) there is an undue delay in initiating an investigation and prosecution; 3) and there exists a bias against the defendant.[17] The purpose of these rules is to "create an incentive for states, and to encourage them to develop and then apply their national criminal justice systems as a way of avoiding the exercise of jurisdiction by the ICC."[18]

Some legal scholars, however, have asserted that the complementarity principle, while important to advancing substantive criminal law, subjects the Court to the "whims of state cooperation."[19] Some have even suggested that it will stratify the ICC's jurisdiction by creating a rigid, juridical "legal order." Whether or not the ICC will, in practice, impose a hierarchical juridical order remains to be seen. However, the prospects for such an order suggest that the ICC's ethical commitment will likely trump any decision to defer to national courts. It is this trumping power that reflects one of most important procedural features of the ICC Statute: namely, the elimination of all forms of national immunity.

[17] The article reads: "(a) the proceedings were or are being undertaken or the national decision was made for the purpose of shielding the person concerned from criminal responsibility for crimes within the jurisdiction of the Court referred to in article 5; (b) there has been an unjustified delay in the proceedings which in the circumstances is inconsistent with an intent to bring the person concerned to justice; (c) the proceedings were not or are not being conducted independently or impartially, and they were or are being conducted in a manner which, in the circumstances, is inconsistent with an intent to bring the person concerned to justice."

[18] Phillipe Sands, "After Pinochet: the role of national courts," in *From Nuremberg to the Hague*, ed. Philippe Sands (Cambridge: Cambridge University Press, 2003).

[19] Cassese, "The Statute of the International Criminal Court," p. 144.

Perhaps the most important provision of the complementarity principle is the thirty-day provision to establish wrongful intent of national courts. Article 18(2), for instance, specifies two conditions under which the ICC may intervene in national judiciary affairs. First, it allows states thirty days to begin their investigation of a case; from the time that they receive a notice from the Prosecutor indicating his or her intent to investigate the international crime. Second, the provision requires the ICC Prosecutor to automatically defer to the state for a period of at least six months. Note that the Pre-Trial chamber can, at any time after the thirty-day period (up to the six-month period), authorize a request of surrender if it deems the investigation to be ineffective or inconsistent with the Court's evidential standards.

But determining the unwillingness of states, as opposed to inability, is certain to be difficult. At minimum, it will require subjective judgments of state intent that may lead to conflicting interpretations of the validity of this intent. Thus, for example, even if the ICC adequately determines that the national court's slow investigative proceedings constitute an unnecessary delay in the process, it is possible that national courts or state leaders will contest this interpretation, especially if it unduly conflicts with their sense of national pride. What this suggests is that the application of the complementarity principle will likely turn on the national government's inability to investigate or prosecute.

Another way that the Court seeks to guard against the potential effects of unwillingness is to stipulate the special exceptions to the *Ne Bis In Idem* rule, which prohibits trying a defendant twice for the same crime. But unlike the double jeopardy rule of domestic courts in most developed states, the ICC reserves the right, under certain extenuating conditions, to suspend the application of this principle. This essentially allows the ICC to address the failure of domestic courts to meet the strict evidential standards of the ICC Statute. The main implication of this rule, however, is that it will result in what Madeleine Morris refers to as the stratification of jurisdiction. Morris, for instance, argues that "the Prosecutor will operate within a structure framed by the Treaty that encourages him or her to be attentive to the interests of the majority of States Parties to the ICC treaty and to certain elements of the Court's broader international audience but much less so to the interests of principally affected states or victims of populations."[20] In her view,

[20] See Madeleine Morris, "High Crimes and Misconceptions: The ICC and Non-Party States," in *International Crimes, Peace, and Human Rights: The Role of the International*

the ICC's focus on state leaders, and not civilians, may end up biasing the Court toward the national population as a whole. Not only will this narrow focus ignore the crimes committed by civilian perpetrators of gross human rights atrocities, but it will also mean that the Court will be able to target certain state leaders for political reasons.

Here Morris distinguishes between what she calls 'active' and 'stratified' concurrent jurisdiction. Whereas stratified concurrent jurisdiction underscores the effects of the imbalance of judicial resources across the international level, active concurrent jurisdiction characterizes the ICC's ability to address effectively the needs and motivations of the affected state (Morris, 2000: 204). Such effects include the limitation on national plea bargaining arrangements and the national judiciary's ability to develop its judiciary after a long protracted civil war. What these effects suggest is that the ICC will need to induce national courts to cooperate with the Court. As Morris (*Ibid.*) points out: "one motive for exercising jurisdiction concurrently with the ICC would be that while the state has a functioning judiciary, the state cannot obtain extradition of those defendants." Given this factor, she concludes that the ability of the ICC to eliminate the effects of stratified concurrent jurisdiction will depend on its willingness to negotiate an arrangement in which national courts are allowed to try some of the gross offenders of human rights abuses in exchange for developing their criminal judicial system.

Accordingly, the complementarity principle holds that states are entitled *prima facie* to investigate and prosecute, but that the Prosecutor reserves the right to launch its own investigation if he or she determines that the national judiciary has not conducted a genuine investigation or trial. Here the Prosecutor must determine whether the state's unwillingness or inability to investigate and prosecute violates the provisions of inadmissibility (see articles 17–20) and if there are admissible conditions for launching a case. Article 17(1), for instance provides the following conditions:

> (a) The case is being investigated or prosecuted by a State which has jurisdiction over it, unless the State is unwilling or unable genuinely to carry

Criminal Court, ed. Dinah Sheldon (Ardsley, NY: Transnational Publishers, 2000) pp. 203–06. Morris also points out that the ICC will prove demeaning to the common people by going after only state leaders and not their followers. But the suggestion that the ICC will demean the common people by devaluing the role or responsibility of the state leader's followers remains a moot point; for it could also be argued that most followers may well see it in their interests to claim that they had no choice in whether they followed or disobeyed the orders of their commanders and state leaders.

> out the investigation or prosecution; (b) The case has been investigated by a State which has jurisdiction over it and the State has decided not to prosecute the person concerned, unless the decision resulted from the unwillingness or inability of the State genuinely to prosecute.

These conditions also provide the basis for minimal threshold of admissibility or a set of criteria for ICC investigation and prosecution. At the Preparatory Committee meetings and Rome conference, ICC authorities and state delegates discussed a set of criteria (i.e. partial state collapse, undeveloped judiciaries) that would necessitate the Prosecutor's *proprio motu* power, while also reinforcing the Court's status as a judicial mechanism of last resort. Carsten Stahn refers to this model of complementarity as a "threat-based" concept or "classical model of complementarity," in which the operation of the Court is tied to state failure, the preservation of domestic jurisdiction, and compliance through threat.[21] The other, more open-ended side of complementarity embedded in the Statute is the Court's positive role in facilitating "burden-sharing" and "assistance from the Court to states." Stahn refers to this side as "positive complementarity." As he points out, positive complementarity, while articulated in the Statute, remains controversial in regards to "a deferral of responsibility" and "consent-based division of labour."[22] These factors raise important normative issues of the Court's impartiality and independence, including whether the Court should defer its so-called "responsibility to enforce" in order to avoid becoming an instrument of despotic national governments, or a potential source of further political instability.[23] Confronting these issues, then, requires us to strike a (evolving) balance between the statism (realpolitik) or political realism of Rawls's Law of Peoples and the cosmopolitan elements of the ICC.

Relevance to Rawls's Law of Peoples

As I have suggested, the ICC's complementarity principle reinforces the principles of social cooperation and decency, which, in turn, link the ICC's efficacy of norms with its evolving procedural power to

[21] Carsten Stahn, "Complementarity: A Tale of Two Notions," *Criminal Law Forum* 19 (2008), pp. 97–98.

[22] *Ibid.*, 98.

[23] William Burke-White, "Complementarity in Practice: The International Criminal Court as Part of a System of Multi-Level Global Governance in the Democratic Republic of Congo," *Leiden Journal of International Law* 18 (2005), p. 568.

investigate, prosecute, and punish (i.e. an effective and consistent application of prosecutorial power and the increasing number of ratifications, which stands at 108 as of February 2009). Moral accountability in this sense ensures that any state that commits genocide or serious crimes against humanity will be investigated and/or prosecuted. This of course does not mean that all states will voluntarily comply with the ICC's demands. Under these circumstances, the ICC will need to consult the UN for strategic guidance on its decisions by sharing information concerning the nature and extent of the security risks.[24] It should be noted here that the ICC remains independent of the UN, but that the UN can refer a case or situation to the ICC pursuant to the ICC Statute (and the UN Security Council can defer a case with a majority vote on a yearly renewable basis).

The ICC Statute also contains several standards of fairness. Perhaps the most notable is the defendant's civil and political rights (Article 55), or the right to a fair and impartial trial. Such judicial proceedings might assure that developing democratic states and non-democratic societies, which are party to the ICC Treaty, will abide by these standards. At the very least, membership will afford these countries the opportunity to participate in the ICC's decision-making affairs or consultative bodies (i.e. the Assembly of States Parties). Given these factors, it is important to stress that state cooperation remains the most crucial link between the institutional power of the ICC and the promotion of cosmopolitan moral ideals, since it presupposes consensus-building and stronger commitments to promoting international legal norms (The World Trade Organization (WTO), for example, contains a dispute settlement mechanism that provides "reverse consensus" which has thus far proved to be one of the most efficacious instruments for enforcing the free trade principles of nondiscrimination and reciprocity).

But it is also true that developing states might try to politicize justice by using the ICC to do its political bidding. In 2003, for instance, Congolese leaders established a new transitional government based on a power-sharing agreement reached in December 2002. Joseph Kabila, the son of Laurent Kabila, who ruled the DRC from 1997–2001, emerged as the new leader of the new transitional government and oversaw the implementation of the new 2006 constitution ("The Constitution of the

[24] See Steven C. Roach, "Introduction: Global Governance in Context" (Oxford: Oxford University Press, 2009), pp. 1–24.

Third Republic"). In an effort to head off the ICC's initiative to launch its own investigation into the situation, Kabila (self-) referred the situation to the ICC in March 2004. The self-referral was somewhat surprising considering that Kabila himself may have been responsible for some of these crimes and could be subject to investigation. But Kabila's decision, while signaling the government's willingness to work with international authorities to end the violence, was with an intent to summoning the ICC's assistance, that is, to have the ICC pay the political and economic costs of trying the perpetrators ("positive complementarity"). As William Burke-White points out, Kabila probably has less to worry in terms of being investigated and prosecuted since "any crimes against humanity committed by Kabila likely occurred before July 1 2002, and as yet, there is little evidence that he has been directly involved in any of the major issues in the Congo within the Court's temporal jurisdiction."[25] If this is true, then it may mean that Kabila enjoys important political advantages that allow him to strengthen the government (legitimacy) and his position in elections, especially where the evidence of crimes committed by his rivals such as Jean-Pierre Bemba Azarias Ruberwa remains strong (In May 2008, the ICC charged Bemba for committing crimes against humanity and arrested him in Brussels, Belgium a month later).

In the case of Uganda's self-referral, the ICC Prosecutor has focused almost exclusively on the crimes of the leaders of the rebel group, Lord's Resistance Army (LRA). In a somewhat surprising move, however, the Ugandan government, in an effort to hold together a ceasefire agreement with the LRA, requested that the ICC drop its arrest warrants against Joseph Kony and his four top commanders.[26] Thus far, however, the ICC Prosecutor, Luis Moreno-Ocampo, has rejected these pleas by Ugandan officials. Meanwhile, the Ugandan government has established its own (national) war crimes court to prosecute these perpetrators in an effort to further pressure the ICC to drop its arrest warrants. In each of these cases, the ICC's actions have had some demonstrable impact on domestic politics, but has yet to produce (enough) evidence of the transformative link between the institutional power of the ICC and the moral ideals of cosmopolitanism. The ICC of course is still young. However,

[25] Burke-White, "Complementarity in Practice: The International Criminal Court as Part of a System of Multi-Level Global Governance in the Democratic Republic of Congo," p. 565.

[26] See Adam Branch, "Uganda's Civil War and the Politics of ICC Intervention," *Ethics & International Affairs*, no. 21 (2007), pp. 179–98.

its actions in these cases do suggest that the institutional power of the ICC has begun to confront the political realities that have, in the past, undermined the ideal of equal moral concern. Here we should note that in light of the apparent attempts by Uganda and the DRC to use the ICC to do its political bidding, the Assembly of States Parties issued several recommendations for sustaining and increasing state cooperation at its sixth Assembly of States Parties meeting. At a minimum, this policy action suggests a responsive set of institutional modes of the ICC whose other institutional benefits include the (cosmopolitan objectives of) procedural rights of victims, local outreach programs designed to raise awareness of its activities (transparency), and, as mentioned above, fair trials for all defendants.

From the Law of Peoples to cosmopolitanism

When situating these evolving institutional modes of the ICC in global politics, then, we also need to stress the constitutive link between the political reality of cooperation and these above cosmopolitan dimensions of the ICC. As noted earlier, most cosmopolitans argue that the Law of Peoples represents an unduly restrictive, realistic framework of international justice in which democratic societies are treated as "closed societies." For many, the Law of Peoples essentially ignores existing forms of global justice, in particular, the democratic and legal freedoms such as refugee rights, environmental law, and economic integration.[27] While I agree with the underlying intentions of this assertion, it is important to defend the Law of Peoples as a minimalist framework for understanding the evolving modes of international criminal justice. Failure to work within this framework only downplays the existing tensions and political realities of the interstate system. As we have seen, the ICC, like many other international institutions, lacks an enforcement mechanism. As such, it relies on voluntary state cooperation, but must enhance its legitimacy through fair trials and the consistent application of its prosecutorial power.

Nevertheless, the main weakness of the cosmopolitan critique of the Law of Peoples is that it overstates the desired effect of norms by

[27] See Thomas Pogge, "Rawls on International Justice," *The Philosophical Quarterly* 51 (2001), pp. 246–53; Kok-Chor Tan, "Liberal Toleration in Rawls's Law of Peoples," *Ethics*, 108 (2008), pp. 276–95; Charles Beitz, "Cosmopolitan Liberalism and the States System," in *Political Restructuring in Europe: Ethical Perspectives*, ed. Chris Brown (London: Routledge, 1994).

downplaying the slowly evolving functionality of global institutions, as a normative component of global constitutional order. As I have argued, I simply do not believe that the principles of equality and freedom have developed to the point where they can be reliably enforced on decent states. Nor that, as Charles Beitz theorizes, "states can and should agree to a set of principles aimed at promoting global justice and that the natural distribution of resources is a principle to which all states are capable of agreeing to."[28] Indeed, when Andrew Kuper argues that "Rawls has begged some of the central questions of global justice by adopting at the outset a thin statist conception of the legitimate divisions between persons who share a world," he surrenders the instructive link between the Law of Peoples and the evolutionary logic of the ICC's proceduralism to an "unmediated access to the original position."[29] This merely replaces one arbitrary starting point with another and does not demonstrate how the ICC arises from an assertive and consistent application of the procedures (of complementarity) discussed in the prior section.

This is not to say that the ICC remains irrelevant to understanding and redressing inequalities. Rather, it suggests that the ICC may begin to reveal the constitutive links between the political ideals of promoting order and the moral elements immanent to the global rule of law. As such, the ICC's evolving modes of governance characterize what I believe are the seeds of a tacit cosmopolitanism in which functional state cooperation will resolve judicial inequalities, while at the same time advancing the ethic of moral accountability. Indeed, if cosmopolitans such as David Held insist that the "advocacy of regional and global governance and the creation of political organizations and mechanisms would provide a framework of regulation and law enforcement across the globe ...," then they will need to show the problematic link between an effective, accountable international military force and the ICC as a dynamic and evolving context of the global rule of law.[30]

Conclusion

In this chapter, I have attempted to use the ICC as a test case for analyzing the merits and weaknesses of Rawls's Law of Peoples and assessing the evolutionary logic of his principles. I argued that Rawls's Law

[28] Beitz, "Cosmopolitan Liberalism and the States System," p. 292.

[29] Kuper, "Rawlsian global justice: beyond the Law of Peoples to a Cosmopolitan law of persons," p. 647.

[30] Held, "Law of States, Law of Peoples: Three Models of Sovereignty," p. 23.

of Peoples provides an important first step in understanding the evolution of the ICC and exposes many important factors of *realpolitik*. Accordingly, it is important to treat the relationship between the ICC and Rawls's Law of Peoples not as stepping off point per se, but as a point of departure in international legal thinking. As we saw, the problematic implications of the principles of complementarity and moral accountability suggest that states and other non-state actors will have more opportunities to shape the principles of international law through greater participation in international law. We not only need to see this as a new trend towards the cosmopolitanization of law, but also as a sign that the evolving procedural logic of global institutions has become increasingly intertwined with the political and social opportunities of states to shape international law. Indeed, it will be this sort of visionary integrative framework that will allow us to extend our reasonable ideas of justice through and beyond the Law of Peoples.

9

An ideal becoming real? The International Criminal Court and the limits of the cosmopolitan vision of justice

VICTOR PESKIN

I Introduction

Although still in its infancy, the International Criminal Court (ICC) has already become a powerful symbol of a long-hoped for international legal order in which universal human rights and cosmopolitan ideals of justice can win protection from the imperatives and intrusions of statecraft. The ICC is a standing institution with wide international backing, far-reaching jurisdiction, and a mandate to prosecute the perpetrators of the world's worst atrocities – those "that deeply shock the conscience of humanity."[1] As such, the ICC stands as a bulwark against the dehumanization of modern warfare and genocidal violence, and as an agent of individual and societal rehumanization.

The ICC represents an unprecedented opportunity to dispense justice globally – and not only to particular victims, particular countries, or at particular moments in time. In this regard, the ICC represents an improvement over international courts constrained by much more limited territorial and temporal mandates, such as the United Nations International Criminal Tribunals for the Former Yugoslavia (ICTY) and Rwanda (ICTR). Even as advocates hail the jurisprudential precedents set by these two UN tribunals – and other more recently created tribunals such as the Special Court for Sierra Leone – there has been unease about an ad hoc political process in which international justice is provided only for some parts of the world. This selectivity can be viewed as discriminatory insofar as it privileges the suffering and targets the wrongdoing only of individuals from certain states. As a

[1] Preamble of the Rome Statute of the International Criminal Court. The political philosopher Michael Walzer wrote about human rights violations that "shock the moral conscience of mankind." Walzer, *Just and Unjust Wars* (New York: Basic Books, 1977), p. 107.

consequence, the integrity of the rule of law, which is founded on the equal application of justice, is fundamentally challenged. As Richard J. Goldstone, the founding chief ICTY and ICTR chief prosecutor, has written, "The essence of justice is its universality, both nationally and internationally."[2] Therein lies the great promise of the ICC, which aspires to institutionalize the ideal of universal justice. In its inclusive notion of human suffering in which "all peoples are united by common bonds,"[3] the ICC embodies the cosmopolitan world view in which all victims are citizens deserving the protection afforded by the rule of law. The Court's intent to treat all people equally and to privilege no one over another is a cornerstone of cosmopolitanism's regard both for "the *moral worth* of persons" [and] the *equal* moral of *all* persons."[4]

The very establishment of The Hague-based ICC constitutes an unparalleled achievement for the international human rights movement. If human rights has become a "worldwide secular religion,"[5] then the ICC has become its secular altar. Indeed, as Payam Akhavan writes, "the ICC has, for some, come to embody the transcendent and sacred."[6] A court with the mission to prosecute the world's worst imaginable atrocities and to do so on a global scale and in perpetuity is elevated to a status above any other court, domestic or international. This has made the ICC judges, as former UN Secretary-General Kofi Annan has said, "the embodiment of our collective conscience."[7]

The ICC has sparked the imagination of so many people because it is a lofty idea grounded in the real world. The ICC has been translated from a moral ideal to an international treaty and finally into a global institution charged with enforcing treaties pertaining to the laws of war and genocide. As Prince Zeid Ra'ad Zeid al–Hussein of Jordan and president of the ICC's Assembly of States Parties explained on the occasion

[2] Richard J. Goldstone, *For Humanity: Reflections of a War Crimes Investigator* (New Haven: Yale University Press, 2000), p. 122.

[3] Preamble of the Rome Statute of the International Criminal Court.

[4] Introduction chapter.

[5] Elie Wiesel, "A Tribute to Human Rights," in *The Universal Declaration of Human Rights: Fifty Years and Beyond*, ed. Y. Danieli *et al.* (Amityville, NY: Baywood, 1999), p. 3, as quoted in Michael Ignatieff, *Human Rights as Politics and Idolatry* (Princeton: Princeton University Press, 2001), p. 53.

[6] Payam Akhavan, "The International Criminal Court in Context: Mediating the Global and Local in the Age of Accountability," *American Journal of International Law*, 2003, p. 721.

[7] Secretary-General Kofi Annan's Statement to the Inaugural Meeting of Judges of the International Criminal Court, March 11, 2003, The Hague.

of the Court's formal inauguration in March 2003: "The international landscape is strewn with treaties ratified but never implemented. It is truly extraordinary that this one was signed scarcely five years ago and is now in force."[8]

The significance of the Court's establishment has been heightened by the fact that it had been so long in coming[9] and seemed an impossibility only a decade and a half ago. First proposed in the aftermath of World War II, the idea for a global criminal court was soon sidelined by the political intransigence of the Cold War.[10] The end of the East–West rivalry and the UN Security Council's establishment of ad hoc tribunals for the conflicts in the former Yugoslavia and Rwanda in the early 1990s, created the political momentum to revive the elusive dream of the human rights movement. Within a few years, an extraordinary coalition of states and non-governmental organizations (NGOs) came together to lay the foundations of the ICC. The statute of the ICC (known as the Rome Statute) was adopted in July 1998.[11] In July 2002, the ICC officially came into being when the requisite 60th state ratified the Statute.

The celebratory mood over the ICC's creation has, in some quarters, diminished attention to the Court's difficult present and uncertain future. The range of obstacles the ICC faces and the highly political context of its operation underscore how far it must travel to achieve its foundational goal, stated in the preamble of the Court's statute, of ensuring "lasting respect for and the enforcement of international justice."[12] Of course, it is too early in the life of this permanent institution to offer more than a preliminary assessment of the ICC's prospects. However, much can be gleaned about the potential and pitfalls of the ICC by examining the legal and political constraints placed on the Court.

The aim of this chapter is to demonstrate how an international court created in the name of cosmopolitan values and meant to operate above

[8] Prince Zeid Ra'ad Zeid al–Hussein Statement to the Inaugural Meeting of Judges of the International Criminal Court, March 11, 2003, The Hague.

[9] Secretary-General Kofi Annan's Statement to the Inaugural Meeting of Judges of the International Criminal Court, March 11, 2003, The Hague.

[10] William A. Schabas, *An Introduction to the International Criminal Court*, 2nd ed. (Cambridge: Cambridge University Press, 2004), pp. 8–9.

[11] For an analysis of the important role NGOs played in creation of the ICC, see Marlies Glasius, *The International Criminal Court: A Global Civil Society Achievement* (New York: Routledge, 2006).

[12] Preamble of the Rome Statute of the International Criminal Court.

politics is deeply enmeshed in and constrained by the political calculus of nation-states. The establishment of the ICC has been spurred, as the preamble of the Court's statute implies, by the memory of the "millions of children, women and men [who] have been victims of unimaginable atrocities."[13] But even as the ICC has ostensibly been created on behalf of individual victims, states have shaped the institution to safeguard key elements of their sovereignty. Upholding state sovereignty helps explain why the blueprint for the ICC that emerged at the end of the Rome negotiations in July 1998 has sharply limited the Court's capacity to dispense justice universally and evenhandedly.

Even as the ICC's jurisdiction is revolutionary in its global reach, it is not yet and may never be a truly global court. That is because of a key provision in the Rome Statute that allows many states to stand beyond the reach of the ICC chief prosecutor. States that do not consent to becoming parties to the Rome Statute will, it appears, usually remain immune from ICC prosecution. However, this immunity is not foolproof. Individuals from non-states parties can become a target of ICC investigation if they commit a violation of international humanitarian law on the territory of a state party. And individuals from non-states parties can fall under ICC jurisdiction if the Security Council directs the Court's chief prosecutor to initiate a war crimes investigation. The Security Council's March 2005 referral of the Darfur situation to the ICC underscores that some non-states parties such as Sudan may not be able to evade the Court. Still, it is uncertain how frequently the Security Council will use its referral powers. In the absence of such Council action, individuals from non-states parties that commit atrocities within their state's territory will remain beyond the reach of ICC prosecution. This loophole will have profound implications for the Court's effort to realize the "all-inclusiveness" principle that is central to cosmopolitanism.[14] The implications of allowing states to consent to the Court's jurisdiction is underscored by the following passage from an Amnesty International statement issued on the final day of the 1998 Rome Conference:

> Saddam Hussein, Pol Pot, Karadzic, Pinochet, Amin, Mobutu. These are just some of the men responsible for the worst crimes in the world whose prior consent would have been required in order for them to be tried under the statute for a permanent international criminal court.[15]

[13] *Ibid.* [14] Introduction chapter.

[15] "International Criminal Court: Crippled at Birth?," Amnesty International Press Release, July 17, 1998, as quoted in Marlies Glasius, *The International Criminal Court*, p. 73.

The promise of the ICC as a legal body independent of and untarnished by international politics is also called into question by a provision of the Rome Statute that allows the Security Council to suspend investigations and prosecutions for renewable one-year periods. Article 16 of the Statute is ostensibly reserved for those situations when the pursuit of investigations and prosecutions is deemed to threaten international peace and security. That the ICC might actually present such a threat poses a challenge to the Court's *raison d'etre* to deter mass atrocity. Yet, regardless of the possible merit of suspending certain prosecutions, this provision gives the Security Council legal license to subvert the ICC. The Security Council's use of Article 16 – and the predictable lobbying campaigns on the part of targeted states to press the Council to suspend prosecutions – may undermine the legitimacy of the ICC by reinforcing the perception that its legal process can ultimately be controlled by Great Power politics.

The politics currently surrounding and embedded in the fabric of the ICC and the Rome Statute presents a serious obstacle to the realization of the cosmopolitan ideals of fairness, autonomy, and universality that are so central to the Court's mission. As I will demonstrate, politics – namely the political interests and actions of states – is an enduring antagonist of the Court. But politics and the nation-state can also prove to be indispensable allies of the Court's quest for legitimacy and longevity. Even as states may imperil the ICC, they also possess the key to its success by virtue of the vital cooperation that states can provide in the investigation and prosecution of war crimes, crimes against humanity, and genocide. For better or worse, politics is and will remain a protagonist in the story of the ICC and its attempt to translate its cosmopolitan vision into a working institution.

II The ICC and the enforcement problem

To understand the distance separating the ideal and reality of the ICC it is necessary to examine the political dimensions of the Court. A logical starting point is the enforcement problem, which poses the most intractable and consequential challenge for the ICC. The enforcement problem is intractable because the ICC is bereft of police powers or an army of its own. It is therefore permanently reliant on the cooperation of a range of external actors – nation-states, international organizations, and NGOs. The enforcement problem is consequential because in the absence of external assistance, the Court will be unable to obtain custody of suspects and fulfill its prosecutorial mandate. The ICC will founder unless external actors take responsibility for ensuring the protection of the Court's war crimes investigators, for the unfettered access to witnesses, mass graves, and archival evidence, and for the arrest and handover of indicted war crimes suspects.

International community actors can play a critical role in directly aiding the ICC's war crimes prosecutions. For example, states with robust intelligence services can share satellite imagery with the Office of the Prosecutor to pinpoint mass graves and bolster criminal indictments. However, the cooperation of states complicit in atrocities is often even more decisive to the prosecutorial objective. Such states are often the only ones in a position to answer the Court's request for crucial elements of cooperation, given their involvement in these crimes, their control of the territories and crimes scenes where atrocities have occurred, and their protection of indicted nationals. Sudan is a case in point.

This is demonstrated by the Sudanese government's ongoing refusal to arrest and transfer indicted nationals sought by the ICC chief prosecutor. As of the beginning of 2010, three Sudanese suspects tied to state-sponsored atrocities in Darfur remain at large, including President Omar Hassan al-Bashir, the first head of state to face ICC indictment. In July 2008, ICC Chief Prosecutor Luis Moreno-Ocampo targeted the top of the Sudanese political hierarchy by requesting an arrest warrant for President Bashir on charges of war crimes, crimes against humanity, and genocide. In early March 2009, an ICC pre-trial chamber issued a warrant for Bashir's arrest and approved the war crimes and crimes against humanity charges against him.[16] In May 2007, an ICC pre-trial chamber approved Moreno-Ocampo's request to issue arrest warrants for the other two suspects; Ahmad Muhammad Harun,[17] a Sudanese government minister, and Ali Kushayb,[18] a leader of the government-backed Janjaweed militia.

Targeted states such as Sudan have the most to lose by cooperating with the ICC. Despite the Court's reassurance that individuals and not states are on trial, complicit states perceive a profound threat from international war crimes trials, particularly when the head of state

[16] See ICC arrest warrant for Omar Hassan al-Bashir; available at: www.icc-cpi.int/iccdocs/doc/doc639078.pdf.

[17] See ICC arrest warrant for Ahmad Muhammad Harun; available at: www.icc-cpi.int/iccdocs/doc/doc279813.pdf.

[18] See ICC arrest warrant for Ali Kushayb; available at: www.icc-cpi.int/iccdocs/doc/doc279858.pdf.

faces indictment.[19] When targeted states defy international war crimes tribunals and contest their legitimacy, they often do so out of fear that criminal indictments will render their regimes illegitimate at home and abroad. Regardless of whether suspects are actually delivered for trial or convicted, the international imprimatur of a war crimes indictment can cause lasting political damage. In this regard, even indictments of low-level suspects can stigmatize and shame a regime in the court of international opinion, casting its high-level political and military officials as perpetrators unworthy of leadership. Even the domestic (and democratic) successors to a complicitous regime may have reason to fear international war crimes indictments and withhold cooperation because of the potential for anti-government backlash if they move to hand over indicted suspects. The prospect of turning over indicted nationals – particularly those hailed at home as heroic defenders of the homeland – may undermine the viability of the new government and spark a destabilizing resurgence of nationalism.[20] Thus, the ICC's bid for universal acceptance and "lasting respect"[21] may often clash with the prerogative and power of the nation-state. Therein lies a fundamental challenge to the Court's quest to overcome its lack of enforcement powers and receive the state cooperation needed to deliver criminal accountability.

The clash over cooperation between nation-state and international war crimes tribunal is by no means unique to the ICC. Even as the ICC is presented by advocates as a superior model of international justice,[22] it is hamstrung by the same reliance on state cooperation that has hampered the ICTY and ICTR and other tribunals, such as the Special Court for Sierra Leone. Indeed, all of today's international tribunals lack the enforcement powers bequeathed to the Allied-run Nuremberg and Tokyo military tribunals in the aftermath of World War II. The dependence of the contemporary tribunals on state cooperation is as starkly apparent for the ICC now as it was for the ICTY and ICTR during their early years. As of the beginning of 2010, the ICC had just

19 Victor Peskin, *International Justice in Rwanda and the Balkans: Virtual Trials and the Struggle for State Cooperation* (New York: Cambridge University Press, 2008), pp. 14–16.

20 Victor Peskin and Mieczyslaw P. Boduszynski, "International Justice and Domestic Politics: Post Tuđjman Croatia and the International Criminal Tribunal for the Former Yugoslavia," *Europe–Asia Studies*, 55, No. 7 (2003).

21 Preamble of the Rome Statute of the International Criminal Court.

22 For instance, see Interview with Philippe Kirsch, President of the International Criminal Court, *International Review of the Red Cross*, 88, No. 861 (2006), 10.

four suspects in custody out of a total of fourteen that have so far been publicly indicted from the four country "situations" under ICC scrutiny. In addition to the three Sudanese suspects at large, the ICC has so far been unable to obtain custody of several indicted Ugandan suspects belonging to the Lord's Resistance Army rebel group, as well as one remaining indicted Congolese suspect. Four Congolese suspects are currently in ICC detention, including Thomas Lubanga, whose trial, the Court's first, began in late January 2009 after significant delay due to a legal controversy surrounding the prosecution's failure to disclose evidence to the defense.[23] Jean-Pierre Bemba, one of the four detained Congolese suspects, faces an upcoming trial for alleged atrocities in the Central African Republic. Court advocates applaud that there are even this many suspects in custody. But some observers take a dimmer view of the Court's promise to fulfill its central function of holding trials, arguing that from a retributivist perspective "the record of the ICC to date looks dismal."[24]

The ICTY and ICTR also had few suspects in custody in their early years. But these numbers increased markedly. This was particularly the case for the Tanzanian-based ICTR, which received custody of numerous Hutu genocide suspects who had been arrested by African states after fleeing Rwanda at the end of the 1994 genocide. Although the ICTY was slower to fill its detention center, the late 1990s brought a significant increase in suspects at The Hague-based tribunal. This was due in large part to the arrests carried out by NATO forces in Bosnia. The following years brought scores of suspects to the ICTY, as the United States and the European Union used significant political and economic leverage to press for cooperation from the new democratic coalitions governments in Serbia and Croatia. In recent years, the EU's policy of conditioning these states' progress toward Union membership on cooperation with the ICTY has been a critical factor in the handover of suspects. In this regard, the ICTY, among today's international tribunals, enjoys a privileged position owing to strong Western support.[25]

[23] Heikelina Verrijn Stuart, "The ICC in Trouble," *Journal of International Criminal Justice*, 6 (2008), 409–17.

[24] Marlies Glasius, "The ICC and the Gaza War: Legal Limits, Symbolic Politics," *Open Democracy*, March 25, 2009.

[25] Victor Peskin and Mieczyslaw Boduszynski, "Balancing International Justice in the Balkans: Surrogate Enforcers, Uncertain Transitions, and the Road to Europe," paper presented at the International Studies Association Annual Meetings, New York City, February 2009.

The victories of the ad hoc tribunals in the area of state cooperation and the establishment of the ICC have fostered the optimistic belief that success is inevitable for this permanent court. "We waited fifty years for this Court and now it has to work, because there will be no second chance," said Phillipe Kirsch, the chief negotiator at the Rome Conference and the founding ICC president.[26] In this expression of destiny, one senses the activist spirit that continues to drive the project of building the ICC and the international human rights movement more generally. Still, the ICC confronts a more difficult and complicated challenge in its quest for state cooperation than its ad hoc predecessors. If the ICTY and ICTR lack enforcement powers, the ICC's problem is even more pronounced.

The ICC's greater enforcement deficit is illustrated by contrasting the relative legal authority enjoyed by the ICC on the one hand and the ICTY and the ICTR on the other hand. The ICC's comparative disadvantage in the realm of state cooperation is manifested in its limited recourse to the Security Council, whereas the ICTY and ICTR – offsprings of the Council and its Chapter VII powers – have the right to register formal complaints of state noncompliance to the Council. Therein lies the tribunals' opportunity to press the Security Council to sanction such violations of international law. These ad hoc tribunals also have the right, indeed obligation, to periodically address the Security Council on their progress toward achieving their mandates. As with legal authority itself, access to the Security Council is not a panacea for the ad hoc tribunals' efforts to wrest cooperation from defiant states. In fact, the Security Council has rarely punished noncompliance on the part of the states of the former Yugoslavia and Rwanda. Nevertheless, these tribunals have strategically used the Security Council forum that is often in the international media spotlight. For the tribunals, condemning state noncompliance at the Security Council represents one of the most effective ways of garnering attention and damaging a state's credibility and its claims of compliance.

Whereas the ICTY and ICTR have a legal right to call upon the Security Council to enforce cooperation, the ICC can only do so in circumstances when the Security Council has asked the Court to launch an investigation in a particular country.[27] Under these circumstances,

[26] Interview with Phillipe Kirsch, President of the International Criminal Court, *International Review of the Red Cross*, 88, No. 861 (2006), p. 17.

[27] When it comes to the Darfur situation, the ICC chief prosecutor is obliged to submit written and oral progress reports to the Security Council twice a year.

the ICC can lodge complaints of state noncompliance with the Security Council because the Council originally requested the ICC to open investigations in that country. Thus, when it comes to Sudan, the ICC, despite confronting defiance from the Khartoum regime, has access to the global stage afforded by the Security Council. That has already proved useful in amplifying the ICC's criticism of Khartoum, as seen in the significant attention the international media paid to Chief Prosecutor Luis Moreno-Ocampo's critical assessments to the Security Council of Sudanese cooperation in December 2007[28] and in June and December 2008.

Whereas all UN members have a binding legal obligation to cooperate with the ICTY and ICTR, only states that have ratified the Rome Statute have such a legal obligation vis-à-vis the ICC. Thus, the ICC's legal right to state cooperation is currently less expansive than that enjoyed by the ICTY and ICTR. This level of legal authority, of course, does not by itself compel a state to cooperate. However, it can create a strong foundation to bolster a tribunal's campaign to obtain cooperation from recalcitrant states. The binding legal obligation on all UN member states to cooperate enables the tribunals to shame defiant states as violators of international law, and to garner international condemnation of such behavior.[29]

For the ICC, the challenge of bringing suspects to trial, at least in the short-term, is likely to remain a formidable one. The ICC's challenge here has been starkly illustrated by the decision of four non-states parties to host President Bashir of Sudan, just weeks after the ICC issued a warrant for his arrest. In the span of one week in late March 2009, Bashir received warm welcomes from allied heads of state in visits to Eritrea, Egypt, Libya, and Qatar. Beyond demonstrating Bashir's defiance of the ICC, his visits to these regional allies highlighted a central weakness in the Rome Statute, namely, non-states parties do not have a legal obligation to arrest Bashir. However, the Security Council resolution that referred the Darfur situation to the ICC does "urge" all states "to cooperate fully" with the ICC.[30] While the ICC aspires to be a global court, the legal obligations pertaining to state cooperation falls far short of what is necessary to realize universality. In this regard, the ICC does

[28] Warren Hoge, "Official Urges Arrest of 2 Darfur Suspects," *New York Times*, December 6, 2007, A10; "Delay, Obstruction and Darfur," *New York Times*, op-ed, December 10, 2007.

[29] Peskin, *International Justice in Rwanda and the Balkans.*

[30] Security Council Resolution 1593, adopted March 31, 2005.

not yet embody the cosmopolitan ideal (as set forth in the Introduction Chapter) in which all members of the world community have an obligation to sustain a particular political or legal project.

III Sovereignty, deference, and the pursuit of trials at the ICC

The contention that the ICC faces comparatively greater obstacles in its quest for cooperation and that these obstacles imperil the fledgling system of international justice is open to debate. It is therefore important to consider the ways in which the ICC may presently, or over time, be favorably positioned in its quest for state cooperation. As discussed earlier, states that do not consent to becoming parties to the Rome Statute are, by and large, beyond the prosecutorial reach of the Court and do not have an obligation to cooperate. In this respect, the ICC, relative to the ICTY and ICTR, may be seen to be a weaker court and one less able to wrest cooperation from states. Yet even as this deference to states is a source of weakness, it may also be a source of strength insofar as the design of the Court reflects the will of states,[31] renders the ICC less of an unwanted imposition and thus may foster a greater sense of ownership and trust among states, ultimately leading to more acceptance and cooperation from them. This, in turn, may create a stronger political foundation for the ICC and render its long-term prospects for additional state ratifications more viable.

At the heart of the ICC's deference to states lies the principle of complementarity which renders the ICC a court of last resort. The ICC chief prosecutor cannot prosecute a state's nationals unless that state is unable or genuinely unwilling to carry war crimes trials of its own. Thus, in order to move forward with a prosecution, the ICC Office of the Prosecutor must undergo an admissibility assessment that determines whether or not a domestic prosecution is a viable option. This assessment is then reviewed by an ICC pre-trial chamber which makes a final determination on admissibility. Complementarity contrasts sharply with primacy, the defining principle guiding the chief prosecutors at the ICTY and ICTR. Under primacy, the ICTY and ICTR chief prosecutors have the sole authority to decide which suspects to

[31] As Phillipe Kirsch has said, while the ICTY and ICTR "were imposed on states … the International Criminal Court was created by states and reflects their will." See Interview with Phillipe Kirsch, President of the International Criminal Court, *International Review of the Red Cross*, Volume 88, Number 861 (2006), p. 10.

prosecute without regard to whether the states of the former Yugoslavia and Rwanda are willing or able to prosecute these suspects domestically. At the ICC, complementarity aims to promote state responsibility for criminal justice, while reserving the ICC for those circumstances in which states have no intention or capacity to undertake credible prosecutions. In ideal circumstances, the ICC will actually conduct few war crimes prosecutions because states themselves will take the lead.

In comparison to the primacy of the ICTY and ICTR, the complementarity of the ICC represents a significant redistribution of power to the state insofar as the ICC is a court that waits in the wings. In this regard, the ICC envisions a more horizontal relationship with states. However, the ICC's relationship with a targeted state takes on a vertical dimension if the Court imposes justice on a state that is unwilling to undertake prosecutions itself. In these instances, the conflict between the ICC and the targeted state may be as intense as those that have taken place between the ICTY and ICTR and the states of the former Yugoslavia and Rwanda. This point is underscored by the acrimonious battle waged between the Sudanese government and ICC Chief Prosecutor Moreno-Ocampo over whether Sudan will comply with its legal obligation to cooperate with the Court.[32]

As a global court, the ICC should find itself well placed to call upon the international community to confront and overcome the defiance of targeted states, such as Sudan. In the absence of enforcement powers of its own, the ICC depends on "surrogate enforcers"[33] – influential international actors that can pressure and persuade targeted states such as Sudan to cooperate. The ICC should be able to count on a multitude of surrogate enforcers. After all, the Court is the product of a multilateral treaty in which 110 states (as of the beginning of 2010) have consented to join through a process of domestic ratification of the Rome Statute. The increase in state ratifications, and the domestic campaigns that often accompany them, should deepen normative acceptance for the ICC. This socialization process should, in turn, solidify the resolve of states parties to provide unstinting backing to the Court, particularly in the critical arena of state cooperation. The Rome Statute requires nothing less.

[32] Victor Peskin, "The International Criminal Court, the Security Council, and the Politics of Impunity in Darfur," *Genocide Studies and Prevention: An International Journal*, 4, 3 (December 2009): 304-328.

[33] Peskin, *International Justice in Rwanda and the Balkans*, p. 12.

The belief in the ICC's resilience in meeting the challenge of state cooperation stems from two related factors; first, the broad international consensus sustaining the Court and second, the range of stakeholders who, by virtue of their role in negotiating the Rome Statute and establishing the Court, feel a sense of responsibility for its success. By contrast, the ICTY and ICTR have a narrower foundation of support, given their establishment by the fifteen-member Security Council. Despite the legitimacy of the Security Council resolutions authorizing these two ad hoc tribunals, the decisions to establish them were made on behalf of the world community, but not actually by it. In this respect, the creation of the ICTY and ICTR was far less participatory than the creation of the ICC. To be sure, states not on the Security Council and influential NGOs weighed in on the question of whether to establish these tribunals and how to design them. But this contrasts sharply with the process of creating the ICC, which was the outcome of a global civil society movement that, as Marlies Glasius writes, "has been almost unprecedented in international treaty negotiations."[34] Indeed, 162 states and hundreds of NGOs gathered in Rome for a five-week conference in which all aspects of the Court's proposed Statute were reviewed and debated. One might expect the political convergence in Rome to have translated into an unflagging commitment to heed the Court's Preamble, "to guarantee lasting respect for and the enforcement of international justice."[35] But the international commitment to the Court, from both states parties and non-states parties, has so far been wanting.

Even as the ICC serves as a testament to the strength of the international human rights movement and cosmopolitan ideals, it currently lacks the necessary political backing to deliver justice on a global scale. The problem lies in the incomplete political foundation currently supporting the Court. That the ICC has 108 states parties at this early stage in its development speaks to the global appeal of this institution.[36] Nevertheless, the ICC has so far fallen well short of receiving the formal backing of all 192 United Nations states.

The ICC's quest for universality and state cooperation is currently undermined by the decision of some of the most influential states not

[34] Marlies Glasius, *The International Criminal Court*, p. xiii.

[35] Preamble of the Rome Statute of the International Criminal Court.

[36] It is important to note that several state parties are micro-states, such as Andorra, Liechtenstein, the Marshall Islands, Nauru, and San Marino.

to join the Court. Most significantly, three of the five permanent members of the Security Council – the United States, Russia, and China – have not ratified the Rome Statute. In addition, such populous states as India, Pakistan, Indonesia, and Turkey have also chosen not to join the ICC. And, with the exception of Jordan, no other state in the Middle East or North Africa belongs to the Court.[37] In total, states representing somewhat more than half the world's population have decided not to join the ICC.

This lack of international support has dealt two major blows to the ICC. First, and most obviously, this has undermined its cosmopolitan vision of delivering justice universally, given the serious limitations placed on prosecuting suspects from non-states parties. To be sure, the Security Council referral of the Darfur situation to the ICC and the arrest warrant issued for President Bashir importantly demonstrate the Court's capacity to target individuals from non-states parties. But there will likely remain an imbalance in the type of non-states parties that will fall under ICC jurisdiction through the route of the Security Council referral process. Powerful states on the Security Council, such as the United States, China, and Russia, will be shielded from Council referrals to the ICC because of their ability to wield a veto. These powerful states, in turn, will likely use their veto to block referrals that could implicate their closest allies. In this regard, the United States would most certainly block any Council move that could lead to ICC investigations of Israeli officials for conduct in the recent Gaza conflict. This built-in deference to the Great Powers casts a long shadow over the ability of the ICC to move beyond victor's justice.

The lack of fuller international backing has further undermined the Court by complicating its bid for influential "surrogate enforcers" of state cooperation. Thus, the ICC has diminished prospects in building and sustaining the crucial backing of some of the most powerful international actors, such as the United States. Washington has done more than just sit on the sidelines of the ICC issue. As is well known, the Bush administration, particularly during its first term, launched strident attacks on the Court, assailing it as an unaccountable institution, a threat to American sovereignty, and a vanguard of world government. This disdain was summed up by Tom DeLay, the former US Republican Congressional leader, who referred to the ICC as a "kangaroo court … a shady amalgam of every bad idea ever cooked up for

[37] A list of all the States Parties is available at: www.icc-cpi.int/asp/statesparties.html.

world government."[38] As a non-state party with the power to veto any Security Council referral to the ICC, Washington would seem to have little reason to fear possible ICC prosecutions. However, such a possibility still exists. The Rome Statute, as stated earlier, grants the ICC jurisdiction over individuals, regardless of their nationality, accused of violations of international humanitarian law that occur on the territory of a state party. The Bush administration went to great lengths to prevent ICC prosecutions of American military personnel, including a concerted campaign to have countries sign bilateral agreements guaranteeing that US citizens would not be extradited to the Court. Its efforts here also include the 2002 American Servicemembers' Protection Act that, with several exceptions, forbids the United States government from lending any support to the Court and provides for the withholding of military aid to governments ratifying the Rome Statute. With such acts, the American political establishment also sought to reverse the political momentum behind the Court by raising the costs of entry for would-be members.[39]

But this stance has incurred costs of its own for the United States by hardening its image abroad as an uncompromising unilateralist and undermining its bilateral relationships with allies. As former Secretary of State Condoleezza Rice acknowledged, the policy of withholding military aid to some pro-ICC allies is akin to the US "shooting [itself] in the foot."[40] As a consequence, President Bush in his second term began to soften his hardline stance toward the Court in a number of ways. The administration indicated that if asked by the ICC it would offer assistance in its investigations of Darfur atrocities.[41] This new change – along with the administration's decision not to block a Security Council vote to refer the Darfur situation to the ICC in March 2005 and its opposition in 2008 to a bid to have the Council suspend the pending case against President Bashir – underscores that Washington's approach has not been set in stone.

For the ICC, the problem posed by having major world powers on the list of non-states parties underscores the need for a strong coalition

[38] "International Criminal Court: Let the Child Live," *The Economist*, January 25, 2007.

[39] Mieczyslaw P. Boduszynski and Kristina Balalovska, "Between a Rock and a Hard Place: Croatia, Macedonia, and the Battle over Article 98," *Problems of Post-Communism*, January/February 2004, pp. 18–30.

[40] "International Criminal Court: Let the Child Live," *The Economist*, January 25, 2007.

[41] Nora Boustany, "Official Floats Possibility of Assistance to Hague Court," *Washington Post*, June 12, 2007, A20.

of states parties to actively support the Court. To be sure, many states parties – particularly such influential ones as Britain, France, Germany, The Netherlands, and Canada – have played a critical role in sustaining the ICC after Rome. Notably, these states have campaigned for additional state ratifications, defended the Court against US attacks, and provided it with much-needed logistical, legal, and financial assistance. Without such backing, the ICC could not have registered the institutional gains it has made in a few short years. However, on the whole, states parties have not been strong and consistent "surrogate enforcers" when it has come to applying political pressure needed to bolster the ICC's quest for the arrest and transfers of suspects and other aspects of vital cooperation.[42] What has gone largely unnoticed in the media and scholarly literature is the reticence of states parties to muster the political fortitude to compel cooperation from targeted states. Instead, states parties in Europe and beyond have often been timid advocates of cooperation.[43] Particularly in the case of Sudan, the ICC's coalition of the willing has been unwilling to consistently and vigorously press the Khartoum government for cooperation or to significantly raise the political costs of noncompliance. For the ICC, this uneven support from many pro-ICC states has made an already difficult path to state cooperation even more so, raising doubts about the commitment of these states to aid the ICC in realizing its cosmopolitan promise.

The lack of state party support on the issue of arrests raises a question, the answer to which provides insight into the limits of the ICC's cosmopolitan vision of justice: why would the most ardent backers of the ICC balk when it comes to throwing their political weight behind the Court's efforts to prosecute some of the world's most egregious atrocities? The answer lies in the real, yet often unacknowledged tension existing within the political establishments of most states parties, including those Liberal democratic states in which support of the ICC is a central pillar of foreign policy and is widely-backed by domestic constituencies. Juxtaposed with a normative desire to see the ICC succeed is a pragmatic concern with the unintended consequences of pursuing international war crimes prosecutions. A central issue for these states is whether the pursuit of international justice will threaten their interests in maintaining stability in the targeted state and surrounding region.

[42] Fieldwork interviews with ICC officials and international human rights activists, The Hague, June and November 2007, December 2008.

[43] Fieldwork interviews with ICC officials, The Hague, June and November 2007.

In other words, will the prospect or reality of indictments, arrests, and trials stymie the efforts of peace negotiators by hardening the resolve of targeted state and rebel leaders to wage war and inflict atrocities?

The ICC and its ad hoc predecessors are founded upon the principle that there is no conflict between peace and justice and that justice is essential to the pursuit of peace. In this regard, justice has been cast as both a moral and pragmatic necessity, as Kofi Annan underscored in his speech at the ICC's inauguration. "There are times we are told justice should be put aside," Annan said. "But we have come to understand that without justice there can be no lasting peace."[44] Yet serious doubts remain, not least among friends of the ICC. The perception that the pursuit of prosecutions may in certain situations undermine the pursuit of ceasefires and peace-treaties – as well as jeopardize related policy goals such as the delivery of humanitarian aid and the deployment of peacekeepers – appears to be a major reason for states parties' lack of resolve as surrogate enforcers. In some cases, deferring prosecutions may be justified if doing so can significantly improve prospects for peace and stability. Still, the firmness of states' commitment to the ICC begins to unravel when the priority of peace over justice becomes too close to the rule than the exception. Knowing this, targeted states and their allies will seek to pressure the ICC's would-be surrogate enforcers to remain mere observers.

The Sudan case is again a prime example of this phenomenon of the international community's conditional commitment to the ICC. The Sudanese government has stirred concern among a range of diplomats and other international actors that the ICC's bid for the handover of Bashir has dangerously antagonized the president, threatening the protracted quest for peace in Darfur, jeopardizing the fragile North–South peace settlement in Sudan, and triggering government retaliation against innocent victims in Darfur. In the immediate aftermath of the March 2009 arrest warrant for Bashir, the specter of government retribution became real. Accusing international humanitarian groups in Darfur of collaborating with the ICC, Bashir expelled thirteen major aid organizations and a few local ones.[45] For the hundreds of thousands of Darfurians living in refugee camps and dependent on humanitarian

[44] Secretary-General Kofi Annan's Statement to the Inaugural Meeting of Judges of the International Criminal Court, March 11, 2003, The Hague.

[45] Lynsey Addario and Lydia Polgreen, "In Aid Groups' Expulsion, Fears of More Misery Engulfing Darfur," *New York Times*, March 23, 2009, A6.

assistance, the expulsion of these aid organizations is potentially life threatening.

For the ICC, the expulsions pose a threat of a different order insofar as it may undercut international support for the Court as states try to assuage Bashir's anger at being targeted for arrest. Since the ICC began its investigations of the Darfur situation, the Sudanese government has sought to manufacture a conflict between peace and justice to deter international support for the ICC's incriminating work. With the government's decision to expel major humanitarian aid organizations that provide a lifeline to vulnerable Darfurians, the government has sought to undercut the ICC further by manufacturing a conflict between *survival* and *justice*. Even as many states parties have called on Sudan to cooperate with the ICC, they appear ambivalent about Bashir's indictment lest it prolong the Darfur crisis.

The obstacles facing the ICC and the constraints it confronts in its quest for state cooperation are due not only to the political interests of states, but also to the law of the Rome Statute itself. There should be nothing surprising about this. The Court's founders designed the ICC to pay significantly more deference to state sovereignty and to have considerably less legal authority to compel states to cooperate than either the ICTY and ICTR have had. In the trajectory of today's international war crimes tribunals, the ICTY and ICTR possess the most legal leverage to wrest cooperation from recalcitrant states. These two ad hoc institutions represent "the high-water mark"[46] of tribunal authority vis-à-vis states, as one senior ICTY official wistfully remarked in an interview not long after the ICC's establishment. And now with the imminent closure of these two ad hoc tribunals, the high-water mark for international tribunals appears to be receding.

IV Conclusion: The ICC as political actor in the quest for state cooperation and the cosmopolitan vision of justice

This chapter has focused on the political and legal constraints that have rendered the ICC's prosecutorial mandate and its vision of justice very difficult to achieve in the short term. Such an inquiry is incomplete without considering how the ICC – and particularly its chief prosecutor – has acted and should act to realize the Court's goals of delivering

[46] Fieldwork interview with ICTY official, The Hague, December 2003.

justice fairly and universally. Here, I turn to examine this critical question.[47]

Because it is not simply a creature of its international creators bound to heed their interests and instructions, the ICC is not powerless to act on its own behalf in the battles for state cooperation. Although the ICC is the offspring of many founders, it is meant to be independent of its sponsoring states. If the ICTY and ICTR have learned anything from their experiences, it is that they themselves are often the only actors willing to keep a state's obstruction of justice in the international spotlight by forcefully calling for compliance. The tribunals – and particularly their chief prosecutors – soon came to realize that cooperation would be impossible without political engagement, which included prodding targeted states and seeking vital backing from would-be surrogate enforcers in the international community. Yet, when it comes to forcefully pressing targeted states and key international community actors, the ICC and its chief prosecutor are at a significant disadvantage, relative to the ICTY and ICTR. As with these two ad hoc tribunals, the efficacy of the ICC's campaign for state cooperation is often shaped by the constellation of international actors willing and able to lend tangible support to the cause of international justice. This constellation has been comparatively strong for these ad hoc tribunals, the ICTY in particular. This has not been the case for the fledgling ICC.

Although the international community frequently disappointed the ICTY and ICTR by failing to press the states of the former Yugoslavia and Rwanda for full cooperation, these international tribunals have had the benefit of being tribunals of the United Nations. This provenance meant that the tribunals were deputized by the UN Security Council to bring perpetrators of atrocities in the Balkans and Rwanda to justice. As arms of the world's pre-eminent international body, the ICTY and ICTR have legal recourse to the great powers to intervene on their behalf with defiant states. Tasked by the Security Council to deliver justice, these tribunals could reciprocally task the Security Council to ensure that justice would in fact be delivered. In short, the Security Council provided a solid legal and political foundation with which the ICTY and ICTR could wage their battles for state cooperation. Moreover, the Security Council's requirement that all UN member states are legally

[47] For an examination of the role of the ICC and its chief prosecutor in the quest for state cooperation, see Victor Peskin, "Caution and Confrontation in the International Criminal Court's Pursuit of Accountability in Uganda and Sudan," *Human Rights Quarterly*, 31 (2009): 655–91.

bound to provide full and immediate cooperation has enabled top ICTY and ICTR officials to confront state defiance head-on, by shaming noncompliant states as violators of international law. The temporary, ad hoc nature of the ICTY's and ICTR's mandates and the pressure from the Security Council to complete all their cases expeditiously have given these tribunals yet more impetus to lobby actively for the arrests and handover of indicted war crimes suspects. As a consequence, these tribunals, and the ICTY in particular, have often taken a sharply adversarial approach to the cooperation issue.

In contrast, the ICC operates from a considerably weaker legal and political foundation in its campaign for cooperation. This disadvantage is an outcome of key provisions of the Rome Statute that, in contrast to the ICTY and ICTR statutes, have diluted the global obligation to sustain the global ICC. Most importantly, non-states parties are exempt from an obligation to cooperate with the Court. And even as the ICC aspires to attain universal state support, it is currently built upon an inchoate political foundation. The political structure supporting the Court is far from complete, given that a number of major states have not joined the ICC. These legal and political deficits have created acute dilemmas for ICC Chief Prosecutor Moreno-Ocampo as they will for his successors.

Two vexing and foundational questions confront the ICC chief prosecutor. First, what strategies can Moreno-Ocampo employ to increase the prospects of receiving the state cooperation he needs to hold trials and obtain convictions? Second, how can Moreno-Ocampo pursue his campaign for state cooperation in such a way that advances, instead of undermines the cosmopolitan vision of justice that lies at the core of the ICC project?

The ICC prosecutor has been under considerable pressure to take an active stance in trying to obtain much needed state cooperation in order to prove the viability of this nascent court. But how exactly should the chief prosecutor act? In their bid for cooperation, the chief prosecutors of the contemporary international war crimes tribunal have developed a range of adversarial and conciliatory strategies.[48] The adversarial approach is more familiar to us, perhaps in large part because it often takes places in the public arena. Here, a chief prosecutor, mirroring the actions of leading international human rights NGOs, will seek to shame a state for its noncompliance in the court of international public

[48] Peskin, *International Justice in Rwanda and the Balkans.*

opinion. But given the inherent limits of shame and its capacity to further antagonize a recalcitrant state, a chief prosecutor will also act in a conciliatory manner. Here, the prosecutor will seek to find common ground with a targeted state by offering concessions, small and large, to leverage some cooperation rather than none at all. The conciliatory measures taken by a chief prosecutor are usually enacted out of public view and are not readily acknowledged. Indeed, maintaining an image of non-negotiable rectitude is integral to maintaining the prosecutor's and the tribunal's moral authority as an institution based on law, not political expediency. Still, the tribunal's enduring dependence on state cooperation may lead a prosecutor to seek behind-the-scenes negotiations aimed at obtaining a measure of cooperation.

There is, however, a fine line between compromises that advance the court's prosecutorial mission and those that compromise its integrity and legitimacy. Eschewing any form of bargaining can undermine a tribunal by failing to reach out to recalcitrant states. But engaging in bargaining can run adrift by subjecting the legal process to an escalating cycle of political calculation. This threat becomes particularly acute when a prosecutor's accommodation to a state leads to granting major concessions, such as forgoing indictments of state officials and limiting prosecutorial scrutiny to the state's enemies. That is what has happened at the ICTR, where its successive chief prosecutors have refrained from indicting members of the Tutsi-led Rwandan government for non-genocidal atrocities committed against Hutu civilians in 1994. In strategically shielding government officials – upon whom the tribunal relies on for vital cooperation in the prosecution of Hutu genocide suspects – the ICTR chief prosecutor has been an enabler of victor's justice.

A parallel process of conciliation appears to be in motion in the ICC chief prosecutor's quest for cooperation from the Ugandan government. In Uganda, Moreno-Ocampo has, so far, only targeted Ugandan rebels for indictment while sparing Ugandans implicated in state-sponsored atrocities. Some analysts contend that this one-sided focus on non-state actors in Uganda is the result of the prosecutor's need to maintain the government's vital cooperation.[49] The prosecutor's perceived indebtedness is heightened, in the view of some observers, because of

[49] For instance, see Phil Clark, "Law, Politics, and Pragmatism: The ICC and Case Selection in the Democratic Republic of Congo and Uganda," in *Courting Conflict? Justice, Peace, and the ICC in Africa*, ed. Nicholas Waddell and Phil Clark (Royal Africa Society, March 2008), p. 43

the government's decision to accede to Moreno-Ocampo's request, in late 2003, to invite the ICC to begin an investigation in Uganda of rebel crimes.[50]

At the time, receiving the Ugandan referral represented an important step forward for the ICC since it paved the way for the Court's first arrest warrants in 2005. Gaining this foothold in Uganda was crucial for the ICC to signal that it could quickly move from utopian ideal to functioning institution. Indeed, if the Court is to move from ideal to reality it must make good on its most fundamental objective, which is to investigate cases, bring indictments, and hold trials. Yet if obtaining an invitation to begin investigations in Uganda was a pivotal first step toward realizing the ICC's judicial mandate, it also demonstrated that the way a chief prosecutor goes about obtaining justice has serious implications for whether the cosmopolitan vision of universal justice will ever be achieved. By apparently aligning itself with a state in order to obtain necessary cooperation, the ICC prosecutor seemed to hold little interest in targeting state actors. (The Office of the Prosecutor has left open the possibility of bringing cases against Ugandans implicated in state abuses, but some analysts doubt this will come to pass.[51]) There may in fact be valid reasons, such as a lack of gravity of state crimes, not to bring a case against state actors in Uganda. However, in the Uganda situation, a perception developed in some quarters that the prosecutor was being one-sided for political reasons.[52] And with this perception, questions were raised about whether the prosecution would remain faithful to the "all-inclusiveness" principle that lies at the heart of cosmopolitanism. The larger question for the ICC is whether the prosecutor's dependence on state cooperation will now and in the future undermine the principle of fairness and universality that is the driving principle behind the dream of a universal war crimes court.

Victor's justice is the antithesis of the cosmopolitan vision of justice that emphasizes "the *moral worth* of persons" as well as "the *equal* moral worth of *all* persons." In this all-inclusive vision, international law is broad enough to include all victims as equally deserving of accountability and narrow enough to ensure that no suspect reaps the privilege of being excluded from the scrutiny of accountability. The fundamental

[50] The alternative would have been for Moreno-Ocampo to open an investigation in Uganda under his own authority, something he appeared reticent to do because it could be perceived as an intrusion of Uganda's sovereignty and a less effective way to garner cooperation from the government.

[51] *Ibid.*, p. 43. [52] *Ibid.*, p. 43.

goal of the ICC – and all of the international tribunals that succeeded Nuremberg and Tokyo – is to institutionalize the ethic of treating all people, whether victims or suspects, as citizens of the world deserving equal protection under the law. Of course, no international tribunal can literally achieve this ideal of equality given the impossibility of prosecuting the legions of suspected perpetrators implicated in mass atrocity. If the ad hoc tribunals carried out too few prosecutions (in the view of many victims), then the ICC will carry out far fewer because of a much wider territorial jurisdiction and the likely economic constraints of prosecuting more than a handful of suspects from each country situation. In this regard, the justice delivered by all tribunals, but perhaps the ICC especially, will be highly symbolic. But in no small part because of this symbolism, the onus is on the ICC chief prosecutor to approach his quest for state cooperation and the related decisions of case selection with regard to the "all-inclusiveness" principle of cosmopolitanism. Of central importance for the prosecutor is to apply an ethic of evenhandedness to his case selection decisions so that no side of an armed conflict implicated in significant atrocities wins immunity from justice.

PART V

International migration

10

Is immigration a human right?

JORGE M. VALADEZ

In recent decades the process of globalization has involved the migration of substantial numbers of people from developing to developed countries and between developing countries. This global development has prompted politicians, civil activists, legal scholars, political philosophers, and others to grapple with issues related to immigration. A view that has emerged from some writers who uphold cosmopolitan ideals is that immigration should be regarded as a human right. My primary purpose in this chapter is to examine from a normative standpoint the claim that immigration, understood as involving eventual full integration into countries of destination, should be regarded as a human right. Even though I will argue that one cannot reasonably claim that immigration is a human right, the moral concerns that motivate this claim should be taken seriously. I therefore propose some moral principles to guide the formulation of just immigration policies that take these moral concerns into account. In arguing that immigration should not be regarded as a human right, I contend that there is a fundamental tension between the cosmopolitan claim that we should show equal moral concern for everyone and the institutionalization of that claim in immigration policies that allow individuals to move freely across national borders.

In the first part of this chapter, I examine what is involved in claiming that immigration is a human right. I discuss the nature and scope of this right and identify the right-bearers and those on whom the right can be claimed. In the second part, I critically examine two arguments that could be used to justify the claim that immigration is a human right. In the third section some moral principles and policy guidelines are presented to guide the formulation of just immigration policies. These principles and guidelines are proposed as an alternative to regarding immigration as a human right. I conclude with some critical comments on Thomas Spijkerboer's paper on the distributive approach to the immigration issue.

The nature and scope of immigration as a human right

From the outset it is important to be clear about the nature of the right to immigrate, its scope, the parties who bear the right, and those on whom it can be claimed, because only then can we properly evaluate its normative legitimacy. I begin by clarifying a common misunderstanding of what is involved in claiming that immigration is a human right.[1] The idea is that national boundaries are artificially imposed impediments to people's movement and that these boundaries should not supersede the right that people have to exercise their natural capacity for movement. According to this view, relocating one's residence to a different geographical location is simply an expression of this natural capacity. That is, to claim that people have a right to immigrate involves nothing more controversial than claiming that people have the right to make voluntary decisions regarding their physical location. Appealing to freedom of movement makes it seem as if immigration regulations are obviously grossly unjust because they restrict the natural right that people have to move about. But if a right to immigrate exists, it surely involves much more than people simply having the freedom to move from one position in space to another and it is a serious misrepresentation to portray it in this manner. Immigration as a human right involves not the freedom to move about or even the freedom to choose where to live. Properly understood, this right involves membership in a political community.

If we understand the right to immigrate in a weaker sense than potential membership in a political union, we run the risk of accepting as legitimate a democratically unsustainable scenario in which some individuals are part of a political body without being able to participate in the process of democratic self-governance. Even though political membership usually comes in degrees and rights of citizenship can be disaggregated into distinct political and social privileges, if a political union or community neglects to eventually fully integrate into its political institutions the individuals living within its boundaries, it creates an unjust situation in which some of its inhabitants will be outside the realm of its institutional framework for self-governance. These

[1] The simple appeal to freedom of movement is used by some immigration activists to justify the right to immigrate (though few philosophers would rely on this idea alone in making a case for this purported right). See, for example, "Freedom of Movement," Human Rights Education Associates, available at: www.hrea.org/abouthrea.html (July 1, 2007).

marginalized people will become "political internal foreigners" who will be unable to fully participate in the democratic self-governance of the political community in which they live. Thus, unless we are willing to accept as legitimate political bodies that are democratically unjust, the right to immigrate when properly understood involves the option of eventual full membership and integration into any political body of one's choice. This is much stronger than the claim that immigration merely involves freedom of movement.

In examining the nature of a right it is customary to identify the right-bearers, that is, those who hold the right, and the parties on whom the right can be claimed. If immigration is a human right, the right-bearers would be every human being on the planet. By its nature as a human right, the right to immigrate would be universal and would apply equally to everyone, like freedom of speech, freedom of religion, or the right to assemble. The cosmopolitan would certainly go along with this latter claim, for it is part of cosmopolitanism to extend basic moral entitlements to all human beings. Unless we introduced distinct and independent moral principles to override the right to immigrate, there would be no special circumstances, such as ethnic background or religious affiliation, which would grant particular privileges in the exercise of this right. On the other hand, the parties on whom the right could be claimed are all of the political communities in the world. Note that I use the term "political community" and not "nation-state" because those political bodies on which this right could be claimed would include American Indian reservations, Maya communities in Chiapas, and semi-autonomous regions such as the Kurdish political community in northern Iraq. Here again, unless additional moral principles are introduced that override the universal right to immigrate, right-bearers could exercise their right to eventual full political membership in any political community of their choosing.

Recognizing that the right to immigrate involves a universal entitlement to eventual full membership in any political community of one's choice helps us appreciate the far-reaching implications of accepting this purported entitlement as a human right. This is not to say, of course, that recognizing this suffices to refute the claim that freedom of movement shows that immigration is a human right. So far I have only shown that it is a misunderstanding to characterize the right to immigrate as involving merely freedom of movement. It may still be the case that freedom of movement is by itself such a strong and unconstrained entitlement that it justifies the option of inclusion into any political community of one's choice. Thus, I need to establish that freedom of movement in itself fails to ground a right to immigrate.[2] This task, which I undertake briefly in what follows, will also provide a transition to other more plausible arguments for the claim that immigration is a human right.

We should begin by noting that there are numerous restrictions and regulations on our freedom to move. We cannot, for example, move into private property without the owner's consent (except perhaps during emergencies or when we have special right of access). And since most property is privately owned, this means that we are in general significantly restricted regarding where we can move. Moreover, even public space is heavily regulated. For instance, we cannot drive our car on the streets in any direction we please or at any rate of speed. Neither can we decide to live on publicly-owned open spaces such as national parks or on publicly-owned buildings such as city libraries. Taking note of these familiar and well-accepted restrictions on movement reminds us that our freedom to move is usually constrained by numerous considerations that involve the individual and collective interests of others. We cannot, in other words, simply assume that we are free to engage in any particular form of movement without taking into account how this might affect others. Appealing to freedom of movement by itself fails to provide a moral ground for recognizing immigration as a human right because physical movement is in general a significantly constrained activity and we cannot automatically assume that relocation to another political community is among those forms of movement that should be unconstrained.

Nevertheless, it remains an open question whether there are other compelling reasons for holding that the privileges that should accompany long-term or permanent residence in a political community are such important goods for people's welfare that they outweigh the reasons political communities might have for regulating membership. Thus, those who reject the claim that immigration is a universal human right need to respond to the arguments made by those who maintain that there are strong reasons, other than the simple appeal to freedom of movement, to grant people the right to immigrate.

[2] Joseph Carens appeals to freedom of movement in making a case for the right to move across national borders, see: "Migration and Morality: A Liberal Egalitarian Perspective," *Free Movement: Ethical Issues in the Transnational Migration of People and Money*, ed. Brian Barry and Robert Goodin (New York: Harvester Wheatsheaf: 1992).

The moral equality argument

Besides the freedom of movement argument, there are at least two other arguments that could be used to justify the claim that immigration is a human right. I will refer to the first of these as the moral equality argument. According to this cosmopolitan line of reasoning, all human beings are moral equals in the sense that they should be the subjects of equal moral concern. This moral equality and concern, moreover, should be granted to all people regardless of their membership in any particular political community, ethnic group, religion, race, or other mode of affiliation. That is, the moral concern we grant to others should extend to all members of the world community, and not merely to the members of those groups with whom we share special affinities. A corollary to the principle of the moral equality is that we should express equal moral concern for peoples' basic interest in leading a flourishing life. If every person is as equally morally worthwhile as every other, then surely his or her fundamental interest in leading a flourishing life should be granted equal consideration. Expressing equal moral concern for their basic interest in leading a flourishing life, moreover, involves providing them, short of significantly compromising our own well-being, with the opportunity to attain such a life, where this opportunity is understood in terms of their chances of enjoying a basic level of security and freedom, having access to medical care, finding a job that provides adequate material compensation, and attaining other goods important for leading a flourishing life.[3] But since different political communities provide vastly unequal opportunities to lead a flourishing life, people should have the right to immigrate to those political communities where they have a reasonable opportunity to flourish. This would be consistent with one of the central defining features of cosmopolitanism that extends equal moral concern for all people, regardless of their national, ethnic, religious, or other form of group affiliation.

This argument explicitly acknowledges that immigration involves not merely freedom of movement or place of residence, but also membership in a political community. While recognizing that there may be

[3] For a defense of an open-border immigration policy based on the equality of opportunity to attain one's life goals, see Joseph Carens, "Aliens and Citizens: The Case for Open Borders," in *The Rights of Minority Cultures*, ed. Will Kymlicka (New York: Oxford University Press, 1995). Even though here Carens appeals to the notion of liberty to ground movement across borders, he evidently considers possessing such form of liberty as essential for human flourishing.

reasons why a political community would want to control membership, advocates of this argument maintain that the right to immigrate has normative priority, because it embodies our commitment to the moral equality of the world's inhabitants. According to the moral equality argument, people should be able to decide for themselves where they can best achieve their life goals and live a flourishing life, because the right to make this decision is meaningless unless they are free to immigrate to the political community of their choice.

In evaluating the moral equality argument we should first note that it is notoriously difficult to establish precisely what we commit ourselves to by regarding all persons as moral equals. Presumably, the cosmopolitan would want to institutionalize this commitment in part by developing immigration policies that provide everyone with an opportunity to flourish by residing in a country that gives them a reasonable chance to attain a decent standard of living. It is certainly possible to understand this commitment in a weaker manner than the cosmopolitan interpretation, say, as involving merely the protection of the negative rights of others (such as their civil and political rights). Here I will not argue in favor of a strong or weak interpretation of the commitment to treat others as moral equals. My point is that if the strong cosmopolitan interpretation of moral equality that the moral equality argument employs is not successful in grounding a universal right to immigrate, it is less likely that arguments based on weaker interpretations of moral equality will succeed.

In any case, the question we should ask at this point is: if, as the moral equality argument maintains, we have a moral obligation to do what we can, short of significantly jeopardizing our own well-being, to ensure that all persons have the opportunity for a flourishing life, is upholding immigration as a human right the best way to fulfill this obligation? I believe the answer to this question is no. There are at least four reasons for answering in the negative, which I discuss in turn.

First, when we expand our focus of analysis and see how others besides immigrants are affected by immigration, we realize that people in countries of origin and destination are affected in positive and negative ways by immigration. By regulating migrant flows, we can maximize the positive benefits of migration while minimizing its negative effects for the vulnerable people left behind in countries of origin. Developing countries suffer significant economic harms by the exodus of some of their most skilled and talented workers. Countries of origin in the developing world also miss out on the positive contributions that their most capable and educated citizens can make in reforming their social and political institutions.[4] Thus, the capacity to flourish of the people in the countries of origin will be diminished by the permanent departure of some of their most capable citizens. As we shall see more clearly later, systematically regulating migrant flows so that both developing and developed countries benefit from the opening up of domestic labor markets promotes human flourishing more than recognizing immigration as a human right, because the latter does not link *strategic and controlled* access to these markets with the alleviation of global poverty and the efficacy of the world economic system. In brief, because the obligation to promote human flourishing is owed to everyone and not just to those willing and able to immigrate, we should try to maximize flourishing for all of those affected by immigration policies. Thus, the moral motivation behind the moral equality argument actually militates against the claim that immigration is a right to which everyone is equally entitled.

Second, because regarding immigration as a universal human right does not prioritize access to political communities based on greatest need, it does not adequately address the situation of persons such as refugees. The United Nations 1951 Convention relating to the Status of Refugees defines a refugee as a person who:

> ... owing to a well-founded fear of being persecuted for reasons of race, religion, nationality, membership of a particular social group or political opinion, is outside the country of his nationality and is unable, or owing to such fear, is unwilling, to avail himself of the protection of that country; or who, not having a nationality and being outside the country of his former habitual residence as a result of such events, is unable or, owing to such fear, is unwilling to return to it.[5]

Refugees are in effect people without a political community, i.e. people without an institutional framework within which they can flourish. Since they are completely bereft of the means through which they can flourish, they should have priority in immigrating, at least temporarily, to a political community that can provide them with shelter and secure their human rights. Though they do not necessarily have access to any

[4] For a discussion of these claims, see Devesh Kapur and John McHale, "Should A Cosmopolitan Worry About the 'Brain Drain'?" *Ethics and International Affairs*, 20, no. 3 (2006).

[5] Office of the High Commissioner on Human Rights, "Convention relating to the Status of Refugees," available at: www.unhchr/html/menu3/b/o_c_ref.htm (accessed 1 July, 2007).

political community of their choice, the world community certainly has a collective responsibility to provide them with temporary or, if circumstances require, permanent residence. This collective responsibility could be reasonably construed as arising not only from the cosmopolitan principle regarding the moral worth of all people but also from the debt owed by all political communities to the world's inhabitants for the latter's legitimization of their territorial rights.[6]

The case of refugees shows that if we are concerned with promoting the flourishing of the world's people, political communities should grant priority in admission to those with the least available means for flourishing. Because there are more individuals (besides refugees) wanting to immigrate to countries providing protection[7] than these countries can reasonably accommodate, formulating immigration policies that grant priority to refugees and other needful groups[8] means that political communities need to retain the right to control their borders and deny entrance to other potential immigrants. Once again, this contravenes the claim that immigration should be regarded as a universal human right to which all are equally entitled.

Third, to the extent that political communities observe immigration as a universal right, they will be unable to honor effectively the moral obligations they may have historically incurred through their past actions or the ongoing commitments to which they have bound themselves through political alliances. Failing to live up to these obligations and commitments can affect negatively the flourishing of the members of other political communities. For instance, a colonial legacy of oppressing other peoples may justifiably prompt some countries, as France has done, to grant priority status to immigration applicants from former colonies. Preferential immigration policies like these could be seen as a form of compensatory justice aimed at partially rectifying, however imperfectly and incompletely, the harms done to the political communities from which these immigrants come. Similarly, nations whose foreign policies have placed some members of other political communities in danger have sometimes granted these threatened individuals priority in their immigration policies. The US, for example, after the fall of Saigon in 1975, accepted 125,000 Vietnamese who had

[6] I discuss this important claim below in the section on moral principles to guide immigration policies (p. 237).

[7] I am assuming here that affluent countries would be among the countries of choice for refugees seeking protection.

[8] I discuss some of these other groups below.

worked closely with Americans during the Vietnam War and who feared retaliation from the communist government. And arguably, the US has a special moral responsibility at present to grant priority in immigration to Iraqis who are threatened because of their close collaboration with Americans. Finally, countries may owe special responsibilities to other political communities with whom they have bound themselves through political alliances. For instance, political alliances such as the European Union can create special obligations between political communities that may entail granting priority in immigration to citizens of alliance members.

Fourth, political communities have a moral responsibility to fulfill the promises they have made to their members. Political communities have a history, and that history should be taken into account in identifying their obligations to one another and to individuals. The history of a political community is a collective process in which its members have made economic decisions and contributions, made personal sacrifices, developed reasonable expectations, made life-long commitments, and so forth. All of these aspects of belonging to a political community play an important role in the flourishing of its members. It is questionable, however, whether a political community would be able to fulfill these promises and expectations if everybody in the world had a right to claim membership in that political body. The feasibility of implementing its social welfare policies, for instance, would be seriously undermined if it accepted an influx of immigrants on the scale implied by a policy of open borders.

Even though it is entirely appropriate to call attention to the legitimacy of the conditions under which a political community was formed, as well as the possible compensatory obligations incurred to other political bodies by its support of an unjust international economic and political system, the obligations to its citizens do not entirely disappear if they were made in non-ideal conditions of justice. This is particularly true if some of the members of a political community (especially those with the greatest social welfare needs) did not have the education or the means to readily access sources of information regarding the support provided by their political community to such unjust institutional structures. Assuming that a political community is doing its part in rectifying unjust inequalities between political communities, it seems legitimate for that political community to limit immigration to be able to fulfill its obligations to its own citizens. This is not to deny that rectifying great global inequalities may in some cases override a country's obligation to fulfill the promises made to its own citizens, particularly if that country has played a major role in sustaining such inequalities.[9] The point here is that once a country recognizes and takes steps to rectify these inequalities, it should be acceptable for it to be able to regulate immigration. A policy of open borders, if truly implemented, would in many cases be unsustainable for a self-determining political community.

Immigration and self-governance

In criticizing the moral equality argument, I presented several considerations to show that political communities have good reasons for controlling their borders by regulating immigration. There is another more general objection to the claim that immigration is a human right that I want to discuss before proceeding to the next section of this essay. The objection is that considering immigration as a universal right undermines democratic self-governance. A self-governing political community is one that can formulate and implement decisions that affect the individual and collective well being and flourishing of its members in a number of areas, such as the making of short- and long-term economic policies, the provision of health care, the formulation of educational policies, the promotion of democratic public deliberation, and the protection of cultural liberty. But in a world in which immigration is regarded as a human right, and in which anyone is able to claim membership in any political community, it is unlikely that political communities will be able to effectively formulate and implement collective policies in areas such as these.

It is difficult to see, for example, how a political community could undertake effective long-term planning regarding the use of its natural resources without being able to control the influx of immigrants into its borders. For instance, indigenous communities, some of which are situated in attractive environmental settings with valuable natural resources, would be vulnerable to the influx of outsiders who could

[9] Among the considerations that should be taken into account in analyzing this issue are the following. What is the magnitude of the advantages that its citizens have gained over the citizens of other political communities as result of these unjust systems? To what extent have the citizens of other political communities been hindered in their capacity to flourish as a result of these unjust systems? Precisely what role have these unjust systems played in the creation of the present state of disadvantage of the oppressed political communities?

eventually outnumber the indigenous inhabitants and make decisions to use those resources in ways that run counter to the indigenous peoples' interests. Indigenous peoples, who have used ecological knowledge acquired over hundreds or thousands of years to protect and manage what remains of lands that have been expropriated by outsiders, live in some of the richest areas of biodiversity in the world. The natural resources of these areas of rich biodiversity would be vulnerable to the ecologically unsustainable practices of outsiders interested in their economic exploitation. Indeed, many of the struggles of indigenous peoples throughout the world have centered on their efforts to retain or regain control of the use of the natural resources in their homelands.[10] Proclaiming immigration as a human right would exacerbate the plight of many indigenous peoples, because then anyone could claim membership in their political communities and the concomitant right to make decisions regarding the use of their natural resources.

The difficulties of effective planning regarding use of natural resources if immigration was a human right could be generalized to nation-state economic policy-making writ large. Aspects of economic planning, such as determining an appropriate national savings rate to finance future needs of the country, would be very difficult if not impossible to carry out without reliable projections regarding the size of the population. Dramatic increases in population, or decreases in the case of sending countries, would likely make prior economic calculations inaccurate if not useless. Making reliable projections about future tax revenues would also be difficult, particularly for countries with numerous emigrates. In addition, problems would likely arise for other forms of policy-making. Strategic investment in research and development, for instance, would be difficult without accurate knowledge of what the needs of the political community would be in the future. The formulating of educational policies would also be greatly complicated by a large and sudden increase in the number of immigrants, particularly if they originate from countries with a different language than that used in the country of destination.

In summary, we should note that democratic self-determination is of central importance for people to lead a flourishing life, because the rights and ideals that make such flourishing possible need an institutional context for their implementation. That is, political, civic, social

[10] Hurst Hannum, *Autonomy, Sovereignty, and Self-Determination: The Accommodation of Conflicting Rights* (Philadelphia: University of Pennsylvania Press, 1990).

welfare, and cultural rights, if they are to contribute to a flourishing life, need to be interpreted and maintained within a stable institutional framework. Self-determining political communities provide such institutional frameworks, which are the concrete expression of the right of the members of these communities to govern themselves. Even though human flourishing has priority as a moral good over self-governance, the latter has pragmatic priority because if self-governance is undermined we also undermine the attainment of human flourishing. As I have emphasized in this section, if a political community does not retain the power to regulate entrance and membership, it will not possess the *institutional capacity* to exercise self-governance, and in turn its important functional role in promoting human flourishing will be seriously hindered.

The global labor market argument

Another argument that could justify the claim that immigration is a human right is based on the role that immigration can play in providing access to the global labor market. I will call it the labor market argument. According to this line of reasoning, in a globalized economy in which national boundaries are of decreasing importance for the movement of goods, services, capital, and information, the right to immigrate is necessary for laborers to compete on fair terms in the global labor market. The establishment of the World Trade Organization and the passage of regional trade accords such as the North American Free Trade Agreement have facilitated the participation of capitalists in the global economy with minimal interference from national boundaries. It is only laborers who in most cases are still severely hindered by national immigration barriers. And since economic well-being is of central importance for survival, such barriers represent a serious obstacle to living a flourishing life. Advocates of the global labor market maintain that it is a gross injustice that only laborers, but not owners of capital, continue to be restricted by national borders in an increasingly globalized economy. Thus, the labor market argument concludes, immigration should be regarded as a human right, for freedom to immigrate to the country of one's choice is necessary for laborers to compete on fair terms in the globalized economy by having the liberty to access the available labor markets.

I believe that the opportunity for workers to compete on fair terms in the global economic system is a serious moral imperative that anyone concerned with social justice should address.

Different countries provide such vastly unequal labor opportunities that one's life chances are greatly affected by the countries in which one can work. To the extent national boundaries hinder the capacity of workers to access those labor markets where they can earn a decent living or employ their skills effectively, they are unable to participate on fair terms in the global economy. Likewise, national boundaries make it hard for workers to engage in effective transnational labor bargaining, which would enhance their chances of negotiating for better wages and working conditions. Fair participation, in short, would enable workers to obtain a fair share of the benefits of global economic cooperation, which affects their well-being in fundamental ways.

The global labor market argument rightly underscores the importance of fair participation for all participants in the global economy, but is declaring immigration as a human right the best way to achieve the objectives that fair participation intends to attain? Presumably the point of fair participation in the global economy is to promote the flourishing of the members of political communities, including not only workers but also those who depend on them for their well being, such as children, the elderly, the infirm, and those primarily engaged in non-wage labor. One could see laborers in purely individualistic terms and focus on how fair participation benefits only them as individuals. However, workers do not exist as isolated units, but are social beings that have important connections to their family and community. The amount of remittances sent by immigrants to their country of origin attests to this fact.[11] Moreover, the permanent exodus of workers from a community can undermine the patterns of interaction and human connection that underpin its social cohesion and stability. Thus, in order to properly understand the meaning of fair participation in the global economy we need to take into account the ways such participation affects communities in countries of origin. We will then be in a better position to determine whether declaring immigration as a human right is the best way for the parties involved to attain the benefits of fair participation.

And more generally, as we shall see in what follows, we should understand immigration policies within the context of global justice, because the dilemmas of immigration inevitably involve transnational relations. This means that we should take into account the impact of immigration

[11] The total amount of global remittances to developing countries in 2005 was $150 billion. "Summary of the Report of the Global Commission on International Migration," Global Commission on International Migration, 13 October, 2005, available at: www.gcim.org (accessed 1 July, 2007).

on the needs and interests of the immigrants themselves, the countries of origin, the countries of destination, and even on the global economy as a whole. Examining immigration policies from this broad global perspective insures that we do not place undue focus on only some of the parties affected or factors involved. But in order to properly assess the impact of immigration on the parties affected, we first need to consider some of the major positive and negative effects of immigration.

Positive and negative consequences of immigration

First, immigration provides significant advantages to both immigrants and countries of destination. Laborers throughout the world often migrate to those countries where there are employment sectors in need of more workers. In some European countries, low birth rates and aging national populations have given rise to the need for additional laborers. In some highly industrialized countries, such as the US, there is a need for high-skilled workers in such areas as the health care industry and information technologies. In situations in which immigrants fill positions that national workers are either unable or unwilling to fill, both the destination countries and the new immigrants benefit. Destination countries will fulfill their labor needs, while immigrant workers will typically earn substantially more in highly industrialized countries than in their countries of origin.

Second, labor-driven immigration contributes to total global economic output and increases efficiency. Some studies have estimated that if global immigration levels between 2001 and 2025 turn out to be similar to those during the period between 1997 and 2000, world income will increase by approximately $350 billion. This additional income would be roughly equally divided among countries of destination, countries of origin, and the new immigrants.[12] Immigration also contributes to the more efficient use of high-level technical skills. Highly educated workers from developing countries such as engineers and scientists, for example, who might not be able to utilize their specialized training if they remained in their countries of origin would be able to use their abilities more efficiently by immigrating and being employed in a technologically-advanced society. There is also evidence that cultural diversity can be economically advantageous for societies

[12] Kapur and McHale, "Should A Cosmopolitan Worry About the 'Brain Drain'?"

that manage to promote cooperation between individuals with diverse knowledge and talents.[13]

Third, countries of origin benefit from the labor-driven migration of their citizens. The remittances from workers who have migrated from developing to developed countries constitute a major source of foreign currency inflow for developing countries. In Mexico, for example, remittances from workers who have immigrated to the US constitute the greatest source of national income after sales of petroleum. And at a global level, The United Nations Global Commission on International Migration estimates that about $150 billion in remittances are sent to developing countries every year. In 2005 this figure was three times greater than the total amount of official development assistance received by developing countries.[14] Fourth, returning emigrants provide financial and social capital to their countries. The knowledge, contacts, and experiences of returning emigrants can provide entrepreneurial impetus to the economy of their home country while improving its institutions.

While recognizing that labor-driven immigration has its positive effects, there are also significant negative consequences of global migration. First, developing nations are harmed by the magnitude of the exodus of their citizens with a higher education. For instance, the emigration rate in 2000 of skilled individuals from the Caribbean region was forty-one per cent, from Western Africa twenty-seven per cent, from Latin America sixteen per cent, and from Central Africa thirteen per cent. The skilled emigration rates for the Caribbean countries of Grenada, Jamaica, and Haiti were above eighty per cent and for the African countries of Cape Verde they were sixty-eight per cent, Mauritius fifty-six per cent, Sierra Leone fifty-two per cent, and Ghana forty-seven per cent.[15] One problem with these high emigration rates for skilled individuals is that the developing countries from which they left lose the investment they made in their educational and human development. Further, as Devesh Kapur and John McHale have pointed

[13] Ajay Agrawal, Devesh Kapur, and John McHale, "Birds of a Feather – Better Together? How Co-Ethnicity and Co-Location Influence Knowledge Flow Patterns" (paper presented at CEA 40th Annual Meeting, Concordia University, Montreal, May 26–28, 2006).

[14] "Summary of the Report of the Global Commission on International Migration," Global Commission on International Migration, 13 October, 2005, available at: www.gcim.org (accessed 1 July, 2007).

[15] Kapur and McHale, "Should A Cosmopolitan Worry About the 'Brain Drain'?" p. 306–07.

out in their empirical and normative study of immigration, it is the more highly educated and talented individuals who are most likely to improve domestic institutions and to promote democratization.[16] It is the better-educated and more internationally marketable individuals who are likely to bring about positive economic, social, and political changes in their home countries. In addition, emigration of some of the most enterprising citizens might lessen the pressure on the leaders of developing countries to carry out much needed economic and political reforms. In short, it is difficult to overestimate the negative impact of immigration on countries of origin, because many developing countries desperately need the contributions of their most skilled and talented citizens.

Second, some of the most negative consequences of immigration take place when it is unregulated, that is, when it is illegal. Human smuggling, the sexual abuse of women, economic exploitation, and injury or death are major ways in which immigrants suffer when they have to resort to illegal means of entrance. Because they are living in the country of destination illegally, undocumented immigrants are often outside of the protection of the law. This means that they are susceptible to abuse by criminals, unscrupulous employers, and others who recognize their vulnerability. Moreover, when immigration is illegal it is more likely to fracture families and undermine community solidarity in countries of origin. Since immigrants cannot readily visit their families and communities because of their illegal status, the social fabric of their communities is often frayed by their extended absence. If countries were to adopt the policy suggestions I make below, illegal immigration would be greatly diminished, because potential illegal immigrants would know that most of the jobs available in the country of destination have already been filled with legalized immigrants.

Third, low-skilled workers in countries of destination are likely to suffer from increased competition from low-skilled immigrants. These are the workers who have less leverage in relation to management and capital and are more readily replaceable. Typically, low-skilled immigrants are willing to work for lower wages than native-born workers since these wages are likely to be substantially higher than what they would be paid for similar labor in their countries of origin. Low-skilled immigrants are also likely to be willing to work under more trying conditions than low-skilled native-born workers. To be sure, there is some

[16] *Ibid.*, p. 312.

disagreement among researchers regarding the extent to which native-born workers are harmed by competition from low-skilled immigrants, but nevertheless there seems to be general agreement that the former lose out when there are more labour-supply factors that place downward pressure on wages.

Moral principles to guide immigration policies

Now that we have observed some of the positive and negative effects of global immigration on the different parties involved, I briefly outline two moral principles that should guide the formulation of just immigration policies. Given limitations of space, here I can do no more than provide a preliminary account of these two principles. The first of these is the principle of the moral equality of all human beings. As indicated earlier, this principle can be interpreted in a number of ways. In contrast to our earlier discussion of the moral equality argument for immigration as a human right, where I used a strong interpretation of this principle, here we need only rely on a weak interpretation.[17] The strong interpretation involved a corollary moral obligation to maximize human flourishing for all people, but I propose that our commitment to treating immigrants as moral equals be more normatively limited and center on the protection of their human rights. If the concept of democratic self-governance is to remain meaningful, we must leave room for the possibility that in some cases we can have stronger moral obligations to our fellow nationals than to those who are not full members of our political community. Setting as a minimal standard the protection of the human rights of all people within the territorial boundaries of political communities indicates our respect for immigrants' moral dignity as human beings while also respecting the capacity of these political communities to determine the scope of democratic governance and accountability. This capacity for self-determination manifests itself in the morally principled determination of rights for immigrants with different legal status.

[17] We will recall that in criticizing the moral equality argument I employed a strong interpretation of moral equality that involved a commitment to do what we can to promote the flourishing of all people. My purpose in using the strong interpretation was to show that if this interpretation of the principle failed to show that immigration is a human right, weaker interpretations were even more likely to fail. Generally speaking, it is harder to defend successfully a strong than a weak interpretation of this principle, so my use of a weaker interpretation here should make it at least relatively easier for my proposals to be deemed acceptable.

The human rights to which long-term or permanent resident immigrants are entitled should include: security rights that protect them against crimes such as murder, rape, and torture; liberty rights that protect freedom of thought, expression, association, religion, and so forth; due process rights that protect them from such abuses as arbitrary detention, denial of legal representation, and discriminatory application of the law; and social welfare rights that involve provision of such goods as medical care, education, and basic food needs. Because denial of the opportunity for citizenship to long-term or permanent resident immigrants is, as we saw at the beginning of this essay, incompatible with basic principles of democratic self-governance, these immigrants should be placed on the road to citizenship. Once citizenship is obtained they should of course enjoy the political rights associated with full membership in a political community, such as voting, establishing political parties, and running for office. Even before citizenship is attained, however, long-term or permanent resident immigrants should be granted political rights as these apply at the local and regional levels, because these rights provide an important degree of self-determination while promoting political integration through the reinforcement of civic responsibility and political identity. Granting such political rights to non-citizens could be seen as a compromise between alien status and complete civic integration into a political community. We should note that countries in the European Union (EU) grant EU nationals from other member countries political rights at the local and regional levels and that certain EU countries – such as Denmark, Finland, and Sweden – even grant some immigrant non-EU nationals voting rights at the local level.[18]

For immigrants who have not been granted the status of long-term or permanent residents, such as guest workers or asylum seekers, it is acceptable for a political community to restrict their access to those specific rights associated with collective self-governance, such as voting in national elections, establishing political parties, and running for office. Since their long-term status has not been determined, a political community does not have the obligation to grant them all of the

[18] Ruby Gropas, "Immigrants, political rights, and democracy in the EU," ELIAMEP, 29 June, 2007, available at: www.eliamep.gr/eliamep/content/home/media/opinions/latest_opinions/immigrants_eu/en/ (accessed 1 July, 2007) and Kees Groenendijk, "Local Voting Rights for Non-Nationals in Europe," MPI, April, 2008, available at: www.migrationpolicy.org/transatlantic/docs/Groenendijk-FINAL.pdf (accessed 28 February, 2009).

same privileges as permanent or long-term members of the community. These immigrants, however, should still be granted the security, liberty, due process, and social welfare rights described above because these are essential for their continual security and well-being.

Regarding illegal immigrants, advocating rights and protections for this group can be a difficult position to take when people in countries of destination see them as threatening outsiders who are breaking the law by invading their national territory to further their self-interest. These negative feelings can be exacerbated if their ethnicity, language, or religion is different from that of the majority society. But it is in situations like these that the commitment by Western societies to human rights is really put to the test. Western nations often severely criticize other countries when they fail to respect the human rights of their minority groups, and implicit in these criticisms is the notion that people are entitled to human rights regardless of their ethnicity, religious background, nationality, or other form of group affiliation. It would therefore be inconsistent for Western countries to refuse to recognize the basic human rights of illegal immigrants. If all people deserve to have their human rights respected, they merit this consideration by virtue of their status as human beings and not because of their membership in a particular political community. This implies that even people who have entered a country illegally should have their human rights respected. The implementation of this normative principle would insure that immigrants, regardless of their legal status in their country of destination, would enjoy the security, liberty, due process, and social welfare rights described above. These protections and entitlements are particularly important for illegal immigrants, who are often vulnerable to exploitation by employers as well as human traffickers and other criminals. Nevertheless, illegal immigrants would still be subject to deportation, but only if their due process rights have been respected.[19]

The second moral principle to guide the formulation of fair immigration policies is what I call the historically-grounded principle of fair participation. As we shall see, violations of the terms of fair participation create moral obligations to address the primary root cause of

[19] Typically, due process with regard to immigration may involve such rights as a hearing before an immigration judge, legal representation, and a reasonable opportunity for evidence review. In the US it also includes in most cases review by a federal court. For a summary of immigration rights in the US, see "The Rights of Immigrants," ACLU Immigrants' Rights Project, 9 August, 2000, available at: www.aclu.org/immigrants/gen/11713pub20000908.html (accessed 1 July, 2007).

immigration pressures, namely, global economic inequalities. Since the global economic system is a cooperative enterprise involving significant benefits and costs, it is reasonable to require that those involved participate on fair terms.[20] The principle of fair participation recognizes that individuals as well as political communities participate in the global economic system and that both individuals and communities gain benefits, bear costs, and make contributions to this system. The moral obligation for all parties involved in this cooperative enterprise to participate on fair terms derives from several considerations. First, the well-being of participants is affected in fundamental ways by their participation in the global economy. In fact, their flourishing and very survival may depend on how they fare within this economic system. Further, global economic integration is now at a point where participation by the vast majority of the world's people in the global economy is hardly voluntary. Under these joint circumstances, requiring fairness in the conditions and rules of participation seems reasonable.

Second, and perhaps more important, the participants in the global economic system owe one another mutual fair treatment because of the moral reciprocity embodied in the conditional legitimacy of the territorial rights of sovereign states. If we start with the eminently reasonable assumption that all people in principle should have access to the world's land and natural resources to satisfy their basic needs and flourish, an important question arises: What justifies the territorial powers of nation-states? What justifies sovereign countries to say to the world community that they have exclusive control of that part of nature that constitutes their national territory and that they have the right to use force if necessary to limit who can access this territory? The territorial powers of nation-states are powerful rights that underpin immigration policies and yet they are rarely critically examined by political philosophers. By neglecting to consider that nation-states were typically formed through conquest, invasive settlement, or bargaining between imperial powers, the legitimacy of the territorial powers of nation-states has remained largely unchallenged. Even on those rare occasions in which such territories were settled peacefully and without the displacement of pre-existing communities, their unconditional legitimacy is still questionable given that the settling political community did not

[20] See Charles Beitz, *Political Theory and International Relations* (Princeton: Princeton University Press, 1989), for a related discussion of global justice based on a scheme of cooperative participation.

obtain the consent of the world's people to validate their exclusive territorial powers.

What do these observations imply about the legitimacy of the territorial powers of nation-states and the concomitant right to police their borders? We could insist on the implementation of ideal justice and demand a global redistribution of land and natural resources to the world's people on an equitable basis. However, even if an ideally fair, equitable basis for distribution could be found (a highly dubious assumption), there are insurmountable practical obstacles to this suggestion. We cannot start from scratch, and at this point in human history it is simply not feasible to carry out a massive global relocation of the world's people to satisfy an abstract ideal of justice. So we must find a morally-principled position that acknowledges that, even though the territorial powers of nation-states are not morally unconditioned, they can play an important functional role in using the resources of the Earth to promote the flourishing of the world's people.

We could maintain that territorial powers enable nation-states to develop and administer the Earth's land and natural resources. A high degree of institutionalized and informal coordination is needed to extract, refine, and utilize the Earth's natural resources. Nation-states make possible, for example, the complex systems of property ownership, finance, and contract law that make efficient production possible. They are administrative units that take advantage of economies of scale while maintaining production processes within manageable institutional contexts. Barring a global government that would control and administer the Earth's land and natural resources, self-governing political communities with territorial powers would appear to be a reasonable alternative.[21] Moreover, nation-states also provide the institutional frameworks within which civil, political, socioeconomic, and cultural rights are articulated and implemented. These institutional frameworks provide the stable political contexts within which people exercise the self-governance needed to deal with the innumerable and sometimes unforeseeable problems they face individually and collectively.

[21] Note that I am not committing myself to the claim that nation-states are the ideal form of political community. Indeed, there are reasons to think that more decentralized forms of political organization would have advantages over nation-states (on this issue, see Thomas Pogge, *World Poverty and Human Rights* (Malden, Mass.: Polity Press, 2002), pp. 181–95). My point here is that since we cannot start from scratch and since nation-states are likely to persist for the foreseeable future, it is appropriate to take them as the relevant units of analysis for a theory of justice that has a realistic chance of implementation.

This instrumentalist defense of the territorial powers of nation-states and of political borders is a move in the right direction. Having nation-states with territorial powers functioning as distinct administrative units to develop the Earth's natural resources for the benefit of their members and, through global trade, for all of the world's people appears reasonable.[22] The next step is to show how this qualified defense of the territorial powers of nation-states generates moral obligations among nation-states that have implications for just immigration policies. We can begin by noticing that this instrumentalist defense does not acknowledge the debt incurred by nation-states to the world community for the latter's recognition of their territorial powers and what this might imply for inter-state moral obligations. Neither does it take into account that nature does not distribute good land and valuable natural resources evenly nor that some nation-states ended up with less valuable natural resources as a result of the historically contingent and the unjust processes of nation-state formation. Also, it does not recognize how a legacy of inter-state domination played a role in bringing about the present diminished capacity of some nation-states to flourish. My suggestion is to regard the territorial powers of nation-states as *conditional* rights, that is, as rights whose legitimacy depends on nation-states respecting certain conditions affecting the flourishing of other political communities and their people. These conditions should take into account the considerations just mentioned. More specifically, the continued legitimacy of the territorial powers of nation-states should be contingent on their observance of at least the following provisions: (1) providing aid to those nation-states and political communities that possess a scarcity of valuable natural resources; (2) compensating nation-states and political communities who were subjected

[22] Perhaps the single most important economic principle justifying international trade is the principle of comparative advantage. According to this principle, countries should produce and sell those commodities that they can most efficiently produce – given their natural resources, technological development, and human knowledge and skills – and use the money to trade for the commodities they need. According to this principle, this global division of labor will work to everyone's advantage since it maximizes efficiency and productivity. There might be reason to doubt whether this principle works to everyone's advantage in the way mainstream economics maintains. Nevertheless, most nation-states and other political communities do specialize in creating those commodities they are relatively better at producing and thus provide the world population with many commodities their own country would not be able to produce in an efficient manner. In this way we could say that nation-states and other political communities contribute to the total available output of commodities (and increasingly, services as well).

to internal and external forms of colonial oppression; and (3) refraining from, and compensating for, the imposition of an unjust international economic system. These provisions could be seen as components of a principle of fair participation to guide the global cooperative enterprise in which all political communities are engaged.

Given limitations of space, I cannot examine these provisions in detail here.[23] The crucial point is that nation-states are bound in a strong *non-discretionary* form of moral reciprocity with the world community by the latter's recognition of their territorial powers, and that nation-states in response have a positive duty to treat other nation-states and political communities in a just manner.[24] The particular form of just treatment to which nation-states are committed centers on safeguarding and promoting the capacity of the members of other political communities to flourish individually and collectively. And this is as it should be, for the purpose of granting nation-states their territorial powers in the first place was to make possible the individual and collective flourishing of their members. Within this framework, immigration policies could be seen as instrumental mechanisms to promote the just treatment and flourishing of the world's people and their communities. Of course, fair immigration policies are not sufficient for bringing about global justice, but they should be systematically integrated into the economic and social development policies for developing nations.

In the next section I describe briefly some of the immigration policy recommendations that can plausibly follow from the moral equality principle we have discussed and a historically-based principle of fair participation.[25] I should emphasize that these briefly-outlined

[23] I discuss these and other provisions in Jorge Valadez, *Deliberative Democracy, Political Legitimacy, and Self-Determination in Multicultural Societies*, (Boulder, CO: Westview Press, 2001), pp. 277–84. For a discussion of similar global obligations of nation-states, see Thomas Pogge, *World Poverty and Human Rights*, ch. 8.

[24] We should note that nation-states could not opt out of this bond of moral reciprocity, for their very status as distinct and legitimate sovereign countries depends on their territorial powers.

[25] Before moving to the next section we should note the advantages of the principle of fair participation as a non-neoRawlsian principle for global justice. First, it is based on the notion of moral reciprocity, which is practically a universal moral notion (see George Lakoff and Mark Johnson, *Philosophy in the Flesh: The Embodied Mind and its Challenge to Western Thought* (New York: Basic Books, 1999, pp. 290–334)). The idea that you owe a moral debt to someone who has given you something of positive value and that you should reciprocate in turn is a central moral principle in all known cultures. This is in stark contrast to the extremely abstract form of moral reasoning grounding Rawls's second principle of justice, which is highly controversial and derives from a very

recommendations are of a preliminary, tentative, and not exhaustive character.

Policy recommendations

Provide compensation to developing countries for the loss of high-skill workers. Since one of the most serious ways in which developing countries are harmed is by the exodus of their high-skilled workers to affluent countries, the latter should provide compensation to the developing countries from which these workers originate. This recommendation can be justified by the principle of fair participation, since under current conditions destination countries benefit freely from the investments in educational and human development made by countries of origin. This recommendation also promotes global productivity and efficiency, since high-level skills that might not be used in developing countries can be usefully employed in developed countries. However, this recommendation needs to be implemented in conjunction with the others proposed here, so that affluent countries do not continuously draw away the most talented and skilled people from developing countries.

Establish procedures to regulate and increase low-skilled immigrant flows. Regulating the immigration of low-skilled workers would grant

specific cultural tradition. Assuming that we are interested in implementing our theories of global justice, it should matter if they complement the ways a culturally-diverse world actually understands morality. Second, a consideration that any moral theorist must take seriously when proposing ways to rectify global economic inequalities is that the global economic system is capitalist and that this fundamental feature of the global economy, while of course amenable to reform, is unlikely to change. A Rawlsian conception of justice, with its emphasis on institutional reforms to redistribute what individuals have attained through their investments, risk-taking, and efforts, runs counter to the central capitalist conviction that people are entitled to what they have worked for. In contrast, a historically-grounded principle of fair participation, by recognizing the conditions of fair participation and the contributions made by different participants to the effective functioning of the economic system, is more compatible with basic tenets of the market system. Third, by focusing on the particular roles played and the different contributions made by different participants to economic systems, the principle of fair participation enables us to identify uncompensated and devalued reproductive labor, which in all societies is performed primarily by women. This form of labor plays a major role in domestic economies, and by extension, the global economic system. The fair participation principle, by emphasizing the empirical conditions of participation in actual economic activity, helps us identify hidden forms of economic injustice by directing our attention to the social systems in which such activity actually takes place. Rawls's theory, by focusing on the highly theoretical scenario of the original position, draws our attention away from the empirical contexts in which we actually identity injustices and *understand their nature.*

them legal status and bring them under protection of the law, thus reducing the potential for their exploitation. Increasing the number of low-skilled immigrants would address the labor needs of Western countries while providing work to some of the many unemployed laborers in developing countries. Care must be taken, however, to provide both the immigrants and national workers with labor bargaining rights so that businesses do not exploit the greater willingness of economically desperate immigrants to work for low wages under poor working conditions. Legalization of all immigrants is justified by the moral equality principle that advocates that everyone's human rights be protected under the law. Moreover, increasing low-skilled migrant flows enhances the fairness of conditions of participation in the global economy for some of the world's poor.

Affluent countries should provide development aid to poor countries. This development aid would help alleviate the economic desperation that often drives immigration, particularly illegal immigration. It would thus address the root cause of labor-driven immigration. Further, this aid could be seen as a form of compensation for the role that affluent countries have played in the creation of this economic desperation. For example, rich countries often provide their farmers with huge subsidies that drive Third World farmers out of business and compel them to emigrate to make a living. Affluent countries also often protect some of their domestic industries from competition from developing countries. Development funds should be tied to accountability measures to minimize the possibility that they will be appropriated by corrupt officials in developing countries and to make such aid more politically acceptable in the affluent countries. This recommendation could be justified by the principle of fair participation, since it involves a form of compensatory justice to developing countries for the harm done by developed countries through their economic policies, which have made it very difficult for poor countries to compete on fair terms. The fair participation principle could also ground the special obligation of some affluent countries to provide aid to former colonies. The reasoning here is that part of the reason former colonies cannot compete on fair terms in the global economy is due to the historical injustices perpetrated against them by some affluent countries.

There should be a greater emphasis on temporary migration. When immigrants return to their country of origin, they help their country greatly with their knowledge, contacts, experience, and capital. When destination countries use fixed-term work visas and immigrants know that they are likely to return, their connections to their families and communities are likely to be strengthened and this will enhance the contributions they can make to their home country. Destination and origin countries should cooperate in devising programs to strengthen the bonds between immigrants and those left behind, such as reductions in the cost of remittances, dual citizenship, and civic improvement programs in which money contributed by immigrants to civic improvements are matched by local, state, and federal governments.[26] This recommendation could be justified by the principle of fair participation, which advocates that we should promote the participation of all countries in the global economy on more equal terms.

In brief, we can observe that these recommendations can harness the potential of global migration to help alleviate the plight of poor countries without having to make the dubious claim that immigration is a human right.

Response to Spijkerboer

I conclude by responding to claims made by Thomas Spijkerboer in his chapter within this book concerning the relevance of the debate between cosmopolitans and defenders of sovereignty over the issue of border controls. Spijkerboer maintains that the real or truly significant issue regarding immigration is not the justification of border controls, but the status of aliens who are already within state boundaries. He argues that by focusing almost exclusively on the issue of whether the control of national borders is justified, cosmopolitans and defenders of sovereignty draw attention away from the truly important issue of how to deal with aliens who are already part of the national community. In support of his position, he argues that the irrelevance of the cosmopolitan/sovereignty debate as a principled and substantive disagreement is revealed by the fact that the cosmopolitan and the sovereignty defender end up in the same place, namely, justifying the status quo of border control. According to Spijkerboer, the cosmopolitan/sovereignty debate leads us to ask the wrong question and to neglect the real issue, which is that of redistribution of rights within national communities.

[26] For a brief discussion of how these measures might be implemented, see Kapur and McHale, "Should A Cosmopolitan Worry About the 'Brain Drain'?," p. 319.

Regarding his claim that the real issue concerning immigration is not the justifiability of border controls but the status of aliens already living within national communities, it should be pointed out that he does not provide compelling reasons for why only the latter issue but not the former is important. We can certainly recognize that the issue of the status of aliens is significant without denying that the justification of border controls is also important. Spijkerboer seems to set up a false dilemma in which only one, but not both, of these issues can be important. He may be correct in insisting that a great deal of attention has been paid to border controls while the question of how to deal with aliens living within our midst has been neglected, but this does not establish that only one of these issues is important.

Evidently, what motivates Spijkerboer to think that only the issue of the status of aliens is important is that the two principal positions in the border control debate end up agreeing with one another. In spite of starting from very different positions with a different set of premises, the cosmopolitan and the sovereignty positions end up supporting the legitimacy of border controls. Apparently he takes this as evidence for the irrelevance and unimportance of the border control issue. I believe, however, that it is a mistake to reach this conclusion from the fact that the cosmopolitan and the sovereignty defender provide support for the status quo position of border control. In the first place, strictly speaking it is not true that the cosmopolitan and the sovereignty defender reach the same conclusion regarding border regulation. While the sovereignty defender would presumably tolerate highly selective or restrictive immigration policies, the cosmopolitan would favor only those immigration restrictions necessary to prevent serious threats to security or public order.

Second, it is crucial to examine more closely the different rationales that the cosmopolitan and the sovereignty defender employ in supporting border controls. While border regulation seems straightforwardly consistent with the position of the sovereignty advocate, the cosmopolitan's recognition that real-world constraints entail the acceptance of border controls reveals a problem with the process of institutionalizing cosmopolitan principles in immigration policies. Simply because both positions end up legitimizing border regulation does not mean that both positions are equally capable of providing a theoretically consistent justification of border controls. Once we see that the rationales for border control employed by the cosmopolitan and sovereignty defender have different degrees of theoretical coherence with the background assumptions of these approaches, we will not be inclined to regard the fact that they both support border regulation as evidence for the irrelevance of the border control issue.

It is also important to recognize that Spijkerboer considers only two possible opposing approaches that can be taken in the border control debate, and that there may be other approaches, such as the one I have formulated here, for justifying the regulation of national borders. My position could be seen as striking a middle ground between the cosmopolitan and sovereignty positions. I maintain that border regulation enables countries to effectively carry out their functions as administrative units to develop the Earth's natural resources within the context of self-governing political communities. I did not employ, however, Walzer's questionable argument that border controls are justified because they are necessary for the maintenance of national cultures. On the other hand, even though I used the cosmopolitan principle of showing equal moral concern for all people as a basis for developing just immigration policies, I argued that a straightforward cosmopolitan interpretation of this principle as implying a universal human right of immigration is a mistake, because, among other things, it would likely worsen the living conditions of some of the world's most vulnerable people. I maintained that numerous historical and existing complexities and inequalities make it unjustifiable to institutionalize immigration policies which treat everyone equally, regardless of their particular needs or our historically-incurred special obligations to them. Just and morally-principled immigration policies presuppose regulated entry and take into account the reciprocal moral obligations which nation-states owe one another.

In summary, Spijkerboer does not establish convincingly that only the issue of the status of aliens living in national communities is relevant and important, while the issue of the justification of border controls is not. He fails to show that the cosmopolitan/sovereignty debate, simply because both position end up legitimizing the status quo, renders the issue of border controls irrelevant. The issue of border regulation is of great significance and, as I have shown here, it is possible to articulate a position on this issue that provides guidance on just immigration policies that grant national interests their proper important place while remaining faithful to the principle that all human beings are worthy of equal moral concern.

11

A distributive approach to migration law: or the convergence of communitarianism, libertarianism, and the status quo

THOMAS SPIJKERBOER

In this chapter, I will argue that the debate about cosmopolitanism vs. sovereignty can only be considered as a relevant debate if the wrong questions are asked – at least in my field of expertise, migration law. The question which is at the heart of this debate in migration law (under which circumstances should aliens be admitted) is a false one. In my view, the issue is not the just distribution of membership. Instead, the debate is mostly about the position of aliens who are in the community already, and whom the community prefers to consider as non-members, or even as non-entities. If it would be acknowledged that the aliens whose position is being discussed are already in the community, it would become clear that their position can either be debated under the rubric of admission, or under the rubric of redistribution. The obsessive way in which the redistribution option is ignored suggests that the (ideological, material, and/or other) stakes for debating migration under the admission rubric are high.

I will start out by sketching very briefly two poles of the debate, namely the communitarians who defend State sovereignty, and the libertarians who defend a basic human right of international migration. At first sight, the libertarians seem to be the real cosmopolitans, because they criticize migration control because it leads to a situation in which the interests of foreigners carry less weight than those of nationals. However, as soon as the libertarians are confronted with concrete border control issues, their initial moral position is compromised by the institutional setting.[1] On the other hand, the communitarians defend state sovereignty on the basis of the equal value of persons, i.e. on a

[1] It might be added that not all self-identified cosmopolitans share Carens' idea that a consistent application of liberal political theories to migration requires open borders, see the contribution of Valades in this volume.

central tenet of moral cosmopolitanism. In other words: both positions are fundamentally unstable.

I will then address two cases. The first one at first sight is about a quintessential admission issue, being the control of European borders. I will sketch the issue, and see what communitarians and libertarians might have to say about it. The second issue is more easily reconstructed as a redistribution issue, being the position of migrant domestic workers. I will again see what the two different approaches have to say about that.

In a final and tentative part, I will argue that the two approaches end up in the same place. They both legitimate existing immigration schemes. The suggestion that there is a principled debate between the two schools while, upon closer look, there barely is one contributes to this legitimation. I will then argue that immigration issues can also be considered as issues of redistribution within communities, and that this change of register substantially affects issues of legitimacy. In short: in the debate as it stands, we are asking the wrong question, and for a reason. The legitimacy of migration controls rests upon a particular construction of the debate.

The debate[2]

Communitarianism: Michael Walzer[3]

In many discussions about migration control from a political philosophy perspective, one chapter from Walzer's *Spheres of Justice* is taken as a starting point.[4] The attraction of his approach lies partly in its context. His view is part of a larger whole, promoting a progressive liberal agenda. Another part of the attraction lies in Walzer's style. He clearly indicates his hesitations and the limits of his theory. This combination

[2] See for another overview, focussing on asylum, Matthew J. Gibney, *The Ethics and Politics of Asylum. Liberal Democracy and the Response to Refugees*, (Cambridge: Cambridge University Press, 2004).

[3] Walzer, *Spheres of Justice. A Defense of Pluralism and Equality*, (New York: Basic Books, 1983). I have also relied on discussions of Walzer in J.H.M.M. Tholen, *Vreemdelingenbeleid en Rechtvaardigheid?* [Justice in Migration Policy?] Diss. KU Nijmegen (1997), esp. ch. 2; Seyla Benhabib, *The Rights of Others. Aliens, Residents and Citizens*, (Cambridge: Cambridge University Press, 2004), ch. 3; Linda Bosniak, *The Citizen and the Alien. Dilemma's of Contemporary Membership*, (Princeton: Princeton University Press), esp. ch. 3.

[4] Walzer, *Spheres of Justice*, pp. 31–63.

of form and content gives him an eminently reasonable persona which is hard to resist.

Nevertheless, his approach is pretty straightforward. Walzer starts from the presumption that the political community, aka the State, is the appropriate framework for realizing a just society. He finds this presumption justified because redistribution presupposes a community within which redistribution takes place, and a community requires boundaries. If such boundaries are not maintained by States, they will be created by local communities. It is preferable that boundaries are put in place at the national level, because that increases freedom of movement compared to the local alternative, and because this allows for a wider community. A community is only a community if its members share a way of life, if it is a community of character. Because the maintenance of such a community requires closure, in principle States are free to control immigration in ways they think fit to maintain the community's nature. There is a limited exception in the case of forced migrants. Especially when they have already reached the territory of a State, they should not be returned to places where they face serious danger (except if they turn up in such numbers that admission would endanger the community). Walzer admits that he does not know why forced migrants who have not yet reached the territory of a country should not be protected. That does not prevent him, however, from concluding that "the right to restrain the flow remains a feature of communal self-determination."[5] The ethical principle he has identified "can only modify and not transform admission policies rooted in a particular community's understanding of itself." Walzer does address the question whether, if the differences in wealth between countries are enormous, communities may be required to admit necessitous aliens because these communities have more wealth than they reasonably need. He argues that if there were an obligation to admit aliens on that ground, communal wealth would be subject to infinite drainage and would, in fact, cease to be communal. Therefore, the obligation he is willing to admit is one to export superfluous wealth, not to limit the right of the wealthy community to decide about admission.

However, once aliens have been admitted, they should be treated as members of the community, and should be granted full rights. Immigrants should be at least potential citizens, and they should be able to become citizens after a relatively short period. Walzer finds it

[5] Walzer, *Spheres of Justice*, p. 51.

unacceptable that people are subject to political decisions in which they cannot participate. Walzer does not clearly address the issue of to what extent an interim status (between alien and citizen) is acceptable. He rejects the notion, but at the same time allows for it because he understands not every migrant can immediately be granted citizenship status.

Walzer's arguments have been debated extensively. Two main lines of critique can be distinguished. First, cosmopolitans have criticized the presumption that justice requires bounded communities. This presumption is a manoeuvre comparable to Rawls's claim that his construction of justice can only function within national States. But in fact, these critics hold, national States can be (and are) instrumental in an unjust distribution of resources among States.[6] A second line of critique accepts that communities are necessary for organized solidarity, but criticizes the thick notion of community Walzer uses. Less substantive, and hence more open notions would lead to different outcomes (Kymlicka[7]).

In our context, however, the most problematic aspect of Walzer's theory is that he stops short of the crucial issue. His picture of some communities possessing infinite wealth, while many other communities face destitution is an accurate description of the background of today's mass migration. He argues that wealthy communities should export wealth. But what if they don't? Walzer develops a plausible approach for a non-existing situation, being a situation in which wealth is distributed among countries in a more or less justifiable way. That is not a situation which actually exists.

Another problem is that Walzer presumes that Western countries are based on Keynesian presumptions. His approach is plausible if one of the main aims of States is the equitable internal distribution of wealth among its members. However, many argue that around 1980 (ironically, the period in which Walzer wrote his book, which was published in 1983) this ceased to be the dominant paradigm. Since then, States have increasingly sought to make their economies competitive compared to others, often at the expense of internal redistribution (e.g. Sassen[8]). If the communities within which redistribution takes place

[6] E.g. Peter Singer and Renata Singer, "The Ethics of Refugee Policy," in *Open Borders? Closed Societies? The Ethical and Political Issues*, ed. Mark Gibney (Westwood: Greenwood Press, 1988).

[7] For example Will Kymlicka, *Multicultural Citizenship* (Oxford: Clarendon Press, 1995).

[8] Saskia Sassen, "*Territory, Authority, Rights: from Medieval to Global Assemblages*" (Princeton: Princeton University Press, 2006).

are not predominantly or not only national, then Walzer's arguments loose much of their force.

Libertariansm: Joseph Carens

In his plea for open borders, Joseph Carens has responded to the main objections to free migration.[9] The first, based on the property rights of settled citizens, is incorrect because the property approach is based on the *individual* right to property. Restrictions on free migration have to be based on the property right of citizens as a collective; as individuals the regulation of migration restricts them in their property rights because in many cases they cannot sell their property to foreigners, they cannot enter into labor contracts, and so on. Individual property cannot legitimate collective protection. Second, a Rawlsian position cannot justify migration controls, because if we did not know our place of birth, or the particular society we are members of, we would agree that there should be no restrictions on migration (because we may fall in love with a foreigner, seek better opportunities abroad, and so on). However, thirdly, if we move from the ideal world of Rawlsian theory to the non-ideal world, Rawlsian ethics may allow for restrictions if there is a reasonable expectation that unlimited migration would damage public order. The exclusion of people on the basis of national security may be justified, according to Carens, but it should be applied restrictively. Also, restrictions on migration may be justified in order to limit the number of immigrants. Free migration might lead to rich countries being overwhelmed by migrants from poor countries. Carens states that this justifies some restriction, but writes (without any indication of the basis of that statement) that this would surely imply a much less restrictive policy than the one currently in force.

In fact, Carens accepts the two crucial arguments for restricting immigration: national security; and economic well-being, including presumably the protection of national welfare arrangements. He seems to find existing migration-control regimes illegitimate, but this seems to be first and foremost an empirical issue. National security should not be used expansively; the economic well-being of Western countries requires less restrictions that the ones that presently apply.

[9] Joseph H. Carens, "Aliens and Citizens: The Case for Open Borders," *Review of Politics* 49 (1987), pp. 251–73.

Carens' approach is vulnerable to two criticisms. First, he presents his critique of existing legitimations of immigration restrictions as a matter of principle. In fact he agrees on the principles but has some reservations about the empirical arguments for the present arrangements. Second, because he does not acknowledge his objections as empirical ones, he does not deign to give empirical arguments. Thus, his critique is unfounded in the sense that he does not provide us with arguments to follow him in his conclusions. Although his tone is quite radical, he accepts the grounds on which immigration is restricted. He thinks they do not apply, but does not explain why. However, the context of his theory becomes clearer when one realises that the focus of his argument seems to be on migration between rich countries. He has argued that the situation for Wisconsin and Illinois (no migration restrictions) is comparable to the situation between the United States and Canada (where there are migration restrictions).[10]

Two cases

After this outline of the two dominant normative approaches to the legitimacy of migration control, I want to look at two concrete instances of migration control, and investigate how communitarianism and universalism relate to them. The two cases are radically different, and intentionally so. The first case concerns the rising number of fatalities resulting from increased border control in Europe. Can these human costs of border control be justified by either approach? The second case concerns the position of domestic workers in Dutch migration law. Migration law weakens their positions vis-à-vis their employers; can this be justified by either approach?

The human costs of border control[11]

Traveling to Europe without the explicit consent of European migration authorities has become increasingly difficult for people who do not have the nationality of a limited number of countries, such as the US,

[10] Joseph H. Carens, "Migration and Morality: A Liberal Egalitarian Perspective," in *Free Movement: Ethical Issues in the Transnational Migration of People and Money*, ed. B. Barry and R. Goodin (New York: Harvester Wheatsheaf, 1992), as quoted in Gibney, *The Ethics and Politics of Asylum*, p. 74.

[11] See more extensively my "The Human Costs of Border Control," *European Journal of Migration and Law*, 9 (2007), pp. 127–39. I will refrain from footnoting this paragraph;

Canada, New Zealand, Australia, and Japan. The introduction of visa obligations for a large number of countries, combined with immigration controls before departure (typically by airline personnel), has made irregular long-distance travel by air difficult, and therefore expensive. This leaves two options: travel by land, which is the obvious route for those coming from the former Soviet Union and the Near East; and travel by sea, which is the obvious route for those coming from Africa. Migrants from places farther away, like Asia, may travel to Africa or the Near East first, and than use the land or sea route for crossing the European border. I will focus on the sea route, because of the availability of data (which are very hard to get by).

When the Schengen Implementation Agreement entered into force in 1995, aliens could circulate more or less freely among the participating European Community states. Border controls between these countries were abolished (and later reintroduced to some extent, but that is another story). The Schengen states felt vulnerable as a result of the abolition of internal border controls, and put more emphasis on controls at their joint external borders. Initially, this was aimed primarily at preventing air travel. At the time, airlines had little incentives to prevent irregular migrants from boarding their planes, because their gains (price of tickets) were larger than the costs (potential of being forced to transport an alien back to the place of embarkation). The Schengen Implementation Agreement contained an obligation for Schengen states to introduce carrier sanctions – penalties for airlines who transported an undocumented migrant to a Schengen state. After some false starts, the practice now seems to be rather effective. Airlines are obliged to make photocopies of the documents of all passengers on so-called "risk flights," i.e. flights on which normally a substantial number of undocumented migrants arrive. Upon arrival, they must submit these photocopies. If they can't, they have to pay substantial fines. This has created

all sources are from this article, unless indicated otherwise. See for more empirical data on the issue Jørgen Carling, "Migration Control and Migrant Fatalities at the Spanish–African Borders," *International Migration Review* 41 (2007), pp. 316–43; Derek Lutterbeck, "Policing Migration in the Mediterranean," *Mediterranean Politics* 11 (2006), pp. 59–82. The issue has been discussed during a hearing of the European Parliament on 3 July 2007, for which the materials were my briefing paper "The Human Costs of Border Control," IPOL/C/LIBE/FWC/2005-32-SC1; Consiglio Italiano per I Refugiati: *CIR Report Regarding Recent Search and Rescue Operations in the Mediterranean*; and Commission of the European Communities: *Study on the International Law Instruments in Relation to Illegal Immigration by Sea*, Brussels, 15 May 2007, SEC (2007) 691. Available at: www.europarl.europa.eu/hearings/default_en.htm, (accessed 3 July 2007).

an incentive to check whether passengers on such flights actually have travel documents; and to prevent passengers from being smuggled into an airplane by circumventing the regular check-in counter.

When the things which could reasonably be undertaken in this field had been done, European states turned their attention to land and sea borders. The land borders are difficult to guard, in part because they are so long, and in part because there is so much small-scale trans-border traffic. A considerable amount of measures has been taken (x-rays of freight trucks; night glasses at places where people walk or swim across borders at night).

Another area of attention was sea travel. Statistics about interceptions suggest that, when border authorities intensify their controls at particular points, migrants shift their travel routes to other places. One example is Italy. In 1998 and 1999, a large number of Kosovars fled to Italy by crossing the Adriatic Sea. Among the migrants who were intercepted, however, there were large numbers of other nationalities as well. In 1999, more than half of them were not from Kosovo. Controls at sea were intensified, and the number of intercepted persons fell, even if the data are corrected for the Kosovo migration flow (which more or less ceased after the NATO intervention in 1999). However, the number of people who were intercepted near Sicily rose, suggesting that they shifted from one route to another. The same phenomenon can be observed in Spain. The number of interceptions in the Strait of Gibraltar peaked in 2000; those attempting to enter Spain via its enclaves in Morocco then peaked in 2004, after which the number of migrants arriving at the Canary Islands peaked in 2006. Because of increased controls by Moroccan coast guards, departure from Morocco became increasingly difficult. Migrants took longer sea routes, sailing from Mauritania and Senegal. Studies show that, whereas earlier people intercepted on sea routes from Africa originated from Africa, in more recent years this route has also been used by Asian migrants (from Pakistan, Bangladesh, India).

Border control has not only been intensified, it is also changing in character. Controls are increasingly high tech and military in nature. For example, the Spanish Integrated System for External Patrols (SIVE) was started in 2002, and was completed in 2008. There were to be 25 detection stations, 71 patrol boats, and 13 mobile radars, along the coasts of Southern Spain and Fuerteventura.

Nothing in the available data suggest that the increasing border controls have the effect of scaring off potential migrants. Intensification of

Table 1: *Documented deaths at the European Borders 1993–2006*

1993	57
1994	**123**
1995	**179**
1996	**457**
1997	**361**
1998	**390**
1999	**516**
2000	**652**
2001	**444**
2002	**820**
2003	**1309**
2004	**898**
2005	**769**
2006*	**207**
total	**7182**

* until 3 May 2006
Source: United, Amsterdam 2006, available at: www.unitedagainstracism.org

border controls does not seem to lead to less migrants, but to them circumventing border controls by the use of ever more dangerous routes. On the basis of an analysis of the scarce and incomplete data about the number of people who die at the European borders, I conclude that more and more people do not survive the risks they take. The data collected by the Amsterdam based European NGO United are the most comprehensive available. This registry is based on press clippings, and is fairly detailed both on the number of persons, their identity, and the sources of the registry. It also includes, for example, people who have committed suicide pending deportation, who are not of interest in the present context. However, it is the most precise set of data available, and it is very precise as to the identity of the persons concerned, the way in which they died, dates, and the sources. Also, the overwhelming majority of the persons on this list did die while trying to cross the European borders. It should be noted that this list is based on press reports. As a result, the larger incidents (such as the 58 people found dead in a truck in Dover in June 2000, or the 283 people who drowned near Malta on Christmas day 1996) will be reported in the list; but for the smaller incidents, press reporting is all but systematic, and depends on the space available on a given day for *faits divers*.

How incomplete these data are, is shown by comparison to other data. For 2003, United reports 1,309 deaths for all of Europe. An Italian study reports 411 deaths in the Sicily Channel alone. For 2004, these numbers are 898 for all of Europe, and 280 for the Sicily Channel. Both sources are based on the same methodology, namely press reports. This means that there is a considerable dark number, which is hard to quantify however. Nonetheless, the trend is clear. If we stick to the data of United, we can conclude that, before the Schengen Implementation Agreement entered into force, border deaths documented by United were below 200, in the first years after they were below 500, and now they are below 1,000 with the exception of 2003. Once more: this is the trend in deaths reported by United. Although it seems plausible that the trend in actual deaths is the same, the level at which the actual numbers are is unclear. The actual numbers may be over half more, but it cannot be excluded that they may be double, triple or quadruple of the United numbers.

I feel that reporting these facts is a decent thing to do in itself. They are barely known, and merit attention just for their own sake. The least we can do as European citizens is to take notice of the people who are dying for the sake of the control of our borders. So although I mention them out of naked moralism, they are also part of my overall argument. The first question I will raise in this respect is to see in which way the two approaches outlined above impact legal reasoning, and whether even apart from legalism they can justify border controls. The second is to see whether European states are accountable for these deaths under human rights instruments, in particular the European Convention on Human Rights.

Legitimacy

How can one assess the European border policies from the communitarian and libertarian perspectives, respectively? From both perspectives, it seems obvious that the number of fatalities has to be as low as possible. However, the problem is precisely that effective border control seems to lead to an increasing number of fatalities. If States would be under an obligation to do whatever they can to reduce the number of fatalities, they should abandon border controls. Hence, the crucial question is whether these border controls in themselves are legitimate.

From a communitarian perspective, border controls are legitimate if they serve to preserve the way of life of the countries involved. Hence, ordinary migrants can legitimately be refused entry. The admission of refugees can be an obligation, unless their numbers threaten the existence of the settled community. The problem is that border controls do not, and cannot make this kind of distinction. The distinction between forced and "voluntary" migration can be made when a person applies for admission; it cannot be made when a person tries to evade the application process by irregular border crossing. In principle, this solves the issue: these migrants evade the procedure in which a legitimate decision can be taken, and therefore they can be subjected to policies which are necessary to prevent this.[12] I can think of one way to modify this conclusion. One may argue that there is no realistic alternative for migrants, whether they are forced migrants or not, to present themselves to the authorities of Western States in order to apply for asylum. The refugee crises in former Yugoslavia apart,[13] forced migrants do not originate from countries adjacent to Western States. By means of visa obligations, carrier sanctions, and other policy measures, States have made it increasingly difficult for forced migrants to reach the West. If forced migrants turn to Western consulates in order to apply for asylum in poor countries to which they have fled, they will be turned away because they already have found protection in those countries. Hence, only irregular means for reaching Europe are available, and it cannot be held against migrants that they use them. However, I do not think this train of thought can affect the communitarian legitimation for border control. If migrants already reside in a third country, they do not need admission to a Western country in order to escape persecution. Their reasons for wanting to migrate will be comparable, from a moral point of view, to those of "voluntary" migrants. Therefore, it is legitimate that they face effective border control if they try to evade the legitimate migration restrictions they encounter at Western embassies.

How would the libertarian perspective address the issue? Unlike the communitarian, this perspective does not start with the idea that

[12] A peculiar thing is that in one passage, Walzer seems to presume that migrants present themselves at our borders, *Spheres of Justice*, p. 51. This suggests that he is not aware of the intricacies of (forced) migration. Because of the unclarity of this passage, I will not try to construct a position on the basis of it.

[13] See on the border policies of European States in that context Nils Coleman, "Non-Refoulement Revised: Renewed Review of the Status of the Principle of Non-Refoulement as Customary International Law," *European Journal of Migration and Law* 5, no. 1 (2003), pp. 23–68.

migration control is legitimate and then enquires as to its limitations, but begins with the notion that border control is illegitimate, and then enquires where it might be legitimate. However, from there on the reasoning is similar to that in the communitarian view. The legitimacy of border control depends on the legitimacy of the migration restrictions it seeks to enforce. European border-control policies are justified by economic well-being, in particular by the aim to maintain the systems of solidarity which require some form of closure of the settled community. Whether the particular level of migration restrictions can be justified in this way is a matter of legitimate debate, but the principle of border control can be justified in this way.

To sum up: the different perspectives of sovereignty (communitarianism) and cosmopolitanism (libertarianism in its Carensian form) have different starting points because one presumes the legitimacy of the protection of settled communities, while the other presumes the legitimacy of international migration. They also lead to different rhetoric, because communitarianism is widely accepted, while libertarianism seems to be more radical. But, at least in the versions of Carens and Walzer, they both end up legitimating the on-the-ground phenomenon of effective border control, including its increasing death toll.

Legality

Border control does not constitute a wrongful act because, in itself, it is a legitimate activity. Under specific circumstances, States may be responsible for the consequences of acts which are not contrary to international law. Specifically, this can be the case if States undertake "an activity which involves a risk of causing significant harm."[14] However, I think the causal relation between border controls and border deaths is not direct enough to allow us to say that they *cause* the fatalities. There are too many other contributing factors (the behavior of the migrants themselves, the behavior of smugglers, the weather) to allow for holding the States involved responsible.

A parallel that is often drawn is that of the Iron Curtain. Between 1961 and 1989, many people lost their lives when attempting to cross the border between East and West Germany because of anti-personnel mines or automatic fire systems or after being shot at by East German

[14] International Law Commission, U.N. Doc. nr. A/CN.4/L.686, 26 May 2006.

border guards. While the official death toll according to the Federal Republic of Germany was 264, other sources quote a number as high as 938. On account of this, East German leaders were convicted as indirect principals to intentional homicide.[15] Analogizing this to the fatalities at the EU's borders, however, is flawed. Anti-personnel mines and automatic fire systems, as well as orders to shoot at fugitives (*Schiessbefehl*) were conscious, affirmative measures that directly led to the deaths of people who tried to cross the border between the two Germanys. There is a distinction to be made between measures that directly result in fatalities and tightening border controls, the effect of the latter being that migrants will use travel routes that are riskier.

The above parallel does suggest, however, that States can be held responsible for fatalities that occur as a direct consequence of particular border control measures, such as shooting at migrants who attempt to cross the border or placing landmines at the border.[16] Because of this, the authority to shoot at irregular migrants should be cancelled, and the minefields between Greece and Turkey should be dismantled. One could argue that this parallel is mistaken. East Germany killed when people tried to leave their country; that is an established human right. Greek minefields kill when people try to enter the country, which is not a human right. The parallel I draw indeed is another one. I argue that, regardless of whether border controls are used to prevent exit or entry, they may not be enforced by using lethal force. Rather than using lethal force, an enforcement deficit should be accepted.

[15] European Court of Human Rights, 22 March 2001, application nr. 34044/96, 35532/97 and 44801/98, *Streletz, Kessler and Krenz* v. *Germany*.

[16] As indicated above, this is not the focus of the present paper. It should be noted, however, that such fatalities occur regularly. According to press reports quoted by United, migrants were shot on 29 March 1995 (Greece), 20 August 1995 (France), 5 September 1996 (Spain), 17 August 1998 (Italy), 10 May 2000 (Turkey, nine people), 15 November 2000 (Turkey), 3 December 2000 (Spain), 16 July 2001 (Turkey), 12 January 2002 (Turkey, two people), March 2002 (Macedonia, seven people), 22 May 2002 (Turkey), 19 June 2002 (Turkey, two people), 23 September 2003 (Greece), 3 October 2003 (Spain), 11 April 2004 (Spain), 17 April 2004 (Slovakia, two people), 10 September 2005 (Greece), 19 September 2005 (Turkey) and 29 September 2005 (Morocco, five people). Migrants died in the minefields between Turkey and Greece on 13 September 1995 (four people), 30 June 1996 (two people), 15 September 1997 (three people), 16 April 1998 (two people), 26 August 1999 (three people), 31 October 1999 (five people), 1 May 2000, 29 August 2000, 1 September 2000 (two people), 29 March 2001 (two people), 21 May 2001, 22 May 2001 (two people), 30 September 2001, 23 December 2001 (four people), 20 March 2002 (two people), 27 March 2002, 28 August 2002, 4 January 2003 (two people), March 2003, 29 September 2003 (seven people), 5 August 2004, 14 November 2004 (three people), 4 April 2005 (two people), 29 May 2005 (two people) and 9 December 2005 (two people).

The fact that States generally cannot be held legally responsible, however, is not the end of the story. Consider the European Court of Human Rights' decision in *Osman*, which involved Article 2(1) of the European Convention on Human Rights. According to Article 2(1):

> Everyone's right to life shall be protected by law. No one shall be deprived of his life intentionally save in the execution of a sentence of a court following his conviction of a crime for which this penalty is provided by law.

Osman involved a stalker who had harassed a family for a number of years and ended up killing a father and wounding a son. The Court held:

> The Court notes that the first sentence of Article 2 § 1 enjoins the State not only to refrain from the intentional and unlawful taking of life, but also to take appropriate steps to safeguard the lives of those within its jurisdiction (see the *L.C.B.* v. *The United Kingdom* judgment of 9 June 1998, *Reports of Judgments and Decisions* 1998-III, p. 1403, § 36). It is common ground that the State's obligation in this respect extends beyond its primary duty to secure the right to life by putting in place effective criminal-law provisions to deter the commission of offences against the person backed up by law-enforcement machinery for the prevention, suppression and sanctioning of breaches of such provisions. It is thus accepted by those appearing before the Court that Article 2 of the Convention may also imply in certain well-defined circumstances a positive obligation on the authorities to take preventive operational measures to protect an individual whose life is at risk from the criminal acts of another individual. The scope of this obligation is a matter of dispute between the parties.[17]

As in the border control cases, *Osman* did not involve a causal relationship between failing to take preventive measures to protect individuals' lives and those individuals' deaths. The obligation of a State to take appropriate steps to safeguard lives is not conditioned on a causal relationship between the State's actions and someone's death. Rather, the

[17] European Court of Human Rights, 28 October 1998, appl. nr. 23452/94l *Osman* v. *United Kingdom*. Comp. ECtHR 1 March 2005, appl. nr. 69869/01; *Bône* v. *France;* ECtHR 9 June 1998; *L.C.B.* v. *United Kingdom*, 23413/94; ECtHR 24 October 2002; *Mastromatteo* v. *Italy*, 37703/97; ECtHR 14 March 2002; *Edwards* v. *United Kingdom*, 46477/99; ECtHR 17 January 2002; *Calvelli & Ciglio* v. *Italy*, 32967/96; ECtHR 21 March 2002; *Nitecki* v. *Poland*, 65653/01; ECtHR 7 June 2005; *Kilinc* v. *Turkey*, 40145/98; ECtHR 30 November 2004; *Öneryildiz* v. *Turkey*, 48939/99.

obligation is triggered by the State's knowledge that a particular life is at risk and that same State's ability to do something about it.

Increases in the number of fatalities of irregular migrants are related to the tightening of border controls. Thus, these fatalities are a foreseeable consequence of this policy. Although this does not lead to State responsibility, it does trigger a State's positive obligation to take preventive measures to safeguard the lives of those who are put at risk. In the context of border control measures, because States' policies foreseeably increase the loss of lives of irregular migrants, they are obliged to exercise their border controls in such a way that loss of lives is minimized. One can doubt whether States have lived up to that obligation.

From a legal perspective, States arguably fail to live up to a positive obligation to minimize the number of fatalities which are the indirect consequence of their border policies. It requires a slightly innovative (but by no means revolutionary) means of interpretation to argue this. For the rest, border control in itself is not a wrongful act, and therefore its collateral damage is not a violation of a fundamental right of its victims.

Domestic work

Domestic work used to be done by housewives and daughters. The extent to which this is still the case is only surprising for those who take the tales of women's emancipation being finished in the West at face value. However, as women increasingly enter the market of paid labor in Western countries, families increasingly rely on domestic workers. Whereas, at least in the Netherlands, child care is arranged for mostly either informally (granny), outside the home (nurseries, after school child care centers), or by classical babysitting arrangements; and the preparation of food is outsourced in some form (take away, delivery, prefab food); laundry and housecleaning are performed increasingly by domestic workers. These are predominantly live-out domestic workers, who work for half a day or one day per week in one household, and combine several 'addresses' in order to make a living.

Of course, live-ins also exist, as do the specific kind of live-ins called au pairs. A live-in is someone with a labor relation with the employer. The specific nature of the live-in is that she resides in her employer's home. This has considerable effects on the relation (in terms of pay in kind, overwork, and the like). An au pair is a young person who stays abroad for a while (usually something like a year) in order to get to know the world better; in order to allow her to do this, she stays with a family, and in return contributes to running the household (she is a temporary member of the family).

Domestic work is predominantly done either in the informal economy, or by migrant women. In the informal economy, migrant women (both with and without residence rights) work along with autochtone women and young people. In the formal economy of domestic work, women who have migrated with the aim of becoming a domestic worker have a prominent place. I will focus on migrant women performing domestic work, both in the formal and in the informal economy.

It is possible for domestic workers to get a working permit, and hence a residence permit. However, in practice this requires they have a full-time job with one single employer. This kind of full-time domestic work job in the formal economy is expensive for the employer even if the work is done for a low wage, hence this is a rare phenomenon, mostly restricted to diplomats and expats. If the work is full time, the domestic worker often is a live-in. Both the live-in nature of the relationship, as well as the fact that the worker's residence permit is dependent on the continued existence of the labor relation, increases the dependency which exists between employer and employee. The position of live-ins is notoriously bad in terms of labor standards. [18]

The other formal possibility is work as an au pair. Under Dutch law, the relationship between the "guest family" and the au pair is not considered to be a labor relation. The au pair lives with the family in the framework of cultural exchange. The residence of the au pair has a predominantly cultural character. The "guest family" provides facilities, in exchange for which the au pair does "light domestic work." This means the au pair should not work more than eight hours per day, for not more than 30 hours per week, and should have at least two days off per week. S/he should not have sole responsibility for domestic chores to the exclusion of members of the "guest family." The au pair should be between 18 and 26; unmarried and not have responsibility for children of her own. The residence permit will be granted for at most one year. The au pair can exchange one "guest family" for another, but will have to request for a change of her residence permit.[19] Thus, au pairs are tied

[18] See *inter alinea* Guy Mundlak, "Gender, migration and class: why are 'live-in' domestic workers not compensated for overtimes," in *Women and Immigration Law. New Variations on Classical Feminist Themes*, ed. Sarah van Walsum and Thomas Spijkerboer (London: Routledge-Cavendish, 2007), pp. 123–41.

[19] Vreemdelingenbesluit (Aliens Decree) 2000, art. 3.43, Vreemdelingencirculaire (Aliens Circular) 2000, B7/2.

to their employer because in practice it is very hard to change "guest families." They get little pay (only pocket money is allowed) and after expiry of their year they will have to choose between either returning home, or staying without residence rights.

Undocumented women (and men) who perform domestic work will do so often at different addresses. Therefore, their dependency vis-à-vis individual employers will be less than that of au pairs for example They can risk a conflict with an employer without risking their income (they will have other addresses), and without risking their residence right (their employer is not necessarily aware of their identity and address; familiarity with a mobile phone number will do). However, they will have to put up with low pay, no job security, and no social security (except the social security provided by their own networks, such as colleagues, churches, family). In respect to undocumented domestic workers, enforcement of migrant labor law is often formally absent.[20] It is debatable whether the grant of a residence right would improve their position vis-à-vis their employers. Most likely, they would have a position comparable to that of others on the informal domestic labor market, which is not radically different from theirs.[21] However, a residence right would give them alternatives to working in the informal economy. This could enable them to choose other work, and to get an education to the extent that the welfare system allows them to. It is unclear to me why temping agencies do not hire domestic workers full-time who are then contracted out to families for a few hours per week; this might allow migrant women to do domestic work with a residence permit, provided no labor supply is available on the domestic market. Possibly, the formal nature of such an arrangement makes the option unattractive to employers, because the informal market is cheaper and more flexible.

Summing up: au pairs and full-time domestic workers get a residence right which ties them to their employer (aka "guest family"). This weakens their position vis-à-vis their employers. This creates a situation in which unpaid overwork, underpayment, harassment, etc. are more likely to occur than in more horizontal relationships. In the case of au pairs, immigration law facilitates a situation which, if the

[20] Dennis Broeders, *Breaking Down Anonimity. Digital Surveillance on Irregular Migrants in Germany and the Netherlands* (dissertation Erasmus University Rotterdam, 2009), p. 89–90.

[21] I am not aware of studies comparing incomes of domestic workers along lines of gender, age, ethnicity, and residence rights.

persons concerned were not migrant women, would be considered exploitative (compare doing "light industrial work" for a maximum of thirty hours per week, with at least two days off in exchange for housing and pocket money). Undocumented domestic workers are part of an informal economy where low pay, lack of social security, and lack of job security are part of the game. It may well be that they are not more vulnerable to this than their documented colleagues. However, their undocumented status makes them more vulnerable to the risks such a situation involves. They do not have access to social security, and they will have trouble in choosing options other than the informal economy.

Legitimacy

What would communitarians have to say about the position of domestic workers? The position of documented migrant domestic workers at first sight seems unacceptable from Walzer's perspective. Their residence position makes them vulnerable in their labor relations, and that is precisely the kind of transfer of inequality which Walzer opposes. A weak residence right may be acceptable, but it should not influence the migrant's position in other spheres – and that is precisely what happens here. However, labor migrants are bound to their labor for a reason. The live-in character of the work implies not only labor standards under the level acceptable in European countries, but also implies a serious limitation of private life. Live-ins cannot bring their own families into the home; the attraction of live-ins is their availability, so working time will be counted in evenings off, not in hours to be available. Workers who have better options will take them, so if one grants a residence right for the purpose of domestic work, tying the worker to the employment is necessary. In this way, the alternative for domestic workers is not a job in Europe, but a life in the country of origin. Immigration law is crucial in manipulating the exit option.[22] If this would not happen, there would not be enough live-in domestic workers, which would affect the attractiveness of European countries for international business. It is conceivable that under those circumstances, the interests of the national community would prevail over the interests of the domestic workers.

[22] Cf. Audrey Macklin "Public Entrance/Private Member," in *Privatization, Law, and the Challenge to Feminism*, ed. Brenda Cossman & Judy Fudge (Toronto: University of Toronto Press, 2002), pp. 218–64.

Some changes might be indicated, such as tying the residence right to the work, not the employment (which might enable workers to change jobs); and allowing workers to change employment after a number of years of legal residence.

For undocumented domestic workers, the illegal nature of their residence disqualifies them from a communitarian perspective. The only way to do away with this source of weakness would be to grant residence right, which would equal abolishing the possibility to protect the community. That is not an acceptable option.

For libertarians, the reasoning on documented migrant domestic workers would run parallel to that of the communitarians. They would start out by finding their position unacceptable. But because of their acceptance of migration control, and hence the right of States to make residence conditional on fulfilling particular conditions (such as performing a particular kind of job), they would end up understanding the present arrangements all too well, while suggesting some changes in the details. Libertarians would take the side of undocumented workers to start with, but would then have to accept that remedying their weak position by granting a residence right would undermine the concept of migration control.

Legality

The legality of the residence position of documented domestic workers is not subject to debate. The legality of the position of au pairs is subject to limited debate. It is argued that they always perform work, hence should be granted a residence right on that basis, which would elevate their residence position to that of documented domestic workers.[23] However, these suggestions have not been received well by NGO's, including trade unions; no litigation has followed. The legality of the position of undocumented domestic workers is not subject to debate. The European Court of Human Rights has found a violation of Article 4 of the European Convention on Human Rights in a case where a state did not take any action when faced with the extremely exploitative labor condition of an undocumented migrant domestic worker.[24]

[23] T.P. Spijkerboer, *Het VN-Vrouwenverdrag en het Nederlandse vreemdelingenrecht*, Adviescommissie voor Vreemdelingenzaken, Den Haag (2002), pp. 31–37.

[24] ECtHR 26 July 2005, Siliadin v France, application 73316/01.

Convergence

In their actual application to the two cases, we have seen that communitarianism and libertarianism may well end up supporting the status quo by and large. Despite their different starting positions (communitarianism requiring justification of migration's infringement on the community, and libertarianism requiring justification of the community's restrictions on migration), communitarians and libertarians will probably agree on the legitimacy of border control, including the fatalities that go with it; and they will probably agree on the legitimacy of the present day regulation of labor migration. I am not arguing that they will necessarily agree on the details. But the significant conclusion in the present context is twofold. First, they will roughly agree with the actual arrangements. Second, libertarians will not necessarily advocate a less restrictive policy than communitarians. The crux in both perspectives is not the starting position. No communitarian will argue that the exclusion of any alien can be legitimate, regardless of the circumstances. And no libertarian will argue that migration control can never be legitimate. The crux of both positions is in the qualifications which can be made to the starting position. The central question for a communitarian will be: is a restrictive policy in this particular case illegitimate (because the communitarian starts out from the presumption it is). The central question for a libertarian will be: is a restrictive policy in this particular case legitimate (because the libertarian starts out from the position it is not). The substantive difference between these two questions is minimal, if there is one at all. In addition, the factors to be taken into account are identical from both perspectives. The main factors are the interests of the receiving society (economic well-being, security) and the interests of the migrant (existential interests of refugees, intimate interests of family migrants, economic interests of others). So, because the two perspectives focus on the same question, and look at the same factors in answering it, it is unlikely that the perspective makes much of a difference. The perspectives do not determine the outcome of the debate, but the starting point from which the different factors are evaluated. For this evaluation, the perspective makes no clear difference.

One might argue that the default option makes the difference between the two. If justification of an exception fails, restrictions are justified for communitarians, and not for libertarians. However, because at the core of both perspectives lies a balance of interests, justification of either free migration or restrictions will only fail if one wants it to fail. A balance of interests makes an outcome somewhere in the middle highly likely, and that is precisely what we see. Therefore, the default option is unlikely to make a difference between the two perspectives, except in the improbable event that justification would fail.

In actual politics we also observe that these positions can change place. Restrictive immigration policies are usually defended in communitarian terms, and liberal ones in libertarian ones. However, campaigns for the regularization of undocumented migrants often rely on communitarian rhetoric (these people are part of our communities, go to school with our children, come to our church), while objections against them are often universalistic (impartial application of rules). This shows that who is a member of the community can be subject to contestation, just as the beneficiaries of universalism can be. Another example of the categories trading places is that many argue that upon closer inspection, asylum law (accepted as a universalistic strand in communitarianism) may serve to select migrants with a view to their adaptability to Western societies,[25] or my be dominated by foreign policy concerns,[26] or may be a covert labor migration channel, not only for the migrants but also for receiving States (Prakash Shah; Hathaway).[27] On the other hand, in fields where national sovereignty seemingly reigns supreme, such as in the regulation of labor migration, one can barely argue that this serves the national community. Since the competitiveness of national economies has replaced full employment as the prime target of economic policy, the regulation of labor migration is dominated by neoliberal concerns, not by community-oriented social democratic ones (Sassen, Harvey).[28] These are further examples undermining the idea that the libertarianism/communitarianism debate about the regulation of migration has much relevance for the actual policies which are found to be legitimate. Communitarianism, libertarianism, and law justify something quite close to existing immigration regimes.

[25] Robert F. Barsky, *Constructing a Productive Other. Discourse Theory and the Convention Refugee Hearing*, (Amsterdam and Philadelphia: John Benjamins, 1994).

[26] Gil Loescher and John A. Scanlan, *Calculated Kindness. Refugees and America's Half-Open Door, 1945 to the Present*, (New York and London: The Free Press, 1986); Thomas Spijkerboer, *Gender and Refugee Status* (Aldershot: Ashgate, 2000).

[27] Prakash Shah, *Refugees, Race, and the Legal Concept of Asylum in Britain* (London: Cavendish, 2000); James C. Hathaway, *Reconceiving International Refugee Law* (The Hague: Martinus Nijhoff, 1998).

[28] Sassen, *Territory, Authority, Rights*; David Harvey, *A Brief History of Neoliberalism* (Oxford University Press, 2005).

Admission or distribution

Communitarianism and libertarianism are hard to tell apart when applied to two radically different migration law issues. Additionally, their outcomes and the legal status quo overlap considerably. This is possible because the question that is asked (should we admit these people to our communities) is based on a metaphor which is dubious both empirically and normatively. The metaphor is that these people are knocking on our doors, and waiting outside for the answer. In the case of border deaths, this is an applicable metaphor only at first sight. Migrants know the answer to their question already, and therefore try to rush into the door through the gaps; the door is then fortified in such a way that this becomes potentially lethal; yet migrants keep trying to find the gaps (which indeed are still there), and often die of the fortifications if they fail. It turns out to be a fact that migrants are willing to run considerable risks. Apparently what they stand to gain is so considerable that the risk seems worthwhile (no doubt, they will underestimate the risk as well). Given this fact, is it acceptable that the risk is actively increased?

In fact, the heart of the matter is what one takes as dependent variable. Does one take migration control as a fixed variable, and is the aim to influence the migration behavior of people from poor countries? Or does one take migration as a given, and is the question how to adapt migration control in such a way that the number of victims can be minimized? Behind this choice lies, I think, the perception of the wider situation. One possibility is that the gap between rich and poor countries is considered as so enormous, that irregular migration will always remain a realistic option. The risks of border crossing are only part of the assessment potential migrants have to make, hence draconic border controls will not scare people off but merely increase the likelihood, and the number, of fatalities. Another possibility is that one is so focused on the protection of European welfare systems, that intentionally reducing the effectiveness of migration control is no option, hence the option has to be enforcement of migration control and influencing migration behavior.

The same is true, in a more blatant way, for migrant domestic workers. If we choose to let migration control considerations dominate our thinking about the position of domestic workers, their situation will remain roughly as it is. However, we might consider the issue primarily as a labor standards issue, or as a gender issue, and then the perspective changes.

However, can one reasonably argue that one should treat migrants as members of a community, as a perspective change presumes? In the footsteps of Linda Bosniak, I want to point out that we already do so in many respects.[29] Migrants within the jurisdiction of a European State (which means: in any case if they are on the territory of a European State) have the right to life, the right not to be tortured, to be free from slavery, not to be detained arbitrarily, the right to a fair procedure, to private and family life. The extent to which they can benefit from these rights is influenced by their residence status, but they are considered as insiders, as community members from a legal point of view. If this is the case in so many instances, then the idea that migration control should take into account the right to life of its subjects, and their right to be free from slavery, to humane labor standards, is not anathema.[30] Of course this is something one may disagree about, but it is not out of bounds. Normatively, the problem with the separation of insiders and outsiders is that the prior existence of the insider group is taken as a given. From a normative point of view, this is arbitrary.

Charles Maier argues that the notion of territoriality as such is something of the past. In his analysis, the world is now entering a post-territorial phase.[31] Around 1860, in various parts of the world a development began in which four related phenomena occurred, which marks the beginning of what Maier sees as the high period of territoriality. First, central government gained strength at the expense of regional or confederate authority; second, internal and external military capacity became continually mobilized as a resource for governance; third, a new ruling cartel emerged, in which the old landed elite was joined by new leaders of finance, industry, science, and professionals; and fourth, an industrial infrastructure was created, based on technologies of coal and iron, characterized by long-distance transportation of goods and people, and mass output of industrial products assembled by a factory labor force. In the bounded space in which these phenomena occurred, "identity space" (the space which is the basis for collective allegiance) and "decision space" (the space in which physical,

[29] Linda Bosniak, *The Citizen and the Alien*: Dilemmas of Contemporary Membership (Princeton: Princeton University Press, 2006).

[30] See in this sense the Inter-American Court of Human Rights' Advisory Opinion OC-18/03, 17 September 2003, on the Juridical Condition and Rights of Undocumented Migrants.

[31] Charles S. Maier, "Consigning the Twentieth Century to History: Alternative Narratives for the Modern Era," *The American Historical Review*, 105, no. 3 (2000), available at: www.historycooperative.org/journals/ahr/105.3/ah000807.html (accessed 3 July 2007).

economic, and cultural security seems to be assured) coincide. Within the boundaries of the newly reconstituted territory, land and population were crucial assets. Territories also had a center and a periphery. Lines of force, consisting of diverse phenomena such as bureaucratic hierarchies, and telegraph, steamboat, and railroad networks, knitted together the territories in unprecedented ways. Although this system began to fall apart around 1970, historians still consider boundary issues (both in the geographical, and in the social and political sense) crucial.

However, territoriality in Maier's analysis now has a different role than it had until around 1970. Present day metropolises are not linked primarily to their hinterland, but to each other; in this way, they constitute a global network of capital and labor. Coal and iron have been replaced by semiconductors, computers, and data transmission. The concept of the hierarchically organized Fordist production in a national territory was replaced (in image, if not always in reality) by the idea of globally-coordinated networks of information, mobile capital, and migratory labor. The major political division of our times, Maier argues, is not between that of capital and labor any more, but that between those who see their future as based on non-territorial markets or exchange of ideas, and those who insist that territoriality be reinvigorated once again as the basis for economic and political security, "Whether by virtue of direct migration or competitive economic exchange, the well-off and educated residents of the West are fated to live in proximity to, and without territorial protection from, peoples of other traditions."

My thesis in this paper is that normative discourse, both in ethics and in law, is caught in the territorial metaphor. The debate presumes distinct national systems, and debates the possibilities of the transfer of people from one system to another. My analysis suggests that the outsiders are inside already, both in fact (undocumented migrants within national systems) as well as normatively (even those who are physically outside territorial space are within the jurisdictions of states of destination). In order to understand the proximity of places which are distant in a territorial sense, new metaphors have to be developed.

Saskia Sassen offers an analysis which may well be compatible with Maier's[32]. She argues that since about 1980, Western states have not been oriented primarily towards full employment (as they had been since at

[32] Saskia Sassen "Territory, Authority, Rights," in *Medieval to Global Assemblages* (Princeton: Princeton University Press, 2006).

the latest World War II), but to giving their economies a competitive position in the global economy. The primary Keynesian focus on citizens welfare has been replaced by a primary focus on global capital. This has led to less rights (think of the downsizing of the welfare state) for citizens vis-à-vis their state, and to a thinner bond between state and citizen. Also, the unitary nature of citizenry has been put into question, partly by subnational claims (Quebec, Northern Ireland, Basques); partly because migration has led to more diversity; and partly because citizenship has been criticized as partial along lines of class, gender, and race. In her analysis, the national state is not losing importance[33] but its function is changing. It now has a crucial role in the functioning of the global market, while before it had a role in the international coordination of national markets. Territory now is less a place than a function.

In the normative debate about migration control, Seyla Benhabib has pleaded for what I take to be a permanent lack of balance on the issue.[34] On the one hand, she is sympathetic to the idea that the democratic ideal of self-governance requires a bounded community. However, she has argued for constant deliberation about the way in which undocumented migrants can be included. In her view, the ideal territorial autochthony should be replaced by the ideal of public autonomy, which allows for more flexibility.

I want to contribute to this debate by pointing out that any choice one makes, both at the abstract-normative level of ethics, and at the concrete-normative level of legislation, has clear and pretty direct distributive consequences. These consequences should be central to the choices that are being made, instead of being ignored, taken for granted, or blamed on the victims. A choice for a distributive approach to the regulation of migration would not per se lead to a plea for 'free' migration. 'Free' migration tends to mean that the State should to a large extent withdraw from the regulation of migration, and leave migration to the other two main institutions involved: the family and the market. In the neoliberal perspective, the role of the State should be restricted to facilitating the workings of a transnational labor market. This would arguably lead to a deterioration of the position of those worst off in rich

[33] As, in our context, among others Soysal has argued, see Yasemin Nuhoglu Soysal, *Limits of Citizenship. Migrants and Postnational Membership in Europe* (Chicago/London: University of Chicago Press, 1994).

[34] Seyla Benhabib. The Rights of Others: Aliens, Residents and Citizens (Cambridge University Press, 2006).

countries. But even if one takes a distributive approach to migration control, one may argue that the State's intervening power, which the neoliberals propose to use for the benefit of the market, may be used to mitigate the effects of the family and the market for those worst off. The choice is not one between State intervention or freedom; maintaining the market requires considerable State intervention, while the family is a Statist structure for human relations. The choice is about the way in which State power is to be used. For this, it is not fruitful to frame the issue as one of admission. The issue is how to regulate the position of people who, whether we like it or not, are already within the reach of our communities. This implies a different imagining of the conflict. The conflict of interests is not between us and them, but runs through the receiving societies. If domestic workers are given a secure and independent residence status, some will lose, and some will profit. I advocate to analyze issues of migration control in such a concrete, non-totalizing way, as to their distributive effect.

The debate between moral cosmopolitanism (in our context: Carens' universalist, libertarian position) and institutional cosmopolitanism (here: Walzer's communitarianism) cannot be resolved. The purely universalist will be contaminated by particularism as soon as it addresses institutional issues of border control. The purely particularist will be contaminated by universalism as long as it is justified by the equal value of each man's life. The impossibility of closure may not be a bad thing. The resulting instability of our position allows us to discuss the consequences of the concrete ways in which migration is regulated. How will a policy affect the number of fatalities at our borders? How will another policy affect the bargaining position of a domestic worker vis-à-vis her employer? The impossibility of resolving the debate on an abstract level forces us to confront what we do to whom. Migration control cannot be, and should not be, something on which we have a moral position which puts our conscience to rest.

PART VI

Conclusion

12

Can cosmopolitanism survive institutionalization?

ROLAND PIERIK AND WOUTER WERNER

> *Today, the question is not whether to be cosmopolitan or not but what kind of cosmopolis one should prefer, against what particularity should one be poised today.*[1]

This book has examined the relationship between cosmopolitanism as a moral standard and the (legal) institutions in which cosmopolitan norms and principles are to be implemented. The several chapters have analyzed five areas of global concern: environmental protection, economic regulation, peace and security, the fight against international crimes, and migration. The question regarding the relation between moral cosmopolitanism and legal institutions has gained renewed attention in the past few decades, mainly for two reasons.

In the first place, cosmopolitan norms affect many areas of contemporary life. As Jeremy Waldron has argued, these cosmopolitan norms have penetrated daily life as "a dense thicket of rules that sustain our life together, a life shared by people and peoples, not just in any particular society but generally on the face of the Earth."[2] Cosmopolitan ideals have also found their way into international legal documents and have inspired the establishment of international institutions. Increasingly, international law has incorporated notions such as "the common bonds" and the "shared heritage" of all peoples,[3] the idea of human dignity, or the notion that environmental protection is a "common concern of humankind."[4] Of course, this is not to say that all international institutions and regimes are now founded upon cosmopolitan principles or moving progressively towards ideals of global justice. Cosmopolitan values are not incorporated by all international legal institutions,

[1] Martti Koskenniemi, *The Gentle Civilizer of Nations: The Rise and Fall of International Law 1870–1960* (Cambridge: Cambridge University Press, 2001), p. 515.

[2] Jeremy Waldron, "Cosmopolitan Norms," in *Another Cosmopolitanism*, ed. Robert Post (New York: Oxford University Press, 2006), p. 83.

[3] Preamble of the Rome Statute establishing the International Criminal Court.

[4] Preamble of the 1992 Convention on Biological Diversity (Biodiversity Convention).

as Tomer Broude's analysis of he GATS regime on labor migration demonstrates. In his contribution to this volume, Broude sets out how the GATS labor mobility regime fails to meet criteria derived from theories of global justice, including cosmopolitanism. This shows that it is not possible to uncritically assume that Waldron's "dense thicket of cosmopolitan rules" extends to all aspects of institutional life. Even where institutions incorporate cosmopolitan values, these values generally have to compete with values derived from competing theories of (global) justice and national interest.

Neither is it to say that the rise of cosmopolitanism is entirely new to international law. On the contrary, the history of international law can be read as a constant wavering between more cosmopolitan-oriented and more state-centric readings of international law, up to present-day discussions about the constitutional or consensual nature of international law.[5] Yet, although debates on cosmopolitanism are far from novel, the unprecedented scale on which cosmopolitanism ideals have become institutionalized nowadays has given them renewed meaning and force. The proliferation of cosmopolitan elements in positive international law has confronted international lawyers and political philosophers with some of the age-old questions in relation to cosmopolitanism. Can cosmopolitanism retain its critical potential when it becomes part of the world of institutions, diplomacy, and power politics? In what ways, if any, does cosmopolitanism affect legal reasoning and the exercise of power? What happens when ideals of moral cosmopolitanism are incorporated in positive international law?

The second reason why the relation between moral cosmopolitanism and legal institutions has gained renewed attention lies in recent developments in political philosophy. A defining moment in this respect was the publication of Rawls's *Law of Peoples* in 1999. In this book Rawls presented his theory of international justice as an alternative for, and a critique of the cosmopolitan attempts to globalize his domestic *Theory of Justice*. Rawls's attempt to set out rules for international cooperation between peoples (or better: states) raised many objections, especially from liberal cosmopolitan thinkers. The

[5] See Martti Koskenniemi, *From Apology to Utopia: The Structure of International Legal Argument, Re-issued with Epilogue* (Cambridge: Cambridge University Press, 2005). For an analysis of state sovereignty and international constitutionalism see Wouter Werner, "The Never Ending Closure: Constitutionalism and International Law," in *Transnational Constitutionalism: European and International Perspectives*, ed. Nicholas Tsagourias (Cambridge: Cambridge University Press, 2007).

publication of the *Law of Peoples* generated a thriving debate on global justice and, consequently, a renewed political–philosophical interest in – liberal – cosmopolitanism.

The quite ambitious program of liberal cosmopolitanism in political philosophy, however, raised an important question: is it feasible to elaborate ideas derived from moral cosmopolitanism into the world of international law and politics? Would that not turn cosmopolitanism into a pie in the sky or a justification for the exercise of imperial power? That is, political philosophers were confronted with questions similar to those that occupied the minds of international lawyers: what is the relation between cosmopolitanism as an abstract moral standard and cosmopolitanism as an institutional practice?

The chapters in this book have examined the questions identified above on the basis of three approaches, which may be called (i) the normative deductive approach (ii) the critical reconstructivist approach and (iii) the critical deconstructivist approach. Below, we will explain the basic characteristics of the three approaches and set out how each approach has dealt with the relation between moral cosmopolitanism and its institutional implementation. It should be clear, however, that these approaches do not exhaust the possible ways in which moral and institutional cosmopolitanism can be studied.[6] Moreover, it should be kept in mind that the approaches are not necessarily mutually exclusive; the critical reconstructivist and the critical deconstructivist approaches especially, may overlap in their analysis of the effects of cosmopolitanism in specific contexts. Finally, it should be noticed that it is possible to find combinations of approaches within one and the same text. The categorization, in other words, is meant as an analytical tool to identify methods and modes of reasoning, not to label authors as belonging to one school or another.

The normative deductive approach

Characteristic of the normative deductive approach is that it starts out from some basic and rather abstract normative assumptions, e.g. the assumption that all human beings deserve equal moral concern.[7]

[6] It is also possible, for example, to use an "inductive method" that tries to identify valid norms and principles based on their actual acceptance by states. For a more elaborated and nuanced discussion of the inductive method see Georg Schwarzenberge, "The Inductive Approach to International Law," *Harvard Law Review* 60 (1947).

[7] Sometimes, cosmopolitan authors attempt to ground this assumption on more basic arguments. Such attempts tend to oscillate between two main types of justifications. The first

Subsequently, it deduces more concrete moral criteria for the guidance and evaluation of conduct from these general assumptions.

The normative deductive approach is predominant in contemporary cosmopolitan political theory and can be found in the work of leading authors such as Buchanan, Pogge, Caney, or Tan.[8] In this volume, the most articulated expression of this position can be found in Caney's chapter on global climate change. Caney starts out from three basic premises regarding the foundation of individual rights, the nature of global climate change, and the proportionality of measures that protect individuals against the ill-effects of global climate change. Subsequently, he tries to invalidate competing normative foundations and sketches the consequences of the adoption of his basic premises. The strength of the normative deductive approach is its analytical rigor and the precision with which the arguments are made. This makes it possible to articulate and critique systematically the normative assumptions underlying legal institutions and international legal discourse. As Rawls famously argued: "The reason for beginning with ideal theory is that it provides, I believe, the only basis for the systematic grasp of these more pressing problems."[9] As was already set out in the introduction to this volume, the normative deductive approach is also helpful in order to identify the structural injustices that are sustained by the international legal system. Caney's analysis, for example, helps to think through the often-made argument that we owe obligations towards future generations and the problem of how the burdens of global climate change should be distributed.

are justifications based on the existence of certain social facts, such as an overlapping global consensus on human rights (see for example Allen Buchanan, *Justice, Legitimacy, and Self-Determination: Moral Foundations for International Law* (Oxford: Oxford University Press, 2004)) or a global structure of interaction and interdependence, see *inter alinea* Thomas Pogge, *World Poverty and Human Rights* (Oxford: Polity Press, 2002), p. 20. The second are justifications based on naturalistic arguments, such as the existence of a natural duty to contribute to the creation of just institutions (Buchanan, *Justice, Legitimacy, and Self-Determination*; Kok-Chor Tan, *Justice without Borders: Cosmopolitanism, Nationalism and Patriotism* (Cambridge: Cambridge University Press, 2004)). It goes without saying that the factual and the naturalist foundations of cosmopolitanism are difficult to reconcile.

[8] Allen Buchanan, "Rawls's Law of Peoples: Rules for a Vanished Westphalian World," *Ethics* 110, no. 4 (2000); Buchanan, *Justice, Legitimacy, and Self-Determination*; Thomas Pogge, *Realizing Rawls* (Ithaca: Cornell University Press, 1989); Pogge, *World Poverty and Human Rights*; Tan, *Justice Without Borders*; Simon Caney, *Justice Beyond Borders: A Global Political Theory* (Oxford: Oxford University Press, 2005).

[9] John Rawls, *A Theory of Justice Review* (ed.) (Oxford: Oxford University Press, 1999), p. 8.

However, the normative deductive approach also has a (potential) downside: its rather abstract character. Cosmopolitan political theory generally operates in the realm of "ideal theory," which deals with the basic moral principles that a just society has to satisfy, on the assumption that members of a society actually live up to these principles.[10] While such thinking may be helpful in identifying and critiquing existing injustices,[11] it has limited value when confronted with actually-existing social contexts in which normative principles are to be applied. More specifically, it generally lacks a focus on the role of institutions, on the question of what it means if moral principles are institutionalized so as to govern a practice that covers many cases.[12]

Several chapters in this volume have sought to answer this question by addressing the problem of how institutions should be designed so as to ensure the realization of cosmopolitan ideals. The chapter by Pogge, for example, contains elaborate proposals for reforms of the international legal regime protecting intellectual property, taking into account cosmopolitan ideals *and* the realities of the global market. The chapter by Valadez provides another attempt at bridging the gap between ideal and non-ideal cosmopolitan theory. Based on principles of moral equality and fair participation, his chapter formulates desiderata for international and domestic immigration policies that do justice to the right of self-determination of peoples and the human rights of individuals.

What lessons can be learned from these attempts of linking cosmopolitan theory to institutional practice? In the first place, they show that cosmopolitan theory can be used in such a way that idealism is coupled with realism: cosmopolitanism can retain its critical potential vis-à-vis real existing institutions and inspire the development of concrete proposals for institutional reform. Pogge's chapter provides the clearest example of concrete recommendations, while other chapters have moved in varying degrees from ideal towards non-ideal theory. The second lesson is that the move from ideal to non-ideal theory quite often results in recommendations that could also have been defended on the basis of overlapping theories of justice. Tan himself,

[10] *Ibid.*, pp. 308–09.

[11] As Rawls has put it, ideal theory should provide "some guidance in thinking about non-ideal theory, and so about difficult cases of how to deal with existing injustices. It should also help to clarify the goal of reform and to identify which wrongs are more grievous and hence more urgent to correct." See: *Justice as Fairness: A Restatement*, ed. Erin Kelly (Cambridge, Mass.: Harvard University Press, 2001), p. 13.

[12] Buchanan, *Justice, Legitimacy, and Self-Determination*, p. 23.

for example, admits that his criteria for the use of armed force in international relations "do not derive specifically from liberal [cosmopolitan] morality but from more widely shared views about the morality of war."[13] Another example is Valadez's defense of self-determination, which is easily reconcilable with a moderate statist approach towards international relations. Of course, the fact that concrete proposals can be defended on the basis of different moral theories does not discount cosmopolitanism as such – it merely shows that cosmopolitan theory can be used to arrive at conclusions that are also acceptable for those who work on the basis of alternative moral theories. Yet, it does raise the question of whether it makes any practical difference whether one starts out from the cosmopolitanism position or from a competing theory of justice. While the majority of contributors to this volume have argued that it *does* make a difference, others have voiced skepticism in this regard.[14] The third lesson is that the best way to serve the ideals of cosmopolitanism may very well be an institutional design that is much more state-oriented.[15] Some contributions to this volume have questioned the wisdom of building international institutions (solely) on cosmopolitan principles. The chapter by Roach, for example, argues that the cosmopolitan ideals that underlie the International Criminal Court can only be realized via institutions that operate on the basis of a more cautious, Rawlsian approach towards international relations. A similar cautious approach towards the codification of moral cosmopolitanism can be found in the chapter by Valadez, who speaks out against an individual right of immigration.

Critical reconstruction

The starting point of this approach is the adoption of cosmopolitan values and ideals in international legal documents and political parlance. A critical reconstruction starts out, for example, from the observation that environmental treaties recognize the existence of "common concerns for mankind" or the observation that the International Criminal Tribunal for the Former Yugoslavia has claimed that, within international law "... a State-sovereignty-oriented approach has been

[13] See Tan chapter, p. 17

[14] For a more elaborate discussion see *Critical deconstruction*, p. 283.

[15] For a discussion see also Thomas Pogge, "Cosmopolitanism and Sovereignty," *Ethics* 103 (1992).

gradually supplanted by a human-being-oriented approach."[16] By contrast to the normative deductive approach, however, it does not aim to deduce more concrete rights and duties from such abstract normative propositions. Neither does it use such observations inductively to identify the existence of rules of customary law or broader trends in international society.[17] Rather, it studies how the promises of cosmopolitanism work out in practice; in a world characterized by power differences and a still pivotal role for sovereign States. An important question in this regard is who has the power to decide in concrete circumstances on the applicability, meaning, and enforcement of cosmopolitan principles. In this context, the contributions to this volume have focused on two possible enforcers of cosmopolitan principles: States and international – or global – institutions.

The relationship between cosmopolitanism and State sovereignty is complex and somewhat paradoxical. On the one hand, cosmopolitanism seeks to go beyond the boundaries of sovereign States, as to include rights and interests of individuals and global society as a whole. In international law, this has found expression in what Simma has labeled "community interests"; interests that transcend the interests of individual States such as the protection of the global environment, human rights, or collective security.[18] In political philosophy the same idea has been voiced in theories that seek *Justice Beyond Borders*, *Justice Without Borders* or "Rules for a post-Westphalian world."[19] On the other hand, sovereign States remain the primary entities that are supposed to act upon and enforce cosmopolitan values. The idea of a world government is rejected by the vast majority of political philosophers, while international treaties that embrace cosmopolitan values tend to endow States with the primary task of guarding the interests of individuals and global society as a whole. States, in other words, are supposed to act as agents of the global community, with the primary responsibility to determine in concrete cases what cosmopolitan justice requires.

Several contributions in this volume illustrate the paradoxical relationship between cosmopolitanism and State sovereignty. Tan's chapter,

[16] Prosecutor v. Dusko Tadic, Decision on the Defence Motion for Interlocutory Appeal on Jurisdiction, 2 October 1995.

[17] For the inductive method see above, supra note 6.

[18] Bruno Simma, "From Bilateralism to Community Interest in International Law," *Recueil des Cours* (1994).

[19] Caney, *Justice Beyond Borders*; Tan, *Justice Without Borders*; Buchanan, "Rawls's Law of Peoples."

for example, shows the still pivotal position of State sovereignty in liberal cosmopolitan political theory. His chapter starts out from the need to restrict the powers of States in order to protect basic human rights. At the same time, however, it advocates a right of humanitarian intervention for other States in case of gross violations of human rights. States thus simultaneously appear as threats to and guardians of human rights. Other chapters illustrate how international law has dealt with the paradoxical relation between cosmopolitanism and State sovereignty. The contribution of Hey, for example, shows how international (or global) environmental law has moved beyond the inter-State paradigm, *inter alia* via the codification of moral cosmopolitanism in substantive legal provisions. Yet, global environmental law still regards States as the primary guardians of the rights and interests of individuals, future generations, and mankind as a whole. Similarly, Tsagourias' chapter shows how the UN system of collective security seeks to go beyond the interests of individual States, yet remains highly dependent upon the cooperation of sovereign States to counter threats to international peace and security. Another example is provided in Peskin's chapter, which demonstrates how strongly the realization of the International Criminal Court's promise of global justice depends on the capabilities and goodwill of States.

The effectiveness of cosmopolitanism, in other words, largely depends on the ability and willingness of States to act as agents of the global community. However, such "cosmopolitan self-disciplining" cannot be lightly presumed, as the different chapters in this volume attest. States often refuse to act upon the promises of cosmopolitan justice laid down in substantive legal provisions, or end up in political struggles on the meaning and force of such provisions in concrete circumstances. Cosmopolitanism then becomes the continuation of world politics with the inclusion of universalistic arguments.

One of the responses to the unresolved tension between cosmopolitan justice and State sovereignty is a turn to international institutions. Since 1945, international law has witnessed a proliferation of international organizations and supervisory bodies that aim to protect cosmopolitan values and foster the disciplining of sovereign States. While such attempts have certainly produced beneficial effects in different areas (see e.g. the European Convention on Human Rights), several contributions in this volume caution against too optimistic a view on global institutions. In the first place, as was set out above, the effectiveness of global institutions still heavily depends on the cooperation of the very same States they seek to discipline. Secondly, global institutions themselves may help to sustain power-structures that run contrary to the cosmopolitan values they claim to protect. An example of the latter can be found in Hey's contribution to this volume, that shows how the lack of procedural fairness in global environmental institutions tends to marginalize developing countries, thus reflecting and reinforcing power inequalities in the world.

The critical reconstructive approach thus reveals one of the basic tensions in cosmopolitanism: that between the presumed moral unity of the world and the decentralized and dispersed structures of authority that are supposed to protect that unity. By focusing on questions of authority, interpretation, and enforcement, a critical reconstructive approach is able to indicate the borders of cosmopolitan justice in practice. It helps to identify obstacles to the realization of cosmopolitan ideals and to expose the potential dangers of the use of cosmopolitan arguments in world politics. In that way, it can also be used to formulate immanent critiques of cosmopolitanism; to confront the promise of global justice with the actual practices to which this promise gives rise. Moreover, it can point at alternative ways of looking at questions of global justice, e.g. by emphasizing the role of procedural fairness, by cautioning against the institutionalization of moral cosmopolitanism, or by advocating a more dynamic perspective on the way in which cosmopolitanism works in international practice.[20]

Critical deconstruction

Roughly put, the term "deconstruction" stands for a series of techniques that can be used to conceal the contingency, fluidity, instability, and incoherence of structures of social meaning.[21] Within international law, insights borrowed from deconstructivism were popularized by scholars such as David Kennedy and Martti Koskenniemi.[22] Both argued that international legal argument lacks a stable and determinate foundation

[20] The issue of procedural fairness figures prominently in Ellen Hey's contribution. Valadez's chapter warns against the translation of moral cosmopolitanism into institutions in the area of migration policies. The chapter by Roach advocates an evolutionary perspective on cosmopolitan justice, while Tsagourias sets out how cosmopolitan principles and ideals are constantly reinvented in the search for legitimacy.

[21] Jack M. Balkin, "Deconstruction's Legal Career," *Cardozo Law Review* 27, no. 2 (1994), pp. 101, 102.

[22] David Kennedy, *International Legal Structures* (Baden-Baden: Nomos Verlag, 1987); Koskenniemi, *From Apology to Utopia*.

as it constantly oscillates between opposing positions: a consensual and a non-consensual foundation for the validity of rules, an emphasis on sovereignty and world order, a factual and a normative foundation for the existence of States, etc. In similar fashion, it would be possible to deconstruct cosmopolitan theories of justice. As the contributions to this volume have demonstrated, cosmopolitanism too rests on potentially conflicting and underdetermined foundations: global justice and State sovereignty, self-determination of peoples and individual freedom, naturalist and sociological underpinnings of basic duties of individuals, etc.

The question is, however, why one would want to engage in such an exercise, what is the point of revealing contingency, indeterminacy, or a lack of coherence. For some, the whole point of deconstruction is just that: to destabilize established concepts, to demonstrate the absence of solid foundations of knowledge and normative theories. However, there is no need to limit the purpose of deconstruction to an entirely negative task. It is equally possible to deconstruct established meanings with a more critical, "constructive" purpose: to identify injustices, to give voice to suppressed narratives, and to open up our mind to alternative ways of acting and thinking.

In this context, it is useful to recall Balkin's idea that conceptual opposites (e.g. sovereign prerogatives and world order) can be understood as being "nested"; as containing both differences and similarities, "which manifest themselves in different contexts of judgment."[23] Analyzing legal categories of theories of justice in terms of nested opposites has an important consequence. It requires attention for the specific context in which the conceptual opposites receive their meaning: in certain contexts concepts may appear to be radically opposed, while in others they may look quite similar. An example is the relation between cosmopolitan justice and the pursuit of national interests. In some contexts, notions of cosmopolitan justice set limits to and are opposed to what States perceive to be in the furtherance of their national interest, e.g. when cosmopolitan justice requires States to take a fair share of the burdens of climate change. In other contexts, however, notions of cosmopolitan justice may foster the pursuit of what States perceive

[23] Jack M. Balkin, "Being Just With Deconstruction," available at: www.yale.edu/lawweb/jbalkin/articles/beingjust1.htm (accessed March 11, 2009), at p. 6. An edited version of the same text was published in: *Social and Legal Studies*, 3, 393 (1994). For a more extensive analysis of nested oppositions see also from the same author: "Nested Oppositions," (1990) *Yale Law Journal* 99: 1669–1705.

to be in their interest, e.g. where issues of national security are mixed with imperial agendas to re-model enemies after the imagery of decent liberal States.[24] This shows once more that the fluidity and indeterminacy of concepts such as "cosmopolitan justice" or "national interest" preclude any grand generalizations. Arguments made in the name of cosmopolitanism can be "inclusive and humane"[25] but also function as the "normative gloss of globalized capitalism at its imperial stage"[26]; depending on the context in which the arguments receive force and meaning. A contextualized approach makes it possible to engage more critically and more constructively in debates on the role of cosmopolitanism, acknowledging both its critical potential and the ever-looming danger that universalism is used to foster imperial ambitions.

Threads of a deconstructive approach can be found in Tsagourias's chapter, especially where he shows how attempts to "constitutionalize" the United Nations are likely to reinforce the pivotal role of sovereign States. A more outspoken example is provided by Thomas Spijkerboer's deconstruction of cosmopolitanism. Spijkerboer takes as his starting point the opposition between State sovereignty and cosmopolitanism in the context of migration. He argues that both positions agree on how the problem of migration is to be defined (as one of admission) and end up defending more or less the same status quo policies. The aim of Spijkerboer is not to deconstruct State sovereignty or cosmopolitanism as such. Rather, he seeks to lay bare the consequences of a particular way of defining the problem of migration, to set out the role of theories of justice in upholding the status quo, and to search for alternative ways of understanding the issues involved. Contextualized analysis of cosmopolitanism can thus contribute to the never-ending debates on the relation between positive laws, moral conventions, and the pursuit of justice. Valadez's highly critical response to Spijkerboer's arguments constitutes a good example of such an ongoing debate in the area of migration. It shows that theories of justice and existing institutional

24 A prime example can be found in the 2002 US National Security Strategy, which aims to combine issues of national security with an imperial agenda framed in terms of universal and allegedly globally-shared values. Available at: www.acq.osd.mil/ncbdp/nm/docs/Relevant%20Docs/national_security_strategy.pdf (accessed 11 march, 2009).

25 Anne Orford, "A Jurisprudence of the Limit," in *International Law and its Others*, ed. Anne Orford (Cambrdige: Cambrdige University Press, 2006), p. 3.

26 Costas Douzinas, *Human Rights and Empire: The Political Philosophy of Cosmopolitanism* (Routledge-Cavendish, 2007), p. 176.

legal frameworks are to be treated as provisional, open to further critique and deconstruction.

Cosmopolitanism and institutionalization: the never-ending story

The chapters in this book have underlined the multi-faceted nature of cosmopolitan thinking in relation to legal institutions. Some chapters have used cosmopolitan theories as a tool for critiquing existing institutional frameworks and as a source of inspiration for international legal reform. Other chapters have focused more on the practical effects of institutionalizing cosmopolitan values in international law. Generally speaking, these approaches take a more critical stance towards cosmopolitanism, while emphasizing the paradoxical relation between State sovereignty and cosmopolitanism, the importance of procedural fairness, and the danger of abuse of cosmopolitan ideals. Yet others have questioned whether, in specific concrete contexts, it really matters whether one adheres to a cosmopolitan position or a more State-oriented position.

Taken together, the chapters aim to contribute to the never-ending debates on the relation between positive laws, moral conventions, and the pursuit of justice. These debates escape definite answers, because, as Balkin has argued, the relation between legal and moral conventions and the idea of justice is of an inherently dialectical nature: "Human law, culture, and convention are never perfectly just, but justice needs human law, culture, and convention to be articulated and enforced. There is a fundamental inadequation between our sense of justice and the products of culture, but we can only express this inadequation through the cultural means at our disposal … Hence, our laws are imperfect not because they are bad copies of a determinate Form of justice, but because we must articulate our insatiable longing for justice in concrete institutions, and our constructions can never be identical with the longings which inspire them."[27]

This means that it is not only impossible, but also undesirable to close the gap between moral cosmopolitanism and actual institutions, ideal and non-ideal theory, cosmopolitan justice and positive

[27] Balkin, "Deconstruction's Legal Career," p. 11. For a more elaborate analysis see from the same author Jack M. Balkin, "Transcendental Deconstruction, Transcendent Justice," *Michigan Law Review* 92 (1994).

law. Cosmopolitanism is always also a "cosmopolitanism to come"[28], a never-fully-realizable promise of global justice. Rather than searching for closure, the promises, gaps, blind spots, and actual effects of cosmopolitanism should be constantly revealed, discussed, and re-examined. Such an endeavor requires multidisciplinary cooperation and openness to insights from different fields. We hope that the chapters in this book have contributed to this enterprise.

[28] Douzinas, *Human Rights and Empire*.

INDEX

Lightning Source UK Ltd.
Milton Keynes UK
UKOW03f1108190614

233714UK00001B/62/P

9 781107 693098